What They're Saying About *Telecom Made Easy*:

"... a basic but thorough guide to phone systems and services, cellular phones, answering devices, paging, on-line services, modems, faxes, and networked systems... geared toward home businesses, telecommuters, and small firms."
— *Nation's Business*

"If you are among the 55 percent of Americans who are still pedestrians on the information superhighway, this book is for you."
— *Orange County Register*

"... contains chapters on every telecommunication device necessary for an office to survive, and explains in simple, non-technical language how to put these technologies to their best use, while tailoring them to individual needs."
— *Pacifica Tribune*

"I used to call Langhoff when I was writing my column and had a question about telecommunications and the home office. Now I can just pick up this book. This is a great resource."
— Alice Bredin
nationally syndicated *Working at Home* columnist

"... for the small business owner who may be confused by the terminology and sales pitches, the book is an excellent reference work and should pay for itself in the money saved with smart purchasing."
— *McHenry County Business Journal*

"(This) book is great! Anyone can learn a lot from it (even me!). What's good about the book is that it is a combination of a reference book, telecom dictionary, a source book and a how-to book."
— Art Rosenberg, Principal
Telemessaging Communications
(a.k.a. the "father" of voice mail)

D1468798

"... a guide to getting the most out of telephone products and services..."
— *Association Trends*

"If you're suffering from technophobia, you'll appreciate this easy-to-understand guide to getting the most out of telephone products and services."
— Barbara Brabec
Self-Employment Survival Letter

"... offers easy-to-understand information for the technologically challenged..."
— *Canadian Communications Network Letter*

"Suddenly, the small-office/home-office market is hot, spawning a number of new how-to books geared toward the soloist. *Telecom Made Easy* is one we like for its thorough coverage of telephones for home and small businesses... Especially helpful for do-it-yourselfers... Just leafing through this 380-page book will prepare anyone for smarter dealings with salespeople or the phone company."
— *INC.* magazine

"... designed to help home offices and small businesses wade through today's technological telecom maze."
— *This Week in Consumer Electronics*

"June Langhoff is your guide through the maze of telephone products and services... provides simple explanations and detailed descriptions of what to look for and why it's important to *your* small business..."
— *Working Solo* newsletter

"... how to streamline a company and its phone use, and how to provide better services through the phone. An excellent, basic guide."
— *The Midwest Book Review*

"... (The book) performs the unusual feat of discussing technical matters without ever falling into technical jargon, (and) also describes how ISDN phone lines work, how to best use voice mail, and what services are on the way... just about everyone will find something of value in Langhoff's breezy exposition of the world of telecommunications."
— *Association Meetings*

Telecom Made Easy

Money-Saving, Profit-Building Solutions
for Home Businesses, Telecommuters
and Small Organizations

Fourth Edition

by

June Langhoff

Aegis Publishing Group, Ltd.
796 Aquidneck Avenue
Newport, Rhode Island
401-849-4200
www.aegisbooks.com

Illustrated by Vicki Zimmerman

Library of Congress Catalog Card Number: 00-45144

Aegis Publishing Group, Ltd.
796 Aquidneck Avenue
Newport, RI   02842

International Standard Book Number: 1-890154-14-8

Printed in the United States of America.
First Edition, 1995. Second Edition, 1996. Third Edition, 1997.
Fourth Edition, first printing, 2000

10 9 8 7 6 5 4 3 2

Library of Congress Cataloging-In-Publication Data:

Langhoff, June.
    Telecom made easy : money-saving, profit-building solutions for home busi-
nesses, telecommuters, and small organizations / June Langhoff —fourth edition
        p. cm.
    Includes index.
    ISBN 1-890154-14-8
    1. Telephone systems. 2. Telecommunication—Economic aspects.
    3. Small business. I. Title

TK6401 .L36 2000
651.7'3—dc21
                                                            00-45144
                                                            CIP

Acknowledgments
. . . .

SOME SUPER PEOPLE HELPED to put this book together, and I'm most grateful. My heartfelt appreciation to:

Bob Mastin, my editor and publisher, for his unfailing support and enthusiasm for this project;

Patrick Rentsch for patiently answering hundreds of technical questions and wading through very rough drafts;

Nim Marsh and Dee Lanoue for copyediting the manuscript with great delicacy and care;

Vicki Zimmerman for the exceptional illustrations that pepper the book and help explain technical stuff;

John Robertson for an outstanding cover design;

Kim Ecclesine for cheerfully snapping my photo for the back cover;

David Joseph Lacagnina for access to Salestar, his company's telecommunications database;

My friends at Pacific Bell for all their support and advice;

The folks that hang out on the Working From Home Forum on CompuServe, who willingly answered my questions and signed up for many of the interviews that are sprinkled throughout this book;

My office mates, Frisby and Marsha, for keeping their muddy paws off the manuscript;

And finally, thanks to my terrific son Nick, for last-minute proofing and for putting up with this mess for months.

Contents

Chapter 5—Stand-Alone Phones   105

Chapter 6—Phone Systems 137

Chapter 7—Mobile Phones   169

Chapter 8—Voice Messaging   199

Foreword

· ·

"MR. WATSON, COME HERE. I WANT YOU."
Alexander Graham Bell to Thomas Watson, March 10, 1876

As an entrepreneur living in an era of instant information, I often wonder what Alexander Graham Bell would think of modern telecommunications. What remarkable changes have occurred since Bell spoke those historic first words!

Imagine Bell's office if he were alive today. Multiple telephone lines would connect him to colleagues around the world by voice, fax, and modem. He'd probably be a master surfer of the Internet, gathering data for new inventions from points around the globe. On his busy travels, he'd stay in touch by cellular phone, having his messages routed from his voice mail system or pager. His laptop computer would be a constant companion, since he'd be using it to exchange e-mail, data files, faxes, and audio and video clips from remote sites as he visited clients around the world. Interested in learning more about his business? You could call his office's toll-free 800 number for general information, use his pay-per-call 900 number to hear valuable details on recent developments, or access his fax-on-demand system for printed reports of his new patents and inventions.

While this imaginary scene may seem a fanciful depiction, it is the everyday realm of millions of 1990s entrepreneurs who employ these technologies on a regular basis in their work. If Bell were alive today, however, it's also likely that he'd be surrounded by fellow entrepreneurs eager to discover how to use telecommunications effectively in their own businesses—and besieging him to help them decipher the confusing array of options and information.

Since Alexander Graham Bell can be our guide only in our imagination, we are fortunate to have June Langhoff's expertise in this book to assist us with our real-world needs. In clear, easy-to-understand language, she demystifies the complexities of this powerful technology. Her straightforward approach is the perfect fit for busy entrepreneurs who are more interested in running their businesses than becoming telecommunication engineers.

Savvy entrepreneurs understand that staying connected is a key ingredient to success—and that telecommunications is at the heart of those connections. Yet who among us has not been overwhelmed at the fast-paced changes and multiple decisions to make regarding this area? Modern technology enables us to appear like and compete with businesses many times our size. Unlike those larger companies, however, we don't have a dedicated staff member to manage this technology. The potential it brings for empowering our business is thrilling, but the details can make us dizzy.

June Langhoff is here to guide us. Consider her your personal telecommunications consultant—at a fraction of the cost! Never before has a single book provided such a valuable overview of the telecommunications information small business owners need to make their businesses succeed. Use it to find the answers you seek today, and keep it close at hand to tackle those telecom challenges you'll face in the future.

More than any other development, advances in telecommunications have fueled the explosive growth of entrepreneurial activity in our country. Recent studies show that more than 41 million Americans are involved in solo businesses, home-based enterprises, and telecommuting arrangements. Booming numbers, however, do not guarantee success for all. To compete successfully, today's entrepreneurs must adapt technology for their own uses and harness it effectively. And to master technology, you must first understand it.

This book gives that power. Let's cheer June Langhoff for bringing us real-world solutions to high-tech confusion. May the information and advice she has gathered here bring you much success.

Terri Lonier
New Paltz, New York

. . . .

Professional speaker and consultant Terri Lonier is president of Portico Press, publishers of books, newsletters, an online network, audiotapes, and other resources for entrepreneurs. She is the author of *Working Solo*, the complete guide to self-employment, which was chosen by *Inc.* magazine as the number-one book for solo entrepreneurs. It is also one of the top three small-business books in the U.S.

As a modern entrepreneur, Terri reports that she runs her business with four telephone lines, voice mail, a dedicated fax line, a cordless phone, an answering service, four online addresses, and several modem-equipped computers. For information on her resources for entrepreneurs, check her website: www.workingsolo.com. Or call Portico Press at 800-222-SOLO and ask for a free brochure.

Chapter

1

Communications Today

. . . .

TELEPHONES. . .YAWN. Telecommunications. . .borrring. If that's how you feel about the subject of telecom, it's time for you to wake up.

No business today, no matter how small, can afford to remain ignorant about telecommunications. If you want to compete with large, resource-laden organizations, you have no choice but to sound like one yourself. You do that by creating a communications system that handles phone calls, messages, fax, and data transfer with ease—one that keeps you instantaneously available.

That's not easy. But it's getting easier. How? Through employing telecommunications products and services such as those outlined in this book.

Look at what's happening in the communications world today:

- Scientists at the San Francisco Zoo are monitoring endangered black-and-white ruffed lemurs in the wilds of Madagascar. The animals are outfitted with radio collars that transmit tracking information to zoo headquarters via satellite.

- Avid windsurfers along the California and Hawaii coastlines can get reports on the latest wind conditions via their "Call of the Wind" pagers. An automatic monitoring system alerts customers when the wind is right.

- A local SuperCuts in Aurora, Colorado, operates a completely equipped hair salon in an RV. In addition to the usual stuff a beautician would carry, the stylist also packs a mobile phone for last-minute appointments and a cellular credit card authorization machine.

- At the High Tech Cafe in Dallas, the maitre d' asks diners if they prefer "smoking, nonsmoking, or modem ready." Tables at the Cafe are equipped with modem jacks and power cords so that patrons can grab a fax, fire off an e-message, continue computing, or charge their batteries as they do lunch.

- A professor at MIT is building a special Internet browser for parrots (they're very smart birds). Evidently, the approximately eight million parrots living in the U.S. are so bored that they get into mischief. The idea is to give them something fun to do, hence the Interpet Explorer Project.

- At a trendy gym in Manhattan, patrons surf the Web or pick up their emails while buffing up on stationary bikes outfitted with a TV, CD player, and Internet-connected computer.

- When wining or dining at a local TGIF, patrons can request service by speaking into their saltshaker. A pager, hidden inside the condiment holder, summons the waiter.

- Using a closed-circuit TV system enhanced by artificial intelligence, casino guards are alerted if someone runs instead of walks to an exit, if a cash drawer is left open, or if a croupier has his hands under the table too long.

- Farmers are equipping their tractors with cellular phones. In the event of a breakdown, they can dial a repair company directly from the field and save a trip to town. Some are even putting pagers on their dairy cattle, summoning them home with a beep.

- Filmmaker Steven Spielberg edited Jurassic Park while working in Poland on his next movie. He used a broadcast video service from Pacific Bell dubbed "Virtual Hollywood." It employs satellite, microwave, and fiber technologies to move huge amounts of digitized film data.

Our world is shrinking. Advances in telecommunications are changing the way we work and the way we communicate. Organizations are doing business in new forms. Virtual organizations, e-commerce, wireless shopping—these are the business innovations of today. Be a part of this telecommunications revolution, and avoid being left at the side of the road. You don't want to be road kill on the information highway.

A 1994 Coopers & Lybrand survey of the fastest-growing small businesses found that revenue per employee is two and a half times higher for companies that use high technology than it is for low-tech companies. A 1998 study for *American City Business Journal* showed that small businesses using Internet or other online connections grew at a rate of 10 percent a year. Those without these links grew only 7 percent in the same period. The fact that you're reading this book suggests you belong in the former category—or you want to get there. Good for you!

WHY JOIN THE TELECOM REVOLUTION?

You can use telecommunications to:

✔ **Provide great customer service**

Set up an 800 number for your customers to call. Create a fax-back service so they can get instant help. Add a click-to-talk button on your website.

✔ **Stay available**

Carry a voice pager or mobile phone to keep in touch. Sign up for follow-me phone service or call forwarding.

✔ **Discover new ways to market**

Create a newsletter and email or fax it to your client list. Advertise online. Network in cyberspace.

✔ **Speed workflow**

Add a network. Use workgroup software, voice broadcast, and email distribution lists to keep everyone focused. Install a high-speed digital phone line for faster Internet access and accelerated file transfer.

✔ **Tap into instant information**

Check out your competition on the Web. Research industry trends and new markets. Stay abreast of breaking news.

✔ **Save money**

Install a telephone system for maximum line usage and to control long-distance costs. Select the best long-distance dialing plan for your business. Learn to use the Internet for faxing and phoning.

✔ **Add to revenues**

Watch orders increase with a toll-free number. Use a faxback service or online catalog to sell information or goods.

✔ **Improve security**

Install an intercom system from your desk to your door. Take a mobile phone with you on the road.

✔ **Save time**

Avoid centralized meetings by scheduling a teleconference or setting up a desktop video connection. Take advantage of broadcast fax services. Speed transaction processing with broadband communications.

✔ **Expand your market**

Set up a remote line to snare business from another community. Use phone company voice mail or targeted toll-

free numbers to widen your cast. Put your business on the
World Wide Web.

✔ **Work smart**

Carry your office with you in a briefcase, backpack, or bag.
Use email or voice mail to communicate with far-flung colleagues and customers. Schedule team meetings online.

When I was conducting research for this book, I found several
books that explained how to save money on telephone service,
but I didn't find any that advised how to *make* money using
telecommunications. That's what I plan to do. In order to make
money using telecommunications, you need to think of your
communications budget as a marketing expense, not as a fixed
overhead expense.

1977. That was the year the first personal computers appeared
on the market. Those chunky Apple computers looked like a
cute fad, didn't they? Then IBM came out with a personal computer, and the fad was taken more seriously. Some businesses
embraced the technology, found new niches for themselves,
and took off—witness desktop publishing, multimedia, and
online shopping services. Other businesses took a wait-and-see
attitude. Some of them are still around. Many are not.

We're at a similar crossroads today in the arena of telecommunications. Organizations that are taking advantage of new developments in telecom are increasing their chances for survival
tomorrow. Plan to be one of them.

Happily, you don't have to be a large organization with
megabucks to spend in order to join the telecom revolution.
Most of the new technologies are well within the budget of
small and solo businesses.

Be glad you're small. Your lean size lets you make quick decisions, implement rapid changes, and embrace new technology
much sooner than the behemoths. Though a couple hundred

dollars spent on communications technology may seem like a lot to you, large organizations need to multiply that amount by thousands.

Consider how much longer it takes these organizations to make technology decisions when faced with that kind of cash outlay. New technologies are often easier to implement in a small organization. You're not burdened by layers of management, acres of paperwork, and tangled lines of communication.

EVALUATE YOUR NEEDS

Do your communications match your customer's expectations? If your customers are used to doing business by fax, you're losing business by not having fax capability. If they are dedicated emailers, make sure you have an email address of your own. If your clients expect to reach you at a moment's notice, figure out how to accommodate them via pager, call forwarding, or a mobile phone. You can upgrade your image by setting up a voice mail system and adding a dedicated line for fax and modem calls.

Have you ever heard one of your customers, vendors, or clients tell you that your office is very hard to reach? Probably not. They usually don't tell you when they call someone else.

It's time to take control of your communications.

When deciding where to invest your telecom dollars, you need to start with a plan. What do you want to accomplish? Increased accessibility? Wider market share? Speedier ordering? Improved customer service? Maybe your current push is to reduce costs and do things smarter.

Communications choices get more complex every day. When you look in the newspaper or scan computer and telecom magazines, you're hit with an incredible selection of products, all clamoring for your attention. Each one has a longer feature list than the last. Most are described in unintelligible techno-talk. How do you sort it all out?

First, write down all your questions. Yes, all of them.

- Will a palmtop be sufficient for my mobile communications needs? Should I invest in a wireless phone with Internet access capability? Can I afford the monthly bills?

- Maybe I should wait before buying that phone system. It looks like there will be a lot of change in the coming months. Could I avoid getting a wired phone system and get along with a cordless system instead?

- It seems as though everyone in the world has voice mail except me. Should I get it, too? Maybe I should get a multifunction device that takes voice, fax, and email messages.

Next, do your homework. You can start by reading the applicable chapters in this book. Once you know what all those features in the ads are about, make a list of the features you want. If the list is long, prioritize it.

Now you're ready to take a trip to a local electronics or telecom store. Alternatively, you could visit a virtual storefront. Either way, make a vow not to buy on this trip. It may be hard to resist the sales pitch, but you need to learn what's available and how everything works before making a decision. If you're at a physical store rather than a virtual one, try stuff out. Ask for demos to see how the features work.

Once you're safely back in your office again, call around to compare prices and features. Look into the mail order catalogs and check websites for bargains. You could consider buying used equipment or take advantage of leasing plans.

Next, do the numbers. What's the payback period? What's the useful life of the product? What are the operating costs? Can you get a multifunction device that handles several of your needs?

Finally, make your decision and then implement it. Don't wait for the next round of technological improvements. If you do, you'll never actually join the telecom revolution. You'll just sit on the sidelines salivating over technical reviews, and most likely suffer from acute PBX, PDA, or PC phone envy.

HOW TO USE THIS BOOK

First, skim the book. Look at the introductions to each chapter. Then take the quick surveys scattered throughout the book. They are designed to help you select technologies.

You certainly don't have to read every word or every chapter to get the information you need. Both the table of contents and the index can point you to areas of interest.

To help you get set up easily, most chapters have a section on getting connected. Often, I've included feature lists, shopping advice, and troubleshooting tips. At the end of every chapter, you'll find a list of resources—magazines, books, newsletters, websites, vendor names, and phone numbers—hopefully, everything you'll need to get additional information on a particular topic or product.

Now, here's a brief rundown of each chapter's contents:

Chapter 1—Communications Today

You're here already. In case you missed it, however, this chapter piques your curiosity about the telecom world by showcasing new telecommunications technology. I explain what's in it for you, provide some advice on determining your needs, and give you an overview of each chapter.

Chapter 2—Connections

This chapter examines the "nuts and bolts" of telecommunications, including wiring plans, connections, tips for getting the most from your current setup, and some troubleshooting advice. Be sure to read this chapter if you plan to add more phone lines to your phone system. What you do now could save bundles in the future.

Chapter 3—Phone Services

I have listed dozens of telephone company services that can improve your communications. You'll learn about caller ID, follow-me phone service, distinctive ringing, call waiting, Internet calling, and all kinds of call forwarding.

Chapter 4—Phone Lines

Here, you'll get the lowdown on money-making services, such as 800 and 900 lines. I explain the difference between analog and digital phone lines, describe line service types (such as POTS, ISDN, DSL, and cable) in detail, and provide tips on ordering phone service. You'll also receive suggestions for improving bandwidth and advice on networking.

Chapter 5—Stand-Alone Phones

This chapter is all about phones—how they work, what all those different features do, and what to look for in a single-line, multiline, or cordless phone. There's advice about troubleshooting and information about selecting and using a headset. Finally, there's a bonus section on teleconferencing.

Chapter 6—Phone Systems

In this chapter, you'll find everything you need to know to choose the right phone system for your business. (Maybe you don't need a phone system at all!) I discuss key, KSU-less, PBX, Centrex, hybrid, wireless, and PC-based phone systems. You'll learn what all those features mean and which ones are most useful to you.

Chapter 7—Mobile Phones

Mobile phones—including portable, transportable, and car phones—are the topic of this chapter. You'll get advice on selecting a mobile phone and carrier plus useful information on keeping your wireless bill under control. In addition, you'll learn about the newest technological advances, such as wireless Internet access.

Chapter 8—Voice Messaging

You'll need a messaging system to keep track of your incoming calls. This chapter covers voice mail systems, voice mail services, and answering machines. Included are helpful tips for setting up user-friendly voice mail, designing a successful voice mail menu, and leaving effective messages.

Chapter 9—Paging

Pagers aren't low-tech beepers anymore. In this section, I discuss various types of pagers, explain pager features, and offer some advice on shopping for a paging service.

Chapter 10—Email

This chapter explains how email works. It also provides tips for managing your e-mailbox and ways to stop spam. There are special sections on transferring files, opening attachments, and protecting against computer viruses. Information on handling email while traveling and tips for writing more effective email round out this discussion.

Chapter 11—Internet

We start with a brief explanation of how the Internet works and what you need to get connected. Several useful services are covered, including newsgroups, mailing lists, mailbots, instant messaging, Web conferencing, and videoconferencing. I also provide advice on searching for information on the Net, plus steps for building your own website.

Chapter 12—Modems

This chapter simplifies the task of choosing a modem. It tells you what all those blinking modem lights mean, and it takes the mystery out of terms such as Ethernet and USB. You'll also find troubleshooting tips, directions for getting connected, and advice for using your modem internationally.

Chapter 13—Fax

This chapter spells out the various types of fax technologies and explains which features to look for when shopping for a fax machine or fax modem. There's also information on fax-on-demand, broadcast fax, Internet faxing, mobile fax, and faxing internationally, with tips for more effective faxing.

Chapter 14—Your Phone Bill

Staying on top of telephone costs and sorting through all those conflicting, confusing long-distance claims can leave you reeling. This chapter helps you get a handle on controlling phone costs and selecting the best calling plan for you.

Additional Resources

You might want to dip into this section for additional telecommunications books, magazines, telecom catalogs, associations, and websites. There's also a comprehensive index.

THINGS CHANGE FAST AROUND HERE

From the beginning of this project, I wanted *Telecom Made Easy* to be a really useful sourcebook, with names, telephone numbers, and even price ranges. I wanted it to contain all the information you'd need to take action, get more information, and make an informed decision. I believe this book achieves those goals.

However, as you know, the telecom world changes rapidly. Companies merge, change their names, add and drop products, revise price lists, get born, die. So, I can't promise that every telephone number listed is still in service or that every product described is still available. I do promise that the information contained is as up-to-date as I could make it.

Chapter

2

Connections

. . . .

NOW THAT THE TELEPHONE COMPANIES have been deregulated, you are responsible for the installation, repair, and maintenance of your own telephone service. Basically, you are responsible for your interior wiring, which comprises the phone lines that run inside your building, while the phone company assumes responsibility for the exterior wiring, which is everything else. You can do the wiring yourself, pay an electrician or contractor to do it, or pay the telephone company to do it.

If you think you'll need to troubleshoot your communications setup or add capacity, it's a good idea to understand how telephone communications work. At the very least, you will want to find out where your responsibility ends. Knowing a few basic facts about your phone system could prevent the unhappy possibility of paying your phone company a whopping service fee to correct a problem caused by a fault in your interior wiring, a shorted phone, or a flaky answering device.

This subject can be intimidating, but, believe me—if I can understand this stuff, so can you. I promise to try to avoid complex electrical wiring diagrams and technical talk. I also promise to tell you only what you need to know and why you need to know it.

THE ANATOMY OF A PHONE CALL

- **Pick up the receiver**
  When you pick up the receiver, a spring-loaded button on

the phone cradle pops up. This allows current to flow into your phone and notifies your telephone central office that you are requesting a line. The central office finds an unused circuit and sends dial tone down the line.

- **Dial the number**
  Once you have keyed in the first three numbers, your central office switch searches for a circuit to connect you to the central office of the number you are dialing. A ringing tone lets you know that your call is being processed, and, at the same time, the phone connected to the number you are dialing also starts ringing. To determine the most efficient route for your call, the central office takes into account the type of call you placed, your service provider preferences, and the location of the called party.

- **Receiving party picks up**
  When the person at the other end of the call picks up the phone, current flows from that phone line to its central office. At this point, the central office stops ringing the phone and sets up the audio connection.

- **At the end of the call**
  After your call is completed, you hang up the phone by placing the receiver back in the cradle, thereby causing a button in the phone cradle to be depressed. Pressing this button down signals the central office to release the circuit and make a record of the call's duration.

LONG-DISTANCE CALL ROUTING

If your call is long distance, the central office switch will recognize it by the number "1" preceding the country code and/or area code. The switch contacts an interexchange carrier (the company you purchase your long-distance service from) and searches for a trunk to carry the call. Your call may actually be routed over several switches on its journey. Most of the time, though, you won't even notice because it happens so fast.

Calls that must cross an ocean or other large body of water may pass their signals over a ground station to a communications satellite or via an undersea cable. Some calls may also travel by way of microwave relay towers.

HOW CALL SWITCHING WORKS

When you make a call, whether a voice call, a fax, or a call to connect to the Internet, your local telephone company works some magic to send that call through its network. This is accomplished in one of two ways:

- Circuit switching
- Packet switching

CIRCUIT SWITCHING

As soon as your Aunt Lizzie in Des Moines answers your call, a circuit is set up—and stays up—for the entire length of the call. This circuit can't be used by anyone else until you both hang up.

The sound waves of your voice are converted into electrical signals and are then transmitted over the circuit as pulses of electricity or light. When they reach Aunt Lizzie's phone, they're converted back into sound waves so that she can understand you. On your end, the same thing happens in reverse.

Circuit-switched calls are very reliable, but they are also costly and inefficient. Though most calls today are handled through circuit switching, tomorrow's calls will undoubtedly be packet-switched. Let's see why.

PACKET SWITCHING

You pick up your phone or use your computer to call Uncle Oscar in Portland. When packet switching is used, the sound of your voice is converted into digital bits (symbolized by a series of zeros and ones), and this data is then divided up into small packets. Each packet is assigned a unique identifier, which contains the digital address of the packet's destination. Though packets from many different computers and phones are sent along the network at the same time, they are grouped by destination. For example, all packets heading for your central office will be grouped together.

When the packets reach Uncle Oscar's central office, those with the same identifiers and addresses are reassembled to form a complete message. In this way, Uncle Oscar can understand what you're saying. Otherwise, all he'd get would be the type of squealing stuff we hear when a modem is connecting.

Packet switching allows lots of traffic to move over the line simultaneously. By speeding up connections, the telephone company saves money, which is ultimately translated into lower costs for you.

Many of the packet-switched networks use a standard known as Internet Protocol (IP). Communications companies rely on IP to move all kinds of digital information—including voice calls, video transmissions, and various kinds of data—in packets across networks. IP is very efficient because the network is only used in bursts of activity.

YOUR CONNECTION

Telephone service is brought to your home or office via underground or overhead cables from the phone company's central switching office. (For more about central offices, see *Your Local Central Office* in Chapter 4.) The line that connects your location to the telephone company is called the "local loop."

Phone service is brought to a box that can usually be found on the outside of your building or in the basement. This box contains a station protector, which is a grounding device that protects against lightning, as well as some circuitry for testing. The

Station Protector

box goes by many different names: access box, service box, station protector, junction box, or demarcation block.

If your phone wiring was done after 1986, you'll most likely find a phone jack inside the access box. This jack, called the network interface jack, is used for testing (more about this later in the chapter). Unless you pay a monthly fee for inside wiring maintenance, this is the point where the phone company's responsibility for your service ends.

In multiunit buildings, phone service is first brought to the outside of the building. Service to individual suites or apartments comes through a riser, which is a bundle of wires either enclosed in a thick cable or grouped inside a raceway. Individual telephone wires are then "peeled off" to supply telephone service to the office suites or apartments. Usually, there is one access box for each floor, often found inside a utility closet or stairwell. It is your responsibility to pay for the wiring (and its maintenance) that runs from the general access box on your floor to your office. In a large building, this could involve a substantial distance.

If your office has multiple lines, your service is probably wired to a punchdown block. The phone company calls this device the "distribution frame." It looks somewhat like a bunch of combs that have been glued teeth up with wires attached to contacts on each side. The phone company installs its lines on one side of the block, and your lines are connected to the other side. The distribution frame will be located in some out-of-the-way place, commonly referred to as the wiring closet.

NETWORK INTERFACE

Types of Network Interfaces

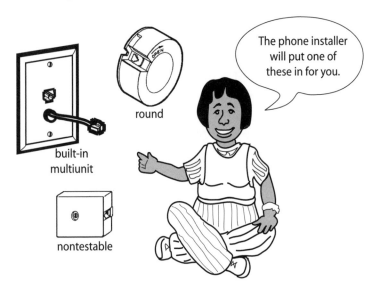

All new telephone wiring installed after January 1987 includes a network interface. This device, essentially a modular telephone jack, is used to help determine whether the source of a given problem exists in your inside wiring or in the outside wiring somewhere in telephone-company land. There is an interface jack for each installed line. Locating this jack is well worth your time because you can use it to troubleshoot your telephone system and save the expense of unnecessary service calls.

Perhaps the easiest way to think about a network interface is to compare it to one of the circuit breakers in your main electrical panel. If you shut off a circuit breaker, electricity to the circuit is shut off. Likewise, if you remove the modular phone plug from a network interface jack, telephone service is shut off on that line. To turn electrical power back on, you just switch the circuit breaker to the "on" position. To restore phone service to a line, you simply insert the modular plug back into the network interface jack.

Unfortunately, not all network interface devices look alike. Some are round plastic boxes, others are oblong boxes, while still others look exactly like the modular phone plugs you probably have along your walls or baseboards. If you have a small office with only one modular jack, it's possible that the jack your phone is plugged into *is* the network interface jack.

2-Line Network Interface (outdoor type)

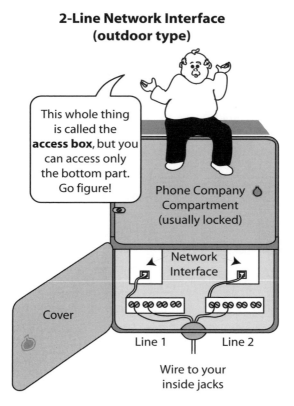

This whole thing is called the **access box**, but you can access only the bottom part. Go figure!

Phone Company Compartment (usually locked)

Network Interface

Cover

Line 1   Line 2

Wire to your inside jacks

If you have more than one line, the network interface jacks will reside in an access box, often shaped like a cigar box and made of gray plastic with a hinged cover. The phone company's lines, some testing circuitry, and a ground wire are located in one compartment, which is sealed by the phone company after installation. The portion of the box that you can access contains your telephone wires (attached to terminals) plus your interface jacks. The wires attach to the interface jack by a very short run of telephone cord, which, in turn, is attached to a modular plug.

The access box is often secured with just a screw. To avoid worrying about vandalism, wiretapping, or pirated long-distance calls billed to you, it's a good idea to install a lock on this box.

Now that you've found the network interface, what can you do with it?

- **Troubleshoot**

  If you are experiencing trouble with your phone service, you can disconnect your service by removing the modular phone plug from the network interface jack. Plug a phone (one that you know works!) into the network interface jack. If the phone still operates, the problem likely resides somewhere in your system. If the phone does not work, the problem is likely caused by something on the telephone company side, and you should contact the telephone repair folks.

- **Prevent shocks**

  If you work on your own telephone wires, you can unplug your network interface and thus avoid all possibility of electric shock. As I mentioned earlier, this is similar to turning off the circuit breaker before beginning to work on an electrical wire.

WIRING PLANS

From the access box, the lines may run inside the walls, along baseboards, under the carpet, in the attic, or through the basement to the individual wall jacks where you plug in equipment. Most homes or small offices utilize one of two wiring plans:

- Series wiring
- Star wiring

Series wiring

In the U.S., most homes and about half the small offices use series wiring. In this wiring plan, the wires run from phone jack to phone jack. If you add a jack to the series, it is wired in line, usually at the end of the line.

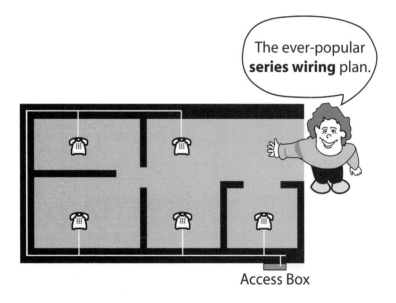

The ever-popular **series wiring** plan.

Access Box

This method saves on wire and installation time, but it has a major drawback—no flexibility. Because all jacks are wired the same, adding a line requires you to rewire everywhere. Also, if a single jack fails, the entire phone system may fail.

For example, if you have five phone jacks and the second jack in the series failed, all phone service from the second jack on would be out. This kind of wiring is akin to those cheap strings of Christmas tree lights that force you to remove each tiny bulb in succession to find the faulty one. Until you find the bad bulb, the entire string is dead. Do you want to do that with your phone service?

Star wiring

Although star wiring uses more wire, it is the preferable wiring solution. Also known as home run or parallel wiring, star wiring runs a separate wire (or wires) from each phone jack back to the access box. Thus, you have the flexibility to route your phone service in a variety of ways.

For example, you might have two lines to your office phones, a separate line to the reception area, and a dedicated line to your copier room for your fax machine. Another advantage of star wiring is that if one jack fails, the remainder of your phones will still operate.

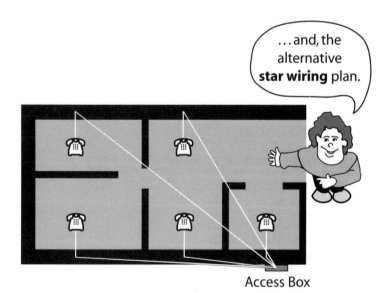

…and, the alternative **star wiring** plan.

Access Box

If you have many lines or you wish to install a telephone system, such as a key system or a private branch exchange (PBX), you should choose star wiring. Additionally, if your building is already wired serially, any new wiring should utilize star wiring to help avoid problems down the road.

PHONE WIRES

Wiring for the majority of households and small offices is composed of twisted-pair wire. If you look at a cross section of a telephone wire, you will find not two, but four copper wires, each wrapped in a protective plastic sheath. A different color sheath—red, green, yellow, or black—is used for each wire. This standardized color-coding makes it easy to rewire or troubleshoot telephone lines.

A telephone needs only two wires to operate, yet almost every set of wires in American office buildings and homes has four wires. Typically, if there is only one phone line, the wires used are the red and green set. What are the other two for? In the past, they were used to supply electrical power to phones that had lighted dials or intercoms. Nowadays, they are simply extra capacity. This is a bonus for you, because it means you can install a second line to your home or office with no new wiring. Just connect the yellow and black wires, order a new line from your phone company, and plug in a two-line phone. Voila! You're in business!

TYPES OF TELEPHONE WIRE

Extension wire
Often called satin wire, this is the line used to connect a modular telephone device to the wall outlet. If you cut this wire, you would see that the color-coded wires inside are aligned side by side. Extension wire is flat, often a silver color, and you can purchase it in reels to make your own custom connections. You can also buy ready-made extensions of various lengths.

Cable wire

This is the line used to run telephone service throughout the inside of your building. It is round, thicker than satin wire, and usually gray. Often called twisted-pair cable, this cable has the same color-coded wires inside, but they are twisted around each other to help minimize interference. This wire is also purchased in reels. If you hire a professional installer to do your wiring, she will use either category 3 cable or category 5 cable.

Category 3 cable is used for standard voice-quality telephone wiring. It may also be used for voice communications and/or Ethernet.

Category 5 cable is a higher-quality telephone wiring that is used for networking or high-speed data needs. It can support high-speed digital circuits up to 100 megahertz.

NUMBER OF WIRES (PAIR)

Today's homes and small- to medium-sized offices normally use 2-pair, 3-pair, or 4-pair wiring.

- **2-pair**—The most common type of wiring found in homes today is 2-pair, and it is used to install up to two lines. If the insulation was stripped off, you'd find four wires inside.

- **3-pair**—Three-pair wire adds two more wires to the cable, thus increasing its capacity to three lines. If you stripped the insulation off this cable, you'd find six wires inside.

- **4-pair**—Similarly, 4-pair wire increases the cable's capacity to four lines. There are eight wires inside this cable.

USE THE RIGHT WIRE FOR THE RIGHT JOB

Some people might be tempted to use flat satin extension wire to replace round phone cable for interior wiring. It is slightly less expensive and works about the same, but is it okay to use?

No! Don't fall into this trap. Phone cable costs more for a reason—it's a heavy-duty wire designed to stand up to years of use, and it is better for transmitting signals over long distances.

Mice and rats love to nibble on insulated wire. A thicker insulation minimizes your chances of having a connection severed by a mouse attack. More importantly, phone cable has twisted wires, which greatly reduces the possibility of line interference or cross talk (a faint conversation heard in the background). Though you can use flat, untwisted wire for short runs between your wall plug and your telephone connection, it is not suitable for longer runs.

Unfortunately, since the deregulation of the telecom industry, the use of non-twisted wire has become increasingly common, especially in prewired new construction. The results can have serious consequences for your business: garbled fax and modem transmissions, security leaks through overheard conversations, and disjointed communications caused by line pops and snaps.

Leaky wires equal lost business

Here's a story that illustrates my point. A decorator lost a prospective customer when her caller, on hold on one line, overheard her discussing wholesale prices with a vendor on a second line. When the decorator came back to her prospect quoting a considerably marked-up price, the caller was livid and told her off in no uncertain terms. The culprit in all this? Cross talk leaking through the cheap wiring.

Fortunately for us, phone system designers have made their wiring systems downwardly compatible. This means you can take advantage of higher-capacity wire and not lose service even if your equipment uses fewer pairs of conductors. For example, you can operate a two-line phone with 3-pair wire, or you can have 4-pair wiring with just one-line service.

SAVE MONEY—INSTALL EXTRA CAPACITY

If you're rewiring your office or wiring it for the first time, use a high-capacity wire. Though you may need only two lines right now, it costs you just a few dollars more to wire with 4-pair wire instead of 2-pair wire.

ALWAYS PLAN FOR MORE THAN YOU NEED

Consider the following scenario. You wired your office for two lines using 2-pair wiring, and you installed four phone jacks—one for your voice line, one for your answering machine, one for your fax machine, and one for the back of the shop. In the San Francisco Bay area, materials are quite cheap, but labor is costly. It costs about $175 to add a cable run to your office and install a new phone jack, so the total cost for wiring two lines and four jacks was in the $700 range. If you had decided to wire for four lines and four jacks, the extra expense for the higher-capacity cable and connectors would have been around $20.

Two years later, you find that you need to add more lines because business is great and you have hired three new associates. By using splitters and switches, you might be able to get by with the same number of phone jacks, but you find your line capacity is still too small. Unfortunately, you now need to replace all the interior cable with 3-pair or 4-pair wire. By "saving" $20 two years ago, you're out another $700.

Four-pair wiring gives you great flexibility. You could, for example, use two lines now for voice and reserve two for future computer networking. Both Ethernet and token ring networks can run on phone lines and require 2-pair wire. Or you could have two voice lines and one dedicated line for fax and modem use. The last line could be kept as a spare, and when you are ready to grow, you just call your phone company. They hook up your service, give you a new number or two, and you're in business. It's that simple.

TYPES OF CONNECTIONS

You'll most likely have one of the following types of phone connectors:

- Modular
- Hard-wired
- Four-prong

MODULAR CONNECTION

Modern telephone equipment uses a snap-together system of plugs and jacks that enable you to connect and disconnect your devices with the telephone wiring. These connectors make it extremely easy to install or move equipment. All you do is press down on the plastic locking lever and insert the plug into the jack until you hear it click in place. That's it—you're connected. To disconnect a device, simply press down on the plastic locking lever and gently pull the plug out of the jack.

Modular Plug and Jacks

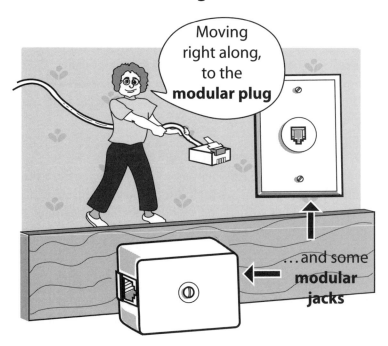

Moving right along, to the **modular plug**

...and some **modular jacks**

HARD-WIRED CONNECTION

This type of connection permanently wires your phone instrument to a wall plug known as the connecting block. To connect another device, you will need to cut the wire and either hardwire the new device or replace the connecting block with a modular jack. If you have this kind of equipment, learn how to replace the connections with modular connections or have someone do it for you.

To replace older permanently wired jacks, you can purchase modular jack kits for about $3. Your local hardware store, electronics store, or telephone specialty shop will have all the equipment necessary for you to perform this task. The flexibility you gain is well worth the effort and minimal cost, especially if you do it yourself.

FOUR-PRONG CONNECTION

Four-prong (or 4-pin) connectors were the first interchangeable telephone connectors. Each plug consists of four long pins set in a particular pattern. To plug the phone in correctly, you align the plug with a four-prong jack. Because this type of connector is quite bulky, it has been largely replaced by the tiny plastic modular connectors you find on today's modems, phones, computers, answering machines, and the like. However, inexpensive adapters are available that convert the older four-prong connection to a modular connection.

NOT ALL MODULAR CONNECTORS ARE EQUAL

Modular plugs and jacks may look alike, and they are interchangeable. Still, there are slight but important differences between them. These differences will dictate how many lines you can connect through one cord.

Plugs

To determine how many lines your connector will support, look through the plastic plug, count the number of colored wires you see, then divide by two. Two wires equals one line; four wires equals two lines; six wires equals three lines.

For our purposes, we'll pay attention to three types of plugs:

- **1-line**—Standard single-line phones, modems, answering machines, and other accessories use the 1-line plug. It has two colored wires, and the phone company calls this connector an RJ-11 plug.

- **2-line**—A 2-line plug supplies phone service for one or two lines. It looks exactly like the 1-line except that you see four colored wires inside the plug. The phone company calls this connector an RJ-14 plug.

- **3-line**—To supply phone service for one to three lines, the 3-line plug is used. It looks similar to the 1- and 2-line plugs, but the cord is wider and it has six colored wires. The phone company calls this connector an RJ-25 plug.

Jacks

When you peer inside a jack, you'll see anywhere from two to eight gold stripes, called pins or contacts. These contacts indicate the potential number of lines this jack can accommodate. To determine how many lines are actually connected at this jack, you'll have to look at a wiring blueprint of your office or take the cover off the jack and count how many wires are connected.

Jacks and plugs must match

The contacts inside the plug must align exactly with the contacts inside the jack. Otherwise, not all your phone service will be able to get through. For example, if you have two phone lines and you use a 1-line plug to attach a two-line telephone to your wall plug, only line one will work. This is because the 1-line plug has only two contacts and is wired for one-line service. While another plug may appear to fit into the outlet, it must have the proper number of contacts aligned the way your system needs them. If not, your service either won't work or won't work to capacity.

MAXIMIZING YOUR CURRENT SETUP

SPLITTER

Would you like to add a phone accessory, such as a caller ID display or an answering machine, at the same location as your voice phone? But you don't have a spare phone jack available? Just use a splitter to convert a single outlet to a multiple outlet. Plug this inexpensive device into your phone outlet; then plug two cords into it—one for your phone, the other for your accessory. Splitters come in two-, three-, and even five-plug combinations, and the price starts at around $3. These devices are known by many names: splitter, outlet coupler, two-and three-way jack, outlet modular adapter, and so on. You get the idea.

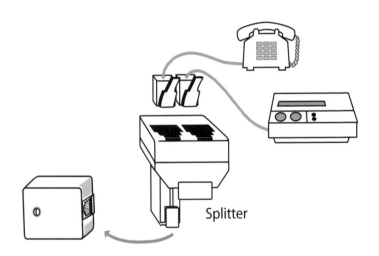

Splitter

WIRELESS PHONE JACK

Do you need a jack somewhere else, but can't have or don't want to have a permanent installation? A wireless phone jack system allows you to plug a jack into any electrical outlet. These systems come with a base unit that plugs into a working phone jack and an extension jack that plugs into an electrical outlet. To use your phone, you just plug it into the extension jack.

When you want to move the jack, simply unplug it. You can find these systems at specialty phone stores or telecom Web sites. Two that I've seen advertised are InstaJack and Wireless Phone Jack. Prices run about $80 for a base unit and one extension jack, plus another $50 for each additional extension. Although these jacks aren't cheap, they sure are easy to set up.

LINE SHARING

Do you have only one phone line to share among your fax machine, answering machine, and telephone? Wouldn't it be great if your line could recognize what kind of call was coming in and route it to the appropriate device? You can now purchase an automatic line-sharing switch that will correctly route voice calls to your phone (or answering machine when on) and make sure those screechy modem tones are heard only by your fax machine.

Loads of companies make line-sharing switches, and they come with different features. Some can work with distinctive ring, a telephone company service that allows up to four different phone numbers to ring on one line (see Chapter 3). Others can specify which phone number should ring at each jack, while still others can distinguish between modem and fax calls.

An inexpensive solution is a manual switch—all you do is turn a knob to switch between two devices on the same single line. Numerous companies make line switches. Check out these handy catalogs for a range of line switches:

- Hello Direct
  www.hellodirect.com
  800-444-3556

- Radio Shack
  www.radioshack.com
  800-843-7422

TROUBLESHOOTING

To troubleshoot a telephone problem, use the process of elimi-nation. Ask yourself these questions:

- ▸▸ When did this begin to happen?
- ▸▸ Have I installed any new equipment?
- ▸▸ Can I receive calls OK, but can't dial out?
- ▸▸ Can I dial out OK, but can't receive calls?
- ▸▸ Has anyone been working elsewhere inside or outside the building? (It's not unusual for phone lines to be acciden-tally cut by electricians, plumbers, street workers, etc.)
- ▸▸ Could weather be affecting service?
- ▸▸ Check the simplest things first:
    - Is the device plugged in?
    - Is the ringer turned down or off?

PAY ATTENTION TO SAFETY

Telephones are electrical devices. Phones always carry low-volt-age electrical current on them, and it is enough to give you a mild shock. High-voltage current is generated when the phone rings. If you're touching a live wire when the device rings, you can get a sizable shock (105 volts). To avoid such hazards, fol-low these simple safety rules when working on telephone equip-ment.

- If you wear a pacemaker, you should avoid all contact with live telephone wires.

- Do not work on active telephone lines while standing in water.

- Do not work where there is a risk of dropping a telephone instrument or wire into water.

- Avoid working during thunderstorms.

- Use shielded tools.

- Unplug your service at the network interface jack or take the telephone off the hook before working on telephone wires. Doing so will "busy-out" your phone line, and you'll avoid the possibility of a dangerous shock should the phone ring.

A FEW COMMON PROBLEMS

Other phones or devices using this telephone line work, but this phone doesn't work

Take the suspect phone and try it out in a working jack. If it works, great! You can assume that the jack at the previous location is bad. If the phone still doesn't work, you now know that there is something wrong either with the phone itself or with the line cord.

Nothing works on your line

If you know where your network interface is, unplug the network interface jack. Then plug a telephone that you know is working into the network interface jack. If you hear dial tone and can dial out, the problem is on your side. If the line is dead, call the phone company repair guys—the problem is on their side.

Shared phone line—one faulty piece of equipment

If you have more than one device on your telephone line (modem, fax, fax/modem, phone, etc.), an electrical short in one device could trip up your entire system. Unplug all the phones and accessories on your line. One by one, replace each device and see if you can get dial tone. Continue until you experience failure—that device is the culprit.

A couple of years ago, I experienced a shorted-out line. At the time, I had four extension telephones on one voice line, and a fax machine shared line two with my computer modem. One day, when I was expecting several calls, I noticed that line one wasn't ringing. When I picked up the line to check for messages, I was surprised to find that my phone company voice mail had several messages waiting for me. This was strange because I hadn't left the office all day, and I hadn't been on the line. So, I called my voice line from my fax line, and guess what? No rings on the line at home, but after four rings, the voice mail picked up.

I called the phone company, but there were no problems reported at its end. The service rep suggested that some of my equipment might be shorting out the line, so I checked each phone in turn. Sure enough, I found that whenever I plugged in a particular cheapo phone, I'd lose all ability to receive calls. Once I unplugged that phone, service was fine. Needless to say, I banished that phone in a hurry.

Of course, you still won't know if the problem resides with the line cord or the phone or the accessory itself. However, if you have a spare working line cord, you can test this out too. Or, you can take the phone, accessory, and line cord to your local telephone accessory store. Many stores offer free testing service for phones and line cords, and it only takes a few minutes.

No ring or soft ring

Sometimes you may not hear your phone ring, or the ring may be very soft. If you've checked that the ringer is turned on, the problem may be that you have too many devices on the line. Your local phone company guarantees you enough power on the phone line to ring the equivalent of five standard telephones. If your phone line has a lot of extensions or other equipment that rings (such as answering or fax machines), you may have maxed out the ringer electronics. To fix this situation, turn off the ringer on one or more devices and see if ringing is restored.

Intermittent problem—sometimes line two doesn't work

This is a rather unusual problem, but it can happen if you have two lines and are using a Princess or Trimline phone. These are the symptoms: When you pick up the telephone, you can make calls normally, but while the Princess or Trimline phone is off the hook, line two acts dead. You can't dial out on it, you can't receive calls, and if someone calls you on the second line, they get a busy signal.

The problem is that Princess and Trimline phones use the wires for your second phone line to light up the phone dial. When you use the phone, all four wires are used. What can you do about it? Replace the old-style phone, use a 2-pair instead of a 4-pair line cord to attach the phone to the wall jack, or convert the phone's wiring to standard 2-pair.

Do-It-Yourself Wiring

Running telephone wire is quite simple. In most systems, you'll find four wires (called a twisted pair) coming to each phone jack, but only two wires are needed for each telephone line. Because phone wires are color coded, it's hard to make a mistake. Be sure to follow safety instructions, however, and use the correct wires, plugs, and adapters for the job.

If you want to do it yourself, you'll find loads of help at your library. I'll mention a few useful resources on the next couple of pages.

RESOURCES

Books
All Thumbs Guide to Telephones and Answering Machines
by Gene B. Williams
Tab Books, a Division of McGraw Hill, Inc., 1994
Blue Ridge Summit, PA 17294-0850

Full of illustrations and refreshingly brief, this guide covers safety, the basic tools you'll need, and basic troubleshooting for telephone wiring, telephones, cordless phones, and answering machines.

Do Your Own Wiring
by K. E. Armpriester
Popular Science
Sterling Publishing Company
387 Park Ave. S.
New York, NY 10016

This publication features an excellent chapter on telephone wiring in an easy-to-follow visual format.

Installing Telephones
by Gerald Luecke & James B. Allen
Radio Shack
Master Publishing, Inc., 1992
14 Canyon Creek Village MS 31
Richardson, TX 75080

This useful booklet contains clear and well-illustrated instructions for making quick modular telephone replacements, adding or changing telephones, running cables, and installing single and multiline telephones.

Installing Your Telephone (video)
Radio Shack, 1994
(same address as above)

The following topics are covered in this half-hour video: modular connections, converting older wiring systems, adding a new outlet, installing round jacks, installing jacks near electrical outlets, running telephone wire, installing wall telephones, and troubleshooting.

Chapter

3

Phone Services

$\bullet \quad \bullet$

DURING THE LAST DECADE, the number and variety of phone services has increased dramatically. You can now discover who's calling (caller ID), have several phone numbers ring on the same line (distinctive ringing), or program your phone to locate you anywhere (follow-me service). Last call return is a service that lets you dial back the person who just called and hung up (though you don't have a clue who it was), and a special ring pattern that lets you know your best customer is calling can be set up via priority ringing.

Perhaps the last time you paid any attention to phone company services was when you initially ordered phone lines for your home, office, or business. You may have signed up for hunting or call waiting—maybe even voice mail. Unless you knew what to ask for, it's unlikely that your sales rep discussed most of the services available. The purpose of this chapter is to explain these services and give you some idea how you might use them in your business.

HOW PHONE SERVICES WORK

Telephone services are mostly computer driven. Because your calls go through a computer switch in the telephone company's central office, it's relatively simple to add services, such as voice mail or caller ID, to your line. The call-handling services supplied to that line are stored on the central office computer.

Most of these central office switches are now fully digital, meaning that telephone conversations are converted into digital form before being passed through the switch. At a later point, they are reconverted to analog and sent on to you.

Digital technology allows local phone companies to process calls faster. It also offers equal access to competing long-distance carriers, and stores more information about each phone line than was previously possible (such as the call handling features supplied to that line). Additions, deletions, and changes to your phone service can be accomplished by changing a few characters in a line of software code. Also, because features are often software controlled, they are much easier to set up and deliver.

Some phone services require extra equipment to take advantage of a particular feature (such as caller ID), but most are designed for use with a standard phone using the Touch-Tone keypad. Many features can be turned on or off by dialing a feature code, usually an asterisk followed by a one- or two-digit number. Rotary phone users prefix their codes with an 11 instead of the asterisk. Many codes require a hookflash. Depending on the type of telephone set you have, you perform a hookflash either by pressing and releasing the receiver button (or switch hook) that sits under the handset or by pressing a flash button.

The codes that activate these special features are not the same throughout the United States. For example, in most parts of the country, pressing hookflash puts your caller on hold and lets you answer a call waiting. However, in parts of New England, you must dial *9 to do the same thing.

You pay for phone services monthly. Often, you'll receive a discounted monthly service fee if you buy more than one service or feature. Or, if you order the services when you initially set up a new phone line, the installation fee may be waived. Removing services down the road does not usually incur a disconnect fee. However, there will most likely be a fee for adding services later.

Of course, these features work on your landlines only. For cellular services, you'll need to check with your wireless vendor to see what is available over the air.

MY FAVORITE PHONE SERVICES

There are loads of phone services to choose from. I'm going to talk about my favorite ones first.

DISTINCTIVE RINGING

This service allows you to assign multiple phone numbers to the same line. Each phone number rings with a different cadence, so you can tell what type of call is ringing in—a business call responding to your radio ad, an urgent personal call (on your special number for emergencies), or a fax transmission. You can then print your fax number, voice number, and emergency number right on your business card. Only you know that they all ring on the same line.

Across the country, this service takes many names, including RingMate, IdentaRing, Ring Master, Personalized Ring, Custom Ringing, Route-a-Call, Teen Service, Multi-Line, and Smart Ring. You pay a monthly fee per number that ranges from $4 to $7 per number. That's a lot less than what you'd pay for a separate line for each number.

If you want to use this service and hang various devices on the line (such as phone, answering machine, fax modem, etc.), you'll need a switch with distinctive ringing capability. This switch plugs directly into the phone line and features several modular jacks for you to plug your devices into. When a call comes in, the switch "listens" to the ring pattern and connects the call to the correct device. Some answering machines and voice mail devices also support distinctive ringing. You can find these switches at any telephone/electronics store or through a telephone supply catalog. Incidentally, if you have call waiting, it will also ring a corresponding distinctive tone (two, three, or four beeps) when a call comes in for the associated number.

A note of caution: If you plan to order this service, you must be very specific with your phone company. Be sure to ask your service rep to explain how it works. Because this service has such a wide variety of names, you may find that your local phone service offers distinctive ringing, but it is not the service we have just discussed. Some telephone companies sell a distinctive ringing service that rings a special cadence, but it is limited to a list of ten special callers that you program into your phone.

CALLER ID SERVICES

Caller ID allows you to see the phone number of an incoming call before you answer the phone. For an extra fee, you can also see the caller's name. Caller ID is usually a combination of two features: calling number delivery and calling name delivery. Calling number delivery displays the 10-digit telephone number of an incoming call, while calling name delivery displays the name (as listed in the directory) associated with the incoming call. Both services display the date and time—this is particularly convenient if you are automatically logging calls. Depending on the provider, the cost of service ranges between $4 and $7.50 per month.

Caller ID is useful for call screening, especially if you link it to an answering machine or voice mail. Then you can minimize interruptions, monitor calls discreetly, and decide which calls to take now and which to return later. Software vendors have developed caller ID applications that feature "screen pops," where a customer's record is automatically retrieved from a company's database and displayed on screen as the call comes in. Information, such as address, order history, and terms, are instantly available to the customer service rep, allowing him to be fully prepared to handle the caller's needs.

Several software vendors sell caller ID products. Some work with contact management software; others let you set up a separate database. Some possibilities:

- Call Editor
  VIVE Synergies (www.vive.com or 905-882-6107). This product works with contact management software such as Symantec's Act!

- Sidekick (Windows and Mac versions)
  Starfish Software (www.starfish.com or 800-765-7839). This well-known personal organizer program now comes with caller ID capabilities. It requires a caller ID interface device.

False delivery orders are stopped cold by caller ID. Delicatessens, pizza parlors, taxicab companies, and the like can verify that the phone number the caller provides actually matches the number displayed. Domino's Pizza reports that caller ID has helped it reduce the amount of bad orders by more than 90 percent.

> ### Fewer robberies
> Mickey Schiavone, manager of Victory Taxi in New Brunswick, said that cab robberies fell more than 80 percent since his company started using caller ID. "It also helps in understanding people who speak another language when they give an address," Schiavone explained. (*Asbury Park Press*, New Jersey Take-Out Services Rely on Caller-ID to Screen Prank Orders, 1/26/95)

To take advantage of caller ID, you need to sign up for the service and install a caller ID translator. This could be a phone with caller ID display capabilities, a separate caller ID device, or a telecommunications board installed in your computer with caller ID software. Prices for phones equipped with caller ID range from $75 to $175. If you don't need a new phone or don't want to pay those prices, you can order an external caller ID display unit from Northern Telecom (800-667-8437) or Hello Direct (800-444-3556).

Caller ID information will display only if the information is available. If the call comes from an area that does not support caller ID, the display will show "OUT OF AREA." When a caller has blocked caller ID by using a privacy code (such as *67), you'll see "PRIVATE." Also, if the call is coming from someone at a PBX, the number displayed will be the customer's main billing number and not the actual telephone number of the person calling.

Note: Caller ID information is delivered between the first and second ring. This means that if you pick up too quickly, you won't get the information. Wait until after the second ring to answer.

The issue of caller ID has long been enveloped in controversy. Oddly enough, both sides cite privacy as one of their principal arguments. Opponents maintain that caller ID takes away their right to make an anonymous call or to remain unlisted. They also say it gives telemarketers and computer databases too much information about them. Proponents include people who want to use caller ID as a call-screening device, as well as businesses that see the advantage of knowing who's calling. To help resolve the issue, the FCC has mandated that caller ID blocking can be enabled prior to any phone call by pressing *67 before dialing out.

FORWARDING CALLS

Call forwarding features allow you to forward (or transfer) your incoming calls to any number you choose—even your cellular phone. Instead of your regular number, all calls ring at the forwarding number you have designated. Use this service to forward calls from your office to home, or vice versa; send calls to a second line; or, forward your fax calls to a fax modem while you're on the road.

When call forwarding is activated, you can still make outgoing calls, but all your incoming calls are immediately forwarded to the number you have programmed. Often, a reminder ring, which sounds like half of a normal ring, will signal you that a call is coming in and is being forwarded. Callers won't get a busy signal when you are on the line, but they will receive a busy tone if the forwarding number is busy.

Call forwarding is available in three main flavors:

- **Forward calls to another line**
  You program your number to automatically transfer all incoming calls to another number.

- **Forward on busy**
  Your calls are forwarded when you're on the line.

- **Forward on delay**
  Your calls are forwarded if you don't answer after a predesignated number of rings. In this case, you have a chance to answer the telephone first.

Note: In most areas, you can program call forwarding remotely by dialing an access code and personal identification number (PIN)—a very handy feature if you're on the road a lot.

If you're absent-minded, call forwarding can be inconvenient. Because you may forget that you've forwarded your calls, they continue to ring at the wrong site until someone notices and cancels the call forwarding instruction. There are some smart phone systems available, however, that have a reminder line or message to alert you that calls have been forwarded.

When calls are forwarded, you pay normal usage charges plus your monthly service charge. Usage charges are based on the distance from your central office to the forwarding number.

TOLL-FREE SERVICE

Providing your callers with a toll-free number encourages incoming business and conveys a professional image. According to Jeffrey Kagan, author of *Winning Communications Strategies*, 86 percent of customers believe that an 800 number connotes high-quality products or services. "No small business should be without an 800 number," he advises. When you see several ads for the same product or service, don't you call the 800 numbers first? I know I do.

By utilizing a prefix, area code, state or, in some cases, nation, your 800 number can be customized to receive calls from a particular area. It's easy to adjust the size of this area whenever you want, which is useful for target marketing and seasonal campaigns. The toll-free number can be programmed to ring in on your current number, commonly referred to as "piggybacking." No on-site installation is required. If you expect a high volume of calls, you can set up a separate line just for toll-free calls.

Some entrepreneurs provide their toll-free number to a select group of customers for premium service. Others print it on their business stationery and display it on every ad.

You can program your toll-free number to route calls to a different location. For example, you could send your calls to your business location during office hours and to voice mail (or your home) after hours. You could even have different routing schemes for different days of the week. When a caller calls an 800 or 888 number, the computer at the central office switch looks up the actual number that is associated with the toll-free number and forwards the call.

Some organizations set up an emergency routing scheme for their toll-free number (which they hope they'll never use). In the event of a natural disaster or other catastrophe that prevents employees from getting to work, you call your phone company and ask that the alternate routing plan be used. This could, for example, send all your calls to a voice announcement service, voice mail, or an alternate location. The alternate scheme stays in memory until invoked.

You can combine toll-free service with distinctive ringing. Depending on the ring, you'll know whether you're paying for the call or they are.

A side benefit of toll-free service is that you are listed in the toll-free database. Customers may locate you by calling 800-555-1212. Many long-distance carriers publish toll-free directories in several different versions, such as international, Spanish language, consumer, business-to-business, and so on. If your number is for private or restricted use, ask for an unlisted number.

During a brief scan of AT&T's toll-free directory, I located a supplier of Amish quilts, a handwriting analysis service, a referral service for black-owned businesses, a 24-hour crab cake delivery hotline, a dial-a-lawyer advice line, a home-for-sale locator service, a network of therapists, and—you get the picture.

Toll-free service costs vary considerably, and rates also vary according to the area covered by your 800 number. Some vendors charge a monthly fee; others do not. Many services come with other attractive options, such as voice mail, fax-on-demand, and follow-you-everywhere service.

In some cases, you can get the best deal from a reseller. A reseller is a long-distance company that does not have its own transmission lines. It buys lines from long-distance carriers at a discount, and then resells them to its customers. Be sure to shop around.

FOLLOW-ME PHONE SERVICE

Portable one-number phone service (sometimes called 500 service) that follows you everywhere is especially useful for road warriors. Your calls can be forwarded to any number that you can directly dial, including cellular phones, fax machines, pagers, and voice mail.

One service, AT&T's True Ties, lets you set up a schedule for call forwarding. For example, you might forward calls to your cellular phone between 8:00 and 9:00 A.M.; to your office from 9:00 to 5:00 P.M.; to your home phone from 6:00 to 10:00 P.M.; and to voice mail after 10 P.M.

<u>On-the-go service</u>
Ron Kopp, a management consultant, is always traveling. His follow-me service has the ability to program three numbers that are tried serially. If there is no answer at any of the numbers specified, his calls are forwarded to his home answering machine. While the phone service is tracking Ron down, his callers hear: "Please stand by, we are trying your party at another location."

Some carriers are offering follow-me services as an 800-service option. For example, MCI offers a service that links all your messaging services—standard telephone, cellular service, fax, voice mail, and paging—to a single 800 number. You can program a desired routing plan for incoming calls using up to three different numbers that will be tried in order. At each stage in the sequence, an automated voice prompt advises callers that the system is still trying to locate you. If your call is a fax, the system recognizes the fax tones and directs the call to a fax mailbox for storage and later retrieval.

You can also arrange with your local telephone company or cellular vendor for follow-me service. It's marketed under a variety of names, including ContactLine, ProLink, New Vector, Total Number, MyLine, and Personal Number.

A PHONE SERVICE SAMPLER

Your local phone company may not offer all the services and features listed here. Some of the more advanced features require digital switches or expensive software upgrades and may not be implemented throughout your region. Those of you residing in urban areas will probably get the newer stuff first. Monthly costs for these services range from $2.50 to $7 per service. Check with your local phone company for the exact price in your area.

Anonymous call rejection

This service works in conjunction with caller ID. It allows you to automatically reject all calls from callers who have activated caller ID blocking. Your caller receives a recorded message advising that blocked calls are not accepted. Some residential subscribers like this service, but it is not too handy for the normal business.

Block call

Depending on your area, this service (1) prevents certain types of outgoing calls, such as toll calls (you can override blocking by dialing a personal code), or (2) allows you to program a list of numbers that will be blocked from ringing on your phone line. See *Call screening*.

Call curfew

This service blocks all calls, both incoming and outgoing, during late night and very early morning hours. It's perfect for parents who want to control their teenager's phone use. You can program a preset schedule or change the schedule according to your needs.

Call on my dime

You can give your preferred customers and business associates a personal four-digit number that allows them to call whenever or wherever they like, and the charge is billed to you. Bell Canada's Call-Me service works in this way. Callers dial zero, then simply key in the four-digit code. Easy!

Call pickup

By dialing the call pickup access code for a particular phone, you can answer a call on that line from another location. This feature is useful if you have a plain telephone set with no special buttons. You can answer calls for coworkers without getting up from your desk and walking over to their phones to pick up.

Call screening

This service is not very useful for most businesses, but some residential customers, home-based businesses, and non-profits use it to get rid of crank callers. In short, you program a list of phone numbers that you absolutely never want to ring on your line again. Screened callers hear a polite message telling them you're not taking their calls. Period. You can also add the number that just called you; you don't have to know the number—just press a special code.

Call waiting

This feature alerts you that someone is trying to reach you when you are already on the phone. A beep tone signals that another call is coming in, and, by pressing hookflash quickly, you can put the first call on hold and speak to the incoming caller. In certain parts of the country, you must dial a short code rather than pressing hookflash. To return to the previous caller, you just hookflash or press the code again.

Some phone companies also offer "talking" call waiting. This service works the same as call waiting, except that the name of the second caller is spoken after the beep tone.

Call waiting has its fans and its foes. Though you gain the capability of handling two calls at once, many people dislike being placed on hold and are especially unwilling to continue holding during a business call. Others think call waiting is tacky and low-budget. This may not be the image you want to portray.

Fax and modem transmissions can be disrupted by call waiting signals, often causing your modem to hang up. This could be a costly problem. If you have call waiting, you should get a separate line for data equipment. At the very least, you should turn off call waiting before initiating a fax or modem call.

Call waiting can also cause problems with the busy call forwarding feature that is used to send calls to voice mail. If you have both phone company voice mail and call waiting, none of your overflow calls will reach voice mail when your line is busy. See Chapter 8 for a complete discussion of this problem and some possible solutions.

You can cancel call waiting before making an outgoing call. Usually, this is done by pressing asterisk (*) 70 before dialing the number. (Rotary phone users can dial 1170.) *Note*: This method only works for the next outgoing call. Also, it does not protect incoming calls (such as faxes) from being disrupted.

Call waiting caller ID

With this service, you can see the number of the incoming call while you're on another call. Then you can decide if you want to take the second call. Caller ID information for the incoming call is displayed at the same time that you hear the call waiting tone. Some phone companies offer additional options that let you forward the second call to voice mail, play a recording of your choice, answer the call, or include it in a three-way call.

Centrex

Your central office provides this phone system. Centrex allows you to purchase business communication features, such as call transfer and night service, as you need them. It is available for businesses with two or more lines. See Chapter 6 for a detailed description.

Complete the call

This service works in conjunction with your phone company's directory assistance service. Callers to directory assistance will hear a message offering to dial the number for them, either free of charge (as a courtesy) or for a stated fee.

Distinctive ring selective call forwarding

Working with the distinctive ringing family, this service forwards only the calls dialed. For example, you could forward faxes to a fax mailbox, business calls to your office answering machine, and personal calls to your mother-in-law's line.

Do not disturb

Now you can get work done without the constant interruption of a ringing phone. By pressing *78, you can turn this service on and off at will, or you can set up a regular schedule in advance. No calls before noon sounds great to me! Also, family members or preferred clients can dial a privileged "caller code" that lets their calls ring through anyway.

Emergency service

If you lose phone service for any reason, emergency service will automatically reroute your calls to another number. Great for disaster recovery! If you rely on your phone service for your daily bread and butter, a service like this makes sense.

Extra line just when you need it

This service lets you expand your phone service on the fly, and you are charged only when you use it. For example, you may use this line exclusively for faxes or to get an outgoing line when all your lines are full. US West offers a service called Stand-By Line, and they provide you with a monthly summary useful for analyzing your call traffic and forecasting future needs.

Hold call

Even if you don't have a hold button on your phone, you can still place a call on hold. First you press hookflash, then dial the call hold code and hang up. In this way, the call is placed on hold, and you can resume the call by picking up the handset at either the original phone or an extension.

Hunting

This service is available only on business lines. If you have more than one line, they can be programmed so that calls ring on another line if the first line is busy. The phone system "hunts" or "rolls over" to another line, but when all lines are busy, the caller hears a busy signal. Also, you're not able to hunt between residential and business lines, even if they are in the same facility. To do that, you'll need to use call forwarding features.

When designed correctly, your hunting system can be a very useful tool. However, if you add features to your line that rely on busy call forwarding technology, such as voice mail, you may get undesirable results. For example, you may have two lines that hunt in sequence. If you put voice mail on the first line, your calls will always go to voice mail when the first line is busy and not roll over to the second line.

Both the hunting feature and the busy call forwarding feature instruct the computer switch on how to handle your busy calls. Only one instruction can "win," and busy call forwarding takes precedence over hunting. If you want to combine hunting with voice mail, your telco rep can help you set up a system that works for you. Prices will vary greatly depending on your region. In some states, it's even free.

Internet call waiting
This software-defined phone service operates like call waiting while you're on the Internet. The name and number of the incoming caller appear on your computer screen. You then have the choice of answering the call, placing the call on hold, forwarding it to a preselected number, or sending the call to voice mail.

Long-distance alert
A special ring alerts you to incoming long-distance calls. This service works with call waiting and can be handy if you need to avoid missing important calls.

Make set busy
Telecommuters needing to ignore incoming calls (while trying to complete a project, for example) will find this service especially useful. Your phone is busied out without having to take it off-hook. Of course, you'll need to have an alternate means of getting messages, such as voice mail.

900 (and 976) service

These services provide a special telephone line that dispenses something people want, such as information or entertainment, for a fee. The 900 numbers are national, while 976 numbers are regional.

Priority ringing

A distinctive ring lets you know that the incoming call is one of a special list of phone numbers that you have selected. In some areas, you can have only ten numbers on this list, but other areas allow more numbers. This service is also known as priority call or call selector.

Priority ringing does not work if the person calling you is using a long-distance carrier because the long-distance call does not carry the coded number in a manner that allows the local switch to read it. Nor does priority ringing work with business lines that are part of a PBX or Centrex system. This is because the number sent to the central office computer is the company's main number—not the number of the extension dialing out.

Repeat dialing

By dialing a code, this service will redial the last busy number you called and keep trying (for up to 30 minutes) until the line is free. When the line is free, your phone will announce the call with a distinctive ring.

Repeat dialing won't tie up your line in the same way as a redialer on your phone does. You can still make and receive calls. When the system detects that the desired party's line is clear, your phone will ring you. This service is also known as continuous redial. *Note*: Repeat dialing will not work if you use a carrier other than your local phone company (such as a long-distance carrier) to place the call.

Return call

Even though you don't know the number, return call service will automatically call back the last number that called you. If the line you're dialing is free, your call will be completed. If busy, this service will check the line for you for up to 30 minutes. When the line is free, you are alerted by a distinctive ring—a nice time saver. Missed calls can easily be returned. This function is also called call cue, call return, and last call return.

Note: Return call does not work in all situations, particularly if the call was not local or if the caller was using a PBX or Centrex phone system.

Select call forwarding

A list of phone numbers that you have selected is forwarded to an alternate number until you choose to restore the line to normal operation. You program the list yourself, and you can update it whenever you want. The calling party is not aware that the call is being forwarded, so select call forwarding can be used for screening calls. This service is also called preferred call forwarding.

Selective call acceptance

You can specify a list of up to 32 phone numbers from which calls will be accepted. When you activate this feature, all other callers hear a polite announcement telling them that you're not accepting their calls. By the way, the operator can always ring through in case of an emergency.

Speed dialing

This feature permits you to program a list of phone numbers that you can be dialed using a one- or two-digit code. Some phone companies allow six numbers only, while others offer 8, 30, or 50 numbers. To use, simply press the code. Frankly, speed calling provided by the phone company is rarely cost effective. If you want speedy dialing, purchase a phone with this feature or, better yet, an autodialer program for your PC.

Three-way calling

Three phone lines—two lines plus your own—can be linked together via this service. For example, your secretary could use three-way calling to send your calls to your home when you're working on a project there. Your office would be billed for the forwarding charges to connect the caller to your home phone.

How it works: Dial the number of the first party you wish to link, tell them what you're up to, then press hookflash quickly. This puts the first party on hold and gives you a second dial tone. Dial the second number, tell them that you're going to connect the first party into the conversation, and press hookflash again. Now you are all linked together.

You can also use three-way calling to make a second call while placing your first caller on hold. In effect, it's as though you had an extra outgoing line.

Transfer call
This feature gives you the ability to transfer a call from your phone to another phone. With this service, there's no need to ask the caller to hang up so that you can dial the other number.

Voice dialing
You can program your own personal telephone directory by saying a name in any language and keying in the corresponding phone number. Henceforth, you just pick up the phone, say the name ("broker" or "mom"), and the call is automatically dialed. No special equipment is needed. This service works with both rotary and Touch-Tone phones.

INTERNET CALLING
Several companies offer voice telephone conversations over the Internet. You can make a phone call to virtually anyone, anywhere, for as long as you wish—and all for the price of a local phone call.

Internet calling requires a multimedia computer with a sound card, built-in microphone and speakers, and a fast modem, plus a subscription to the Internet and calling software. To make a call, you log on and select your phone software. Then click on the name, phone number, or email address of the person you want to talk with. For some software programs, both parties must be logged on at the same time and using the same software to complete the call. Other programs have the ability to call a conventional telephone at the other end.

There are several software vendors that provide Internet phone software. Often you can download a free trial version from the Internet. Check out:

- Dialpad   www.dialpad.com
- Vocaltec, Internet Phone   www.vocaltec.com
- Wincroft.Inc., DigiPhone   www.digiphone.com
- Microsoft, NetMeeting   www.microsoft.com

If Internet calling sounds too good to be true, you may be right. Though the technology is rapidly improving, its sound quality often resembles a half-duplex speakerphone. Two people speaking at the same time can cancel each other out. To ensure better sound quality, get software with full-duplex capability.

During high-traffic times on the Internet, you'll also have to contend with delays of up to one second between the time you speak and the time you hear yourself speaking. Speech breaks up, syllables are dropped, and the sound can get very choppy. Still, if you want to chat with someone across the world and you're not fussy about sound quality, the price is right.

To obtain a good Internet phone connection, you'll need to have a high-speed computer, a very fast modem, a good sound card, and a headset. For top-quality connections, sign up for ISDN, DSL, or cable service (see Chapter 4).

Internet phoning will surely improve with the advent of voice over IP (VoIP), a technology that transmits voice information via Internet Protocol (IP). Voice calls are digitized and then sent in packets over the network. One advantage of VoIP will be a significant reduction in the cost of calling.

RESOURCES

Books
Phone Company Services:
Working Smarter with the Right Telecom Tools
by June Langhoff
Aegis, 1997
800-828-6961

Phone company services are described in detail with advice on how to put them to best use in real-life applications.

Websites
Telephone companies add phone services frequently. Check their websites to see the latest.

- Ameritech　　　　　www.ameritech.com
- Bell Atlantic　　　　www.bellatlantic.com
- Bell South　　　　　www.bellsouth.com
- Pacific Bell　　　　　www.pacbell.com
- Southwestern Bell　　www.swbell.com
- USWest　　　　　　www.uswest.com

Chapter

4

Phone Lines

. . . .

IT USED TO BE SO SIMPLE. All phone lines were the same. You just plugged in your phone, and you were ready to make a call. Today, you have more choices. Now you can arrange for a line that will turn one little pair of copper wires into two lines (ISDN) or 24 lines (T1). You can set up a line that rings in two locations (off-premises extension) or gives you a branch office without moving an inch (remote line). And, for a premium, you can set up super-fast connections.

LINE SERVICE TYPES

You can sign up for a variety of line services. They break down into two main categories:

- **Analog**
  Analog services are commonly used for voice services, fax, and low-volume, low-speed data transfer.

- **Digital**
  Digital service is commonly used for high-speed data exchange and for multiplexed voice service, where one pair of wires is used for multiple voice channels.

ANALOG SERVICES

The majority of local phone lines today are analog. These are the lines that go from your home or office to the telephone company's central office. Basically, an analog line transmits the signals of your voice in a way that is similar (analogous) to your original voice waveform. If you want to send a fax or computer data over an analog line, you'll need a modem to change the signal from digital to analog. The receiving end needs a modem, too, to change the signal back to digital.

POTS

This acronym stands for "plain old telephone service." POTS lines are analog, and this is the service used by most businesses and homes today. These lines allow you to hold a voice conversation, use a modem, send a fax, hook up an answering machine, or add on voice mail.

Foreign exchange line (FX)

A POTS telephone line provided by a central office that is outside, or foreign to, your local exchange area is known as a foreign exchange line. These lines can be useful in a couple of ways. They let you provide local call service to your customers, and they can give you the appearance of doing business in another area. If you work out of your home, but don't want your customers to know it, this feature of an FX is desirable. In addition, a foreign exchange number provides dial tone in the foreign area. Calls to and from phones in the foreign area are charged as if you were actually located there, so you save money.

Off-premises extension

You can request that your phone number ring in two locations, such as your home and your business. A separate dedicated POTS phone line is run to each of the two locations. The off-premises extension can be used to provide answering service to a phone line, though call forwarding is the preferred method these days. Installation costs are usually high, and there are also restrictions regarding how far apart the two locations may be. The least expensive option is when the same central office serves both locations, a service called secretarial line or half-tap.

Remote line

To have a local telephone number in a distant city, you can set up a remote line. Whenever someone calls the remote number, the call is automatically forwarded to your telephone number. The remote line exists only in the computer at the telephone company's central office, but it allows you to maintain a working telephone number when you have no physical location at which to terminate normal telephone service. Also, even though you don't have an actual office or telephone at the remote location, you can still list the remote number in the both the white and yellow pages directories.

By using a remote line, you can keep your business number after you have moved out of an area, or you can create the appearance of a branch office (or several offices) in other cities. For example, a talent agent located in Fresno uses this service to maintain a Hollywood telephone number.

This service is also known as remote call forwarding or market expansion line. You pay for all local and toll charges from the remote number to the terminating number. Your caller only pays the local call charge, while you pay the direct dial long-distance charge.

A remote line differs from a foreign exchange line in two ways: (1) a foreign exchange line is more expensive than a remote line, and (2) you can dial out from a foreign exchange line, but not from a remote line.

DIGITAL SERVICES

More and more organizations are changing to digital lines these days. Digital has become the preferred medium for computerized telephone applications, such as data transfer or online communications. Due to the high-speed transmission rates of digital lines, you can send more information in less time, which saves you money on phone charges. Digital lines are also cleaner than analog lines, resulting in better sound quality for voice conversations and clearer connections for fast data transfers.

Digital allows multiple telecommunications channels over a single twisted-pair copper line. For example, your telephone company could expand your one digital circuit into 24 circuits via multiplexing technology, thus giving you the capacity to handle 24 voice phone calls simultaneously over only one phone line. Or you could use 18 lines for voice, four for fax, and two for data modems—you get the idea.

Unfortunately, analog telephone devices are not compatible with digital lines. You must use telephone equipment specifically designed for digital lines or invest in a converter.

RAMPING UP BANDWIDTH

Bandwidth refers to the speed at which data moves, and sufficient bandwidth becomes an important issue when you want to access the Internet, check your email, or transfer files. Simple text applications require far less bandwidth capacity than multimedia stuff, such as Web radio or streaming video. However, even downloading an image onto your computer screen or sending data somewhere (uploading) can tie up your computer for extended periods of time if you have insufficient bandwidth.

The most popular technologies available for improving your bandwidth include:

- ISDN
- DSL
- Satellite
- Cable

I'll discuss each of these technologies later on in this chapter.

YOUR MILEAGE MAY VARY

Several elements control available bandwidth. They include: the power of your computer processor, the amount of RAM and disk space available, the capability of your access equipment (modem, router, or dish), the rate of speed provided by your Internet service provider (ISP), and network traffic (how many others are trying to move data at the same time).

Upload and download speeds vary depending on the setup you have. For example, 56 kbps modems can download at 53 kbps, but uploads won't travel faster than 33.6 kbps. Cable can download up to 3 Mbps, but uploads are poky—only 33.6 kbps—unless the cable system has been upgraded for two-way transmission. Today, the fastest uploads are available from ISDN at 128 kbps and DSL at 384 kbps.

Some of the faster options require you to give up flexibility for speed. Analog modems, ISDN, and satellite service allow you to access more than one destination; in contrast, DSL and cable are always-on, dedicated connections that link to the same location every time. This will work fine if you only want to reach the Net, but it may be limiting if you need high-speed access to other sites, such as your company network, videoconference sessions, or other online services.

Your bandwidth choices may also be restricted by your location. Although ISDN has penetrated about 90 percent of the U.S., DSL, satellite, and cable are still limited in their distribution. Even if you can arrange for a higher-speed connection, you might not be able to find a local Internet service provider or online service that can support the higher bandwidth speeds. Once you do locate one, be prepared to pay a premium for faster access. Nevertheless, if your keyboard seems to be growing cobwebs between screen updates, you'll be glad you did.

ISDN SERVICE

Integrated services digital network (ISDN) is a service from the phone company that carries data at speeds of 128 kbps over traditional copper telephone lines, the kind most people have in their homes. ISDN service turns your normal phone line into three digital channels, or virtual phone lines). Two of the channels are 64 kbps channels; the third channel ranges from 8 to 16 kbps. This third channel is used for sending information, such as caller ID, via packet-switched transmissions, which are short bursts of encoded information.

Because ISDN service lets you combine voice and data traffic on the same phone line, you can use one channel as a normal voice line and the other for Group IV fax. Or you can combine the two channels for high-speed Internet access. All this can be accomplished without any new wiring.

ISDN requires a special modem that will run you from $100 to $300, and you will pay approximately $100 to $150 for service installation. Depending on where you live, monthly service costs range from $60 to $125. Often, there is a per-minute charge as well.

Look at what people are doing with ISDN lines:

- A gas station runs credit card authorizations over the smaller channel of its ISDN line. The two remaining voice lines are used for the station's direct line and a pay phone. According to Pacific Bell, tests conducted by major credit card companies show that using ISDN to access credit card data cuts the response time down to four to seven seconds versus the 12 to 40 seconds required for an ordinary connection.

- Realtors are using ISDN-enhanced multiple listing services for fast access to full-screen color images of available properties.

- The local school district in Huntsville, Alabama, employs ISDN in its security system to monitor voices and sounds in every school in the city.

- A Hollywood-based music producer sends digitized music across the world at breakneck speeds, using Dolby Fax and an ISDN line.

- Doctors in Palo Alto, California, are able to view X rays remotely via ISDN-provided telemedicine links.

- Freelancers working for the *San Francisco Examiner Magazine* upload stories, photos, and layouts, and then download edited copy each week over an ISDN line.

- Telecommuting scientists and engineers at Lawrence Livermore National Laboratories in California use ISDN for remote access to their office LANs (local area networks) and file servers.

- A sports photo agency uses ISDN to offer an online catalog of over 10,000 images.

- Executive search firms and headhunters conduct virtual job interviews via ISDN-enabled videoconferencing.

CONFIGURING ISDN

ISDN can be configured in several ways, but small businesses most commonly use one of the following three combinations:

Single line—mixed equipment

If you use a "digital modem," such as Motorola's BitSurfr or 3Com's Impact IQ, you can attach your regular telephones and fax machine to the ISDN channel.

Single line—all ISDN

All telephones and fax machines must be ISDN-compatible, or you can use a special terminal adapter. If you plan to go without a modem, your PC must have an ISDN card.

ISDN as your second line

Your voice line remains a standard POTS line, and you put ISDN on the second line.

ORDERING ISDN

When ordering an ISDN line, you'll need to answer the following questions:

- What hardware will you be using?
  Not all hardware will work on the ISDN lines that are available in your area; much of it is switch dependent.

- Do you plan to combine the two ISDN channels?
  If the answer is yes, you'll want to order a BRI line that is capable of inverse multiplexing, multilinking, or bonding.

- How many telephone numbers do you want?
  If you plan to use your ISDN line with your fax and analog phone, you'll definitely want at least two.

PREPARING FOR INSTALLATION

Most vendors will provide ordering information that can make your installation much easier, so it makes sense to buy your equipment before ordering the line.

However, you'll want to do some research before you go out and buy equipment, especially if you plan to buy from a mail order firm. You'll need the following information:

- **Your central office switch type**—Your telephone company will tell you what type you have when you sign up for ISDN. Don't lose this information. It's critical!

- **The telephone number (or numbers) that are assigned to your ISDN line**—Depending on your equipment and your telephone company's capabilities, you can have up to 16 different telephone numbers. The most common configuration, however, is two numbers. You'll also need to know how you plan to configure your lines. For example, you might use one line for Internet calls and the other line for fax calls.

- **The service profile identification numbers that are assigned to each number**—These identifiers tell the central office switch how to talk to your ISDN terminal. Sometimes, you'll hear these numbers referred to as SPIDs.

It's also handy to have the customer service phone number of your equipment vendor—just in case.

Note: If you're not technical or don't have time to mess with all this, you can get help from your vendor or a consultant. See *Resources* at the end of this chapter for some useful contacts.

DSL SERVICE

Digital subscriber line (DSL) is a service provided by the phone company and also by some Internet service providers. Like ISDN, it employs traditional copper phone lines to carry data. There are a bunch of different DSL types that include ADSL, HDSL, IDSL, and SDSL. Depending on the flavor of DSL you install, download speeds reach up to 8.5 megabits per second (Mbps). Upload speeds are often less. ADSL, one of the most common DSL offerings, is ten times faster than ISDN.

With a DSL line connected to your PC, you can send and receive just about anything—including documents, full-motion video, CD-quality audio files, voice—and at very high speeds. DSL service is capable of dynamic bandwidth allocation. This is a fancy way of saying that you can make a data call using the entire bandwidth and, if a voice call comes in, the system automatically shrinks the first call's bandwidth so that it can handle the second call without breaking your Internet connection. Once the call is over, the original bandwidth is restored automatically.

Remember that DSL is an always-on service and provides a connection to just one number. In most cases, that number will be to your Internet service provider. Some organizations use DSL to provide a remote connection to their office network. If you want high-speed connections to a variety of locations, consider ISDN, fractional T1, or another switched service.

ORDERING DSL

To operate DSL, you'll need a special modem and an Ethernet card that goes inside your computer. You must also be located within a certain distance from a telephone company central office—3.3 miles is about maximum. Naturally, costs vary depending on the amount of bandwidth you order and where you're located. Service charges range from $30 to $150 per month; equipment will cost from $150 to $200; and installation can set you back another $100 to $200.

DSL LEXICON

Some of the most common varieties of DSL include:

ADSL

Asymmetric digital subscriber line (ADSL) is a technology used to transmit digital information at high bandwidths over existing phone lines to homes and businesses. Unlike normal dial-up phone service, ADSL provides a continuously available, always-on connection. ADSL divides the line channel asymmetrically, using a larger portion of the channel to download information and a smaller portion of the channel to upload information. ADSL can handle both voice and data uses on the same line. The most common ADSL offering has downstream data rates that range from 512 kbps to about 6 Mbps.

DSL Lite

This service (also known as Universal ADSL, splitterless DSL, or G.Lite) offers Internet connections to home and business computers over regular phone lines. Transmission speeds can reach up to 1.5 Mbps (millions of bits per second), but the most common offering provides downloads of 384 kbps. Still, that's about seven times faster than regular phone service using a 56K modem and three times faster than an ISDN connection. Most services offer upload speeds of 128 kbps.

HDSL

High-bit-rate DSL is most often used for digital transmission within a corporate network, or between the phone company and a large business customer. HDSL is symmetrical, meaning that you get an equal amount of bandwidth in both directions. HDSL can carry up to 2,320 kbps on a single twisted-pair line.

IDSL

If you live beyond the 3-mile radius from your central office, you may be able to get IDSL (ISDN DSL). The speed is slower than the other DSL offerings, but you can obtain data rates of 128 kbps.

SDSL

Symmetrical DSL is quite similar to HDSL. A single line can carry up to 1.544 Mbps of data.

VDSL

Very high-data-rate DSL is a new technology that features much higher data rates over short distances than other DSL flavors. So far, it's the fastest DSL technology. Downloads achieve 13 to 52 megabits per second downstream and uploads from 1.5 to 2.3 megabits per second. The maximum distance from the central office to the user must fall between 1,000 and 4,500 feet. This technology is still in the development stage, and not all the standards have been worked out. One expectation is that when phone companies extend fiber-optic lines to neighbor-hood hubs, home users will also have access to these very high speeds.

VoDSL

Voice over DSL derives voice lines onto a copper line that is DSL enabled. This means that a single phone line can carry up to 16 separate voice channels plus a high-speed data connec-tion, all at the same time. Hardware companies are offering new products that will allow you to provision several voice lines over one DSL connection, but this is a new technology only beginning its rollout. Rhythms NetConnections, Coppercom, and Jetstream are among the hardware companies that are pro-viding VoDSL equipment.

xDSL

This acronym refers to the entire family of DSL services.

☎ In my office

As soon as ADSL became available in my area (California's Pacific Bell territory), I signed up for ADSL. Now I have a voice telephone line, unlimited access to the Internet at speeds from 384 kbps to 1.544 Mbps, and download speeds of 128 kbps. Whenever I need to check on an order or do some research, I just type in the Web address, and the information appears about as quickly as changing a TV channel. There's no setup time, no modem squealing, no waiting, period. Large file transfers that took ten minutes or more with my 56 kbps analog modem now take less than a minute.

For $39.95 a month, I get unlimited Internet access as well as voice service. Because my local phone company was running a promotion, the $198 installation fee was waived and the DSL modem was free. I dropped a second phone line that I maintained just for data ($13.95 per month) plus my former Internet service provider ($20 per month), so I now spend only $6 a month extra for all this speed. What a deal!

SATELLITE SERVICE

Satellite connections can beam Internet data to your computer at speeds of up to 400 kbps. That's three times faster than ISDN and a tad faster than ADSL. The principal provider of this service is DirecPC.

To use a satellite service, you must have a Pentium-class PC and a clear line of sight to the south. Plus, you'll need to install a 21-inch dish antenna, a controller, and some software. In addition, an analog modem and a phone line are necessary for functions such as sending out requests for URLs or uploading email. Equipment will run you about $300 and the setup fee is $50. Monthly service rates start at $29.95 for 25 hours; additional hours are billed at around $2 per hour. If you need help installing the dish, add another $250 to the price tag.

CABLE SERVICE

This service works over conventional television lines, just like the ones that deliver CNN and MTV to your TV. It is available through subscription to a cable data service. Instead of connecting your cable jack to a TV, you link a cable modem to your computer.

Transmission speeds range from 1.5 to 3 Mbps, which is 50 to 100 times faster than a 28.8 modem. However, because cable is an always-on shared service, speeds will slow down as more people in your neighborhood sign on.

The industry leaders in cable modem service are @Home, Media One, and Road Runner. It will cost you about $400 to buy a cable modem, or you may choose to lease one. You'll also need an Ethernet networking card ($100) that goes into your computer and a cable to run to your PC. Monthly costs for Internet access range between $30 and $50, and you will be charged another $100 to $175 for installation.

SPEED TEST

In an independent test performed by Keynote Systems, DSL provided a slightly faster pipeline to the Internet than a cable connection from @Home. During peak traffic hours, DSL was 11 percent faster than cable, though cable is advertised to be twice as fast as DSL.

The reason, according to Keynote, is that cable modem service slowed down in the evening when hundreds of cable customers shared the same line. During the day, cable proved faster because most home users were off the system.

FASTER SPEEDS

Although most small offices won't need anything faster than DSL, I want to include a brief description of some of the other technologies that can "get you there fast."

T-CARRIER SERVICES

T-carrier systems provide voice transmission over digital lines, and there are several offerings. The most common are:

T1

A T1 line provides a point-to-point digital transport capacity of 1.544 Mbps. Though it is a dedicated high-speed data connection, it can be converted into 24 voice channels by multiplexing the circuit. (Multiplexing is the term used to describe different methods of adding channels to a single pair of wires.) Each channel can then be used to carry a typical voice conversation at 64 kbps. (In telecom land, 24 channels at 64 kbps each equals the total bandwidth of 1.544 Mbps). To carry data, the same channels may be combined in a variety of ways to create higher-speed channels that are multiples of the basic 64 kbps voice channel. For example, two voice channels could be combined to create one 128 kbps data channel.

T1 doesn't come cheap. Each month you pay for a local channel, an access connection fee, access coordination, and multiplexing charges, as well as mileage charges. You will also need special equipment at each end of the circuit. According to industry sources, a standard 24-channel connection will cost about $2,800 in fixed monthly charges plus $3.95 per mile. When comparing the options of a T1 line versus simply adding separate lines, the break-even point is about 12 lines.

T1 is not cost effective unless you use it three to six hours a day. If you have heavy digital transport needs that require more capacity than ISDN can offer, but you don't need full T1 bandwidth, you can arrange for fractional T1 service in multiples of 64 kbps.

Fractional T1

This service allows you to lease a portion of a T1 line. Typical fractional T1 uses include videoconferencing and data backup services. Depending on the amount of bandwidth you need, fractional T1 can support speeds from 128 kbps to 768 kbps.

T2

These lines provide data rates of 6.312 Mbps, which are four times the capacity of a T1. One T2 line could carry 96 separate channels—voice or data.

T3

Data rates up to 44.736 Mbps are obtained with these lines—seven times the capacity of T2, so that one T3 line could carry 672 separate channels.

T4

The data transmission rates of a T4 line can reach 274,176 Mbps, 168 times the capacity of a T1. This means that one T4 line could carry 4032 separate channels.

ASYNCHRONOUS TRANSFER MODE (ATM)

This is a line transmission standard that can support voice, data, and video equally well. Internet service providers often use ATM as a backbone technology.

ATM backbones can be found in large multimedia networks, such as medical imaging, group videoconferencing, and high-end design applications. Data rates are either 155.52 Mbps or 622.08 Mbps. Speeds on ATM networks can reach up to 10 gigabits per second (Gbps).

SYNCHRONOUS OPTICAL NETWORK ACCESS SERVICES (SONET)

The American National Standards Institute (ANSI) has adopted SONET as the standard for fiber-optic transmissions in the United States. SONET data transmission speeds range from 51.84 Mbps to 13.22 Gbps. It is most often used as the backbone for very large networks, and it underlies the transmission technology used in many telephone company networks.

Most SONET networks are designed as rings to provide redundancy. In this way, if one fiber fails, the transmission can still be completed.

Data Speed Comparison

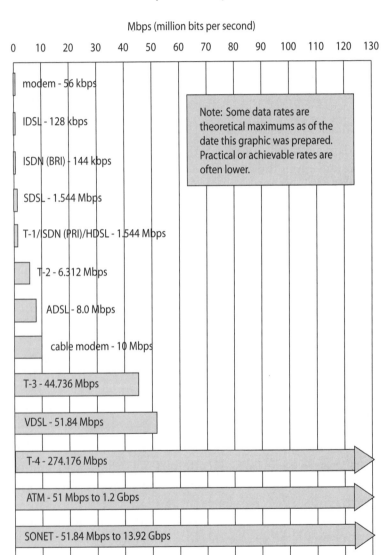

Mbps (million bits per second)

0 10 20 30 40 50 60 70 80 90 100 110 120 130

modem - 56 kbps

IDSL - 128 kbps

ISDN (BRI) - 144 kbps

SDSL - 1.544 Mbps

T-1/ISDN (PRI)/HDSL - 1.544 Mbps

Note: Some data rates are theoretical maximums as of the date this graphic was prepared. Practical or achievable rates are often lower.

T-2 - 6.312 Mbps

ADSL - 8.0 Mbps

cable modem - 10 Mbps

T-3 - 44.736 Mbps

VDSL - 51.84 Mbps

T-4 - 274.176 Mbps

ATM - 51 Mbps to 1.2 Gbps

SONET - 51.84 Mbps to 13.92 Gbps

NETWORKING

If you have more than one computer at your home or office, they can all share one modem by using a network. Other peripherals, such as a printer or plotter, can be shared in the same way, and, if you have a high-speed DSL or cable connection, networking will allow you to tap into that speed from anywhere in your home or office. Networked DSL or cable gives all family members or employees the same connection, thus eliminating the need for each to wait their turn.

Networking can be a cost-effective alternative to purchasing separate modems for each computer. Also, it is often cheaper to network an Internet connection than pay for separate phone lines for each computer. The cost of connecting each computer will set you back about $50 to $100.

There are several networking options:

- **USB network**

  For relatively new computers, you can network two together simply by connecting them through their universal serial bus (USB) ports. If you've run out of USB ports on your computer, inexpensive USB hubs from Netgear (www.netgear.com) or Belkin (www.belkin.com) are available.

- **Ethernet network**

  To access the same-high speed connection, you can connect your computers to an Ethernet hub (router) and then connect the hub to your DSL modem. Some DSL modems include an Ethernet hub, or you can purchase a separate one. Many companies, including Netgear and Netopia (www.netopia.com), make Ethernet routers.

  Ethernet networks support speeds of 10 Mbps to 100 Mbps, but they may be hard to set up. For starters, you'll need to install Ethernet wiring throughout your home or office to connect the computers. However, many of the "smart home" developments come with Ethernet wiring built in.

- **Power line network**
  You can also use the electrical wiring and outlets of your home or office to create a network. PassPort from Intelogis (www.intelogis.com) allows you to link PCs and other peripherals through the AC outlets in your walls. Here's how: Plug one end of the PassPort into the parallel port on your computer and the other into an electrical outlet. Do the same with your second computer. Voila! You now have a LAN. You can expect to get up to 500 kbps over this network.

- **Phone line network**
  This type of network uses your telephone wiring and outlets to connect your devices. Although your modem and your telephone share a single phone jack, there's no interference with phone calls on the same wires. However, installation may be a bit difficult. You'll need to install PC cards and drivers to make the whole thing link properly. Check out Intel's AnyPoint Phoneline Home Network (www.intel.com), 3Com's HomeConnect Home Network Phoneline Kit (www.3com.com), or Netgear's Netgear Phoneline 10X. Phone line networks can transmit data at speeds of approximately 1 Mbps.

- **Wireless network**
  These networks send your data over two-way radio waves that are transmitted through the home or office. Leaders in this area are Proxim's Symphony (www.proxim.com), Diamond Media HomeFree Wireless (www.diamondmm.com), and WebGear's Aviator (www.webgear.com). Network speeds are about the same as phoneline networks, but analysts are expecting a tenfold improvement in speed as soon as second-generation devices reach the marketplace.

CENTRAL OFFICE SECRETS

Have you ever heard the term *G.U.*? It's short for "geographically undesirable," and it refers to a guy or girl who lives too far away to be considered appropriate date material. Local phone services frequently classify particular business locations as G.U. Here's why:

Your local phone service comes into your home or office from the telephone company's central office, where you are assigned a telephone number with an exchange prefix (the first three digits of your seven-digit telephone number). There is a physical limitation on the quantity of phone numbers available from an individual exchange. Depending on the switch type at your central office, there may be 30,000 to 130,000 phone numbers that can be assigned. Smaller central offices may have just one exchange prefix per office; larger ones may have several.

So what, you say? Well, getting the wrong exchange may do serious harm to your business communications plans, because older telephone exchanges cannot provide the calling features you may need. Read on.

• A photographer wanted to add call waiting to her phone service. When she called her phone company, she found that call waiting was not available on her exchange because the switch did not contain the proper electronics to service it. The only solution was to change her exchange, but that would involve changing her telephone number, reprinting business stationery, and notifying all her clients—a very costly proposition. She was lucky, in a way, because her central office did have more than one exchange with call waiting available. If her central office had just one exchange, her only option for call waiting would be an expensive foreign exchange line. Or she could move across town.

• An architect, specializing in CAD/CAM renderings, wanted to relocate to a country setting. Because the majority of his work was done via telecommuting, he felt he could basically settle anywhere in the country. All he needed was a telephone line. He found an idyllic spot and set up shop. Things were fine until he wanted to expand. He decided to add a third line to his setup with call hunting capability. This service, you may recall, groups telephone numbers so that if the first line is busy, the next line in the hunt group rings, and so on. Unhappily, his central office had only one exchange, which could not support hunting unless the numbers were physically located next to each other in the switch. Unfortunately, the numbers needed were assigned years ago, so he was out of luck.

- A small manufacturer was negotiating a major contract with a certain company that insisted all its vendors support EDI (electronic data interexchange). EDI requires digital service, which the manufacturer didn't have. Upon checking with the local telco, the manufacturer learned that the local central office could not provide digital service because its ESS (electronic switch system) was an earlier non-digital version. That was the end of the contract.

- A lawyer wanted to telecommute from his home office, which was located in the suburbs of a major city. Because he wanted speedy access to upload and download large files, he decided to order DSL. Unfortunately, he lived more than three miles from his central office, and DSL wasn't available at that distance. Sorry.

And, finally, woe betide those of you that live in lovely remote areas far from the central office. Even inexpensive services, such as voice mail, become very costly when you have to pay mileage rates.

When you are considering a business location, it's prudent to find out what type of phone switch your telephone company uses for that exchange. Call the local phone company, give them the address of the property you are considering, and ask for the type of switch. If the switch is a stepper or crossbar exchange, you won't be able to do much more than add Touch-Tone dialing. You want an ESS, or better yet, a DMS (digital multiplex system) switch.

If the service agent doesn't know the switch type, ask what kinds of services are available on the exchange. A limited list of services (no call waiting, no call forwarding) means you're out of luck. Additionally, if you are planning to use advanced communications services such as DSL, be sure to find out if they're available in your area or how soon they will be. You'll be glad you did your homework.

ORDERING SERVICE

When you're ready to order a new line, arm yourself with information before calling your business office. Your class of service (CS) determines the types of services available and the rates you will pay for local service. Often, each different class has different features and services associated with it.

- **Residential**
  If your office is in your home, you may qualify for a residential CS. These rates are often considerably lower than business rates.

- **Business**
  A business CS is charged a higher rate than the residential rate, but you receive a free listing in the yellow pages.

PAYMENT PLANS

Most telephone companies offer a variety of payment plans. These are the most common:

Measured service

You pay a lower monthly access charge, but each local call is billed. The cost of the call often varies by the time of day. Some measured rate service is not timed, but the majority is timed—the shorter and fewer the calls, the less you pay.

Flat-rate service

Some areas of the country allow you to pay a fixed monthly sum for an unlimited number of local calls. Flat-rate service is usually available with residential services only. If it's available in your area and you qualify for residential service, get it—it's a bargain.

Party line service

Believe it or not, there are still some areas of the country that offer party line service. This type of service groups two or more separate subscribers on one line. It's usually available in remote areas of the country where the cost of stringing copper wire makes dedicated service prohibitively expensive. If you find your business located in such an area and you don't yet have service, consider moving or look into wireless services (see Chapter 7).

OTHER FACTORS

In addition to your class of service and the features you want on your line, you'll also need to consider other factors:

Touch-Tone

Yes, you have to order Touch-Tone service. In many areas, you also have to pay a small monthly fee for the service. You should definitely order Touch-Tone—without it, you can't take advantage of such powerful features as on-demand call forwarding or voice mail.

Your new number

You do have some control over the number you are assigned. If you want a particular number, say 355-SAVE or 4APIZZA, ask your phone company if that number is taken. The phone company may charge you a research fee plus a monthly charge for the vanity phone number. Still, it might be worth the extra cost.

Hint: You'll want to take a look at the PhoNETic Web site (www.phonetic.com). This interactive site lets you test out different phone number combinations by converting letters to numbers.

Inside wire maintenance

For a monthly fee, often as low as 50 cents per line, the phone company will provide you with a repair service and maintenance plan. Under this plan, a phone company repairperson will come out to your site when you report a phone problem. If the problem turns out to be faulty wiring inside your facility, they will repair the line at no extra charge. Also, if the problem is caused by your equipment, you won't be charged for a "needless visit."

There's a good chance you might not need this service. According to the authors of *The Complete Guide to Local & Long Distance Telephone Company Billing*, inside wire breaks on average only once every 14 years. On the other hand, just one mistake with inside wire will cost you a minimum of $35 for an onsite visit—that's a lot of maintenance payments.

Your listing

If you have business service, you're entitled to a free listing in the business white pages and, in many parts of the country, a free listing in the local yellow pages. You might want to investigate the cost of a display ad, or at least boldface type. Check out your competitor's ads, and consider listing in more than one phone book.

If the bulk of your business is by phone, it makes sense to increase your exposure. For advice on writing an ad, take a look at *Getting The Most From Your Yellow Pages Advertising* by Barry Maher. In his book, you'll learn how to design ads that pull the best response, thus getting the most mileage out of your advertising dollars.

RESOURCES

Books

Demystifying ISDN
by Rick Arnold
Wordware Publishing, 1999

DSL for Dummies, second edition
by David Angell
IDG Books, 2000

Getting The Most From Your Yellow Pages Advertising,
second edition
by Barry Maher
Aegis, 1997

IP Telephony—The Integration of Robust VoIP Services
by Bill Douskalis
Prentice Hall, 1999

The Guide to T1 Networking
by William Flanagan
Miller Freeman Books, 1998

The Essential Guide to Telecommunications
by Annabel Z. Dodd
Prentice Hall, 1999

Chapter

5

Stand-Alone Phones

. . . .

NOT TOO LONG AGO, IF YOU NEEDED a phone, the most important decision you had to make was whether the color should be black, white, or ivory. Later, feature phones added Touch-Tone capability, memory dialing, redial, and the like. Now phones come in a range of styles with hundreds of features—speakerphones, cordless phones, conference phones, fashion phones, clock-radio phones, Internet phones, videophones, even a wrist phone (shades of Dick Tracy).

Today's phones also differ in how they send their signals. Landline phones use telephone wire; cellular phones use air-waves; and cordless phones use a combination of landlines and airwaves. A phone may be classified as stand-alone, meaning it needs only a phone line to operate; or a phone may be part of a phone system, such as a key system or PBX.

This chapter is all about stand-alone landline phones. I'll discuss how they work, what all those different features do, and what to look for in a single, multiline telephone or cordless model. There's advice about troubleshooting, plus information on selecting and using a headset. Chapter 6 will cover phone systems, and Chapter 7 will discuss wireless phones.

HOW PHONES WORK

When you were a kid, did you ever build a play telephone using two tin cans connected by a long string? Ideally, your friend spoke in one can and you could hear her from the other, right? Guess what? Phones work like that, sort of.

The handset of a modern telephone contains a microphone in its mouthpiece that amplifies the sound of your voice. As you speak into the mouthpiece, your voice creates air vibrations. These vibrations cause a membrane stretched across carbon granules in the mouthpiece to move. In turn, the movement of this membrane creates a resistance that directs the current containing your voice waves to flow down the telephone wire. Another vibrating diaphragm and a tiny loudspeaker are located in the earpiece, which may or may not be connected to the handset.

When you dial a telephone number, the instructions are sent through a network of exchanges, which finally result in the phone ringing on the other end. Once that phone is picked up, the two handsets are electronically connected. The sound your caller hears is actually the series of electrical signals that your voice has been converted into. The cracks, pops, and other weird sounds you sometimes hear are electrical interference on the line. With digital lines, you don't experience all that interference.

Interestingly, the ring sequences you hear while waiting for a call to be picked up do not match the ring sequences heard by the dialed party. On early phones, there was dead silence until the phone was answered. This drove people nuts, so the phone companies now add a ringing tone to the calling party's line. The ringing you hear is put there by your phone company only to let you know that the call is being processed. Often, the rings at the dialed end are one or two less than the number of rings you hear, so be patient—six rings to you may only be four rings on the other end.

SINGLE-LINE CORDED PHONES

You can get a simple single-line corded phone with nary an extra button for less than $20. Or you can spend over a $100 for a phone crammed with features. Phone manufacturers are adding an incredible array of functions these days. Is it progress or creeping feature-itis? You decide.

PHONE FEATURES—DIALING

Alphabetic keypad
In addition to the standard numeric keypad, some phones provide a separate 26-key alphabetic keyboard. Handy, if you do a lot of phone programming.

Automatic redial
The last number you dialed is redialed automatically. Some phone models will keep trying if the line is busy.

Note: This is also called last number redial.

Chain dialing
This feature automatically dials a sequence of numbers with appropriate pauses. It's useful for bank-by-phone, voice mail, and other applications that require a sequence of numbers. For example, you dial your bank's phone number, then key in your account number after the call is answered.

Dialing mode selector
If your local service doesn't support Touch-Tone, and you need tones to access a voice mail system or other computerized service, this feature can be useful. It allows you to change from pulse dialing to Touch-Tone.

To do this, you dial the service with pulse dialing, then switch over to tone to communicate properly with the call processing computer.

Emergency dialing
Some phones come with prelabeled buttons for fire, police, and ambulance services.

Jog dial
This feature allows you to scan quickly through your entire speed dial directory. If you have caller ID service, you can scan through your caller ID log, too.

On-hook dialing

Now you can dial without picking up the handset. If you use a headset, you'll definitely want this feature because it saves you the trouble of picking up the handset every time you make a call.

One-touch save

The last number you dialed is saved in a scratch pad, but it will be erased the next time you save a number. If you have to dial the same number several times during a particular day, this feature could save you time.

Programmable soft keys

You can assign certain features to certain keys. For example, you might program one key for last-number redial and another for three-way conferencing.

Speed dialing

Frequently called numbers are assigned a one-, two-, or three-button code that is programmed into your phone. Make sure the phone's memory can accommodate the longest number you want to store, including country code, area code, and long-distance access number. Eleven digits are the bare minimum these days. If you dial internationally, you may need 16-digit capacity.

Note: This feature is sometimes called one-touch speed dialing.

Voice-activated dialing

Some advanced phones let you assign a voice tag to a programmed list of numbers. When you want to place an outgoing call, you just speak the name: "delivery service," or "taxi."

Voice response dialing

As you dial a call, your phone repeats the number in either English or Spanish—may be useful for the dialing-challenged.

PHONE FEATURES—DISPLAY

Call forwarding light
The name says it all. A display light reminds you that you for-warded your phone calls, but you'll need a corresponding ser-vice from your phone company for it to work.

Call waiting display
If you receive a call when you're already on the line, call wait-ing display will show you the name and number of the second caller. Both caller ID and call waiting service are required to utilize this phone feature.

Caller ID compatible
Caller ID compatibility allows a local caller's telephone num-ber (and sometimes the caller's name) to be displayed if the information is available. First, however, you must sign up with your telephone company to get caller ID service.

Some phones also have the memory capacity to store a running list of incoming caller's numbers. This memory feature even records the phone numbers of callers who hang up before you answer.

LCD display
This feature displays the number being dialed, the date, and time. Some phones also monitor the elapsed time of the call, which is useful if you are watching those long-distance minutes or need to rebill your time on the phone.

Visual ring indicator
An indicator lights up when the phone rings to alert you that a call is coming in. Visual ring indicators are especially useful for the hearing disabled, as well as for anyone using a phone in very noisy conditions.

PHONE FEATURES—CONTROL

Busy supervision
If the number you dial is busy, phones featuring busy supervision will automatically hang up for you.

Feature keys
Each key gives you one-button access to phone company features such as call return, repeat dial, three-way calling, call forwarding, and the like.

Flash
This is a useful button for those of you with phone company services, such as call waiting or three-way calling. Pressing the FLASH button works the same as pressing the hookswitch, except you're not able to accidentally hang up on your caller. If you have a tendency to be "heavy fingered," this is definitely a useful feature.

Hold
Holding allows you to keep a caller on the line, but you can't hear him and he can't hear you. It is especially thoughtful to put a caller on hold if your workplace is noisy.

Intercom
The intercom feature lets you talk with other extensions in your facility. If coworkers or family members occasionally answer your line, you'll want intercom capability. In this way, they can call you to the phone by ringing your extension.

Message waiting light
As the name implies, an indicator lights up if there is a message from an unanswered call—especially useful if you have phone company voice mail.

Mute
When you press the MUTE button, you can still hear your caller, but your caller can't hear you. This feature can be handy

if you are working at home or in a noisy setting and need to ask your kids or coworkers to quiet down. It's also handy if you can't stop a sneeze.

Security
By setting up a security code, you can lock your speed dial directory and thus prevent outgoing calls (except for emergency numbers).

PHONE FEATURES—COMFORT

Handset volume control
Adjustment controls located on either the phone or the handset can raise and lower the volume of each caller's voice. Nice if you're stuck with a shouter (or a whisperer).

Hearing aid compatible
Because a hearing aid is a microphone and your phone earpiece is a speaker, putting the two near each other can cause painful electronic feedback. A handset compatible with hearing aids has circuitry that cancels the feedback.

Ringer
You can get all kinds of ringers. Some phones quack, others chirp, while still others play music instead of the standard ring. There's even one that tells you, in English, that you have a phone call. Whatever ringer you get, you'll want to control the volume and maybe even turn it off.

Speakerphone
These phones have a built-in speaker that lets you talk without holding the handset next to your ear. The built-in microphone is omnidirectional, so it is able to pick up your voice wherever you may be in relationship to the phone. This type of mike also picks up every other sound in the room, including the echoes and reverberations that your voice generates as it bounces around the walls. The echo effect can be very annoying to the person at

the other end of the connection. You sound as though you are speaking from the bottom of a well.

Many inexpensive speakerphones are half-duplex. This means that only one party can talk at a time without clipping off the other person's voice. If you need speakerphone capability for conference calling, get a full-duplex phone or consider getting a conferencing system, which is discussed later in this chapter.

To improve your speakerphone's sound quality, use it in a room with lots of cushioning, such as carpets, drapes, and books. Place the phone on a wooden surface, not on metal or glass. If your tabletop is glass, put the phone on a thick pad, telephone book, or other sound cushion.

Speakerphones aren't private. Unless you inform your caller, he or she has no idea who else is within hearing distance of your conversation. Combine this situation with echoing sound quality, and you can definitely put people off.

Computer-based speakerphone

Polycom makes a speakerphone for use with the Internet. It also works with many videoconferencing systems, such as Intel's ProShare. The Polycom SoundPoint PC plugs into your computer's sound card to provide a full-duplex speakerphone. This setup comes with a built-in speaker and microphone for hand-free talking, plus a handset, so you can take a call privately. If you have nosy officemates, you'll appreciate the handset feature.

☎ In my office

Mostly, I use my speakerphone for dialing or when I'm placed on hold, so that I can keep on working until someone comes on the line. At that point, I turn off the speakerphone and use the handset. On very rare occasions, I continue using the speakerphone during the conversation if I need to take copious notes, but only with permission. I also like to use my speakerphone while listening to a menu of voice choices from an automated voice response system.

MULTILINE PHONES

Multiline phones allow you to juggle multiple phone calls, place a caller on hold while dialing out on another line to get needed information, or even conference callers together.

If you have more than one voice line coming into your workplace, you should invest in a multiline phone. The alternative is a real time-waster—a desktop arrayed with single-line phones with you guessing which line is ringing. Multiline phones come in two-, three-, four-, and even five-line models. Depending on your wiring configuration, you can have just one line cord between your phone and the wall jack for each two lines. (*Note*: Most homes and offices are already wired for two lines.) Once you've reached five lines, or even before, you're ready to graduate to a phone system—a key set, hybrid, PBX, wireless, or Centrex. (See Chapter 6 for details.)

☎ In my office

I have a two-line phone in my home office. I use line one for incoming voice calls and line two for outgoing calls, as well as fax and modem calls. A single line cord (called a 2-line or RJ-14 cord) runs from the phone to the wall jack.

MULTILINE FEATURES

Multiline phones come with many of the features of a single-line phone. In addition, they have special features designed for handling more than one phone line. Some of those features are:

Conference button

You can connect the caller on the first line with the caller on the second line by pressing the CONFERENCE button. This is a very useful feature—it allows you to have a three-way conference call without paying extra for the kind the phone company offers.

"Do not disturb" mode

When you need an uninterrupted chunk of time to complete a project or to hold an important conference that can't be disturbed, this feature will make your phone busy without being off-hook.

Intercom capability

Some models allow you to page more than one phone set at the same time.

Line buttons and status lights

Naturally, it will be important to know which phone lines are in use. All multiline phones have lights or a display panel that will indicate which lines are active, which lines are on hold, and which line has a call ringing in. The methods for selecting a line are similar for all models.

Number of lines supported

The most common multiline phone supports two lines. Usually, these phones have two incoming jacks: one for line one, and one for lines one and two. In this way, you can use the two-line phone as a single-line instrument. Three-line phones may have two jacks—the first jack gets a single-line connection, while the other jack gets lines two and three. Alternatively, if your wiring supports a three-line connection, you can attach just one three-line cord. The two jacks that support four-line phones each have a dual-line connection. Five-line phones use a two-line connection for one jack and a three-line connection for the other.

Ringer control

You may want to selectively turn off the ringer on one or more lines, especially if you have that line backed up with voice mail or an answering device. Ringer control lets you do just that.

Speed dial portability

Now you can transfer the contents of your speed dial directory to another phone set. If you need to share a common set of speed dial numbers with others in your organization, this is certainly a convenient feature.

CORDLESS PHONES

Do you walk while you talk on the phone? If so, consider getting a cordless phone. Cordless phones permit you to get up from your work area, pull files, answer the door, or walk outside, and still be connected. Though earlier cordless models were noted for their poor audio quality, most models today operate at or near corded phone quality.

Cordless phones are a combination of wired and wireless technology. They consist of two parts:

- **Base station**
  The base station plugs into a telephone jack and an electrical power outlet, and then stays put.

- **Portable handset**
  The handset contains the mouthpiece, earpiece, and battery. A few cordless models come with an optional headset as well.

The cordless handset communicates with the base station via radio waves. Both sides of the conversation are beamed between the handset and the base station. Until recently, cordless phones were limited to only ten frequency channels. With so few channels, the chances of a neighboring phone using the same frequency channel was high. If more than one caller happened to be using the same channel at the same time, each could hear the other's conversation. The only recourse was to switch channels, and, if all channels were in use, you just had to wait. Now, higher-end cordless phones support over 100 channels, thus reducing the possibility of channel contention.

Have you ever heard a crying child on your cordless? If you have an older cordless phone in your home office and there is a baby monitoring system in your home or a neighbor's, don't be surprised to hear a baby crying over the phone some day. Room monitors and cordless phones operate in the same frequencies.

Earlier cordless phones had one major problem. Anyone with any type of handset could dial expensive long-distance calls over your base station that would be billed to you. Happily, phone manufacturers have curtailed this fraud by adding encoded digital security systems.

Cordless phones have a restricted operating range. Those with 46/49 MHz handle distances up to 150 feet, while the 900 MHz phones claim a range of up to half a mile. The 2.4 GHz phones can handle distances up to 4 miles. Keep in mind that the ranges quoted by manufacturers are optimum figures. Your actual range will be considerably shorter. Obstacles, such as walls or metal shelving, and interference from other electrical appliances, such as computers and fax machines, will affect the range of your phone.

The communication between the handset and the base depends on the power of your batteries. As they fade, the effective range of the phone will be affected. Your batteries are recharging each time you replace the handset in the base station, but if you forget to replace the handset, your batteries will begin to lose power.

Unlike a corded phone, you have to turn a cordless phone on to place or receive calls. Cordless phones will not work if there is a power outage, so don't rely on a cordless phone as your only phone.

Because a cordless phone is so portable, it's easy to leave it lying around wherever you finished your last phone call. Try to avoid this. It's not much fun hunting madly for the handset when the phone rings. Invest in a model that has two-way paging. By pushing the PAGING button at the base station, the handset will ring and you'll be able to track it down.

Note: If you plan to use more than one cordless phone in your workplace, check with your vendor to find out how many cordless phones can be used in the same environment and how far apart the base stations must be situated. Also, be sure to set each phone to a separate channel or, better yet, get a wireless phone system. See Chapter 6 for more information.

CORDLESS FEATURES

Because cordless phones share many features with the corded variety, I'll mention only those features that are unique.

Antenna

Flexible antennas are less likely to snap than the telescoping metal kind. A few cordless models use your hand and arm as the antenna. Incidentally, if your antenna is broken, you can buy an inexpensive clip-on replacement at most phone stores.

Auto answer

By picking up the handset at the base unit, you can receive a call without having to press the TALK button.

Audio encryption

To prevent electronic eavesdropping and ensure privacy, various systems are available that will scramble the voice signal. Anyone listening in will hear only garbled speech.

Backup power

A few cordless phone sets come with built-in backup power, which allows you to make phone calls even during a power failure. An extra charged battery is stored in the base unit of the phone. Backup power can be crucial, especially if you have no corded phones.

Battery life

Battery life is usually measured in two modes: talk time and standby time. Talk time between battery charges can vary considerably, depending on the battery type. Standby times of 14 days are not unusual. Some models come with an extra battery stored in the base that is always charged up and ready to go.

Digital

Unlike analog cordless phones, digital phones convert the sounds of your voice to electronic signals for transmission, then reconvert the signals to voice waves so that you can hear the caller's words. Digital phones promise less interference and static, as well as greater security.

Digital spread spectrum

Some cordless phones are designed to change frequencies frequently, as often as 100 times per second. One result of employing digital spread spectrum is that electronic eavesdropping becomes nearly impossible.

Fast-charging battery

The idea is to get your battery back in business faster. Some systems can reduce recharging time to a little over an hour.

LCD display

These displays show the number dialed, channel, range, and battery status. Some also clock the elapsed time of the phone call.

Lockout feature

To help prevent phone fraud, the lockout feature stops other cordless phone users in the neighborhood from dialing out on your phone line. See *Security codes* below.

Low-voltage meter

This indicator displays a visual status of your phone's battery life.

Number of channels

I have already mentioned that where channels are limited, your phone conversations could be overheard on a neighboring cordless phone. Most cordless phones today offer 10-channel capability, but higher-end 900 MHz and 2.4 GHz phones offer up to 100 channels. To change channels, you can let the phone scan to find the clearest channel, or you can change channels manually at the handset.

Out-of-range indicator
A beeping tone or alarm will let you know if you are roaming close to the limit of the cordless phone's range.

Paging capability
This feature allows you to ring the other half of the phone. It is useful for intercom purposes or for locating a missing handset. Two-way paging allows you to fully use the intercom capability, but some sets only offer one-way (base to handset) paging.

Radio frequency
Cordless phones are available in several frequencies: 46/49 MHz, 900 MHz, and 2.4 GHz. The 46/49 MHz frequency provides a range of up to 1,000 feet, but because this frequency has a wavelength of 18 feet, the effective indoor range is often less than one-fifth of the maximum range. It is most effective in uncluttered open spaces or single rooms.

The 900 MHz frequency allows a range of up to half a mile. It deals more effectively with interference than the 46/49 MHz frequency because its wavelength is just one foot long. The 2.4 GHz frequency handles interference even more efficiently than the other two because its wavelength is much shorter. It has a transmission range of up to four miles.

Ringer
A ringer in the base unit is handy, especially if you have a speakerphone. As with a corded phone, you can adjust the ringer's volume or turn it off completely.

Security codes
Each cordless phone comes with a number of security codes designed to help prevent phone fraud. Early models featured

only a few, but today there are anywhere from 1,000 to 100,000 plus. Most models will randomly change the security code for you.

Speakerphone

Some cordless speakerphones come with a speaker built into the base unit, while others have a keypad in the base as well as the handset, thus giving you the capabilities of two extensions. You can conduct a three-way conversation among a caller, a coworker, and yourself by using the speakerphone and the handset. There are other cordless phones that don't have fully functional speakerphones; these are used for intercom functions only. Be sure to ask.

TROUBLESHOOTING TIPS—CORDLESS

✔ Make sure your base station is situated in a central location. A high shelf is preferable, far away from interference from other electrical appliances.

✔ For best reception, raise the antenna on both the base unit and the handset.

✔ Don't plug the base unit into a circuit that also powers a major appliance. Doing so will probably cause interference and greatly limit your range.

✔ Radio interference may be caused by such things as a TV, refrigerator, vacuum cleaner, computer, fax machine, fluorescent light, or an electrical storm. You can do something about the electrical stuff in your office, but if Mother Nature is active, your best bet is to use a corded phone.

✔ If you experience noise on the line, select a different channel or let your phone automatically search for a clear channel. If you still experience static, move closer to the base unit.

✔ No dial tone? It could be many things. Is the phone in STANDBY mode? (If so, select TALK.) Is the phone switched off? Are the batteries low? Is the telephone cord detached from the base unit? Is the base set plugged into electrical power? Or perhaps the security codes in the handset and base unit have gotten out of sync. Try placing the handset back onto the base and see if that corrects the problem. If you've checked all this out and the phone still doesn't work, it's possible that your phone line is bad (see Chapter 2 for suggestions).

TROUBLESHOOTING TIPS—OTHER PHONES

Static on the line

Many things can cause static on corded phones. Electrical storms, crummy wiring, and damp connectors are among the culprits. If none of these things seem to be at fault, try this old trick: Tap the mouthpiece with the palm of your hand. This shakes up the carbon granules inside the mouthpiece and re-aligns them. High humidity can make the granules stick together, thus creating interference.

Read your manual

This story really happened to me. One day my two-line phone started acting wacky. I first noticed the problem when I called 411 for information and got two information operators on the line. Then, when I called my voice mail provider to get a telephone number, I was connected to two service agents. However, the phone worked fine for incoming calls. Strange.

This Panasonic Easa-Phone had been in my family for about three years, so I thought perhaps it was just getting old. Or maybe the lines got crossed up somehow, and I was dialing out on two lines. It turned out I was correct about this, but my next thought was not so correct. I thought it must be a low-battery thing. So I dug around, found three OK-looking batteries, and swapped them. No luck. I tried changing line cords. Nope. Then I replaced the phone with a working single-line phone. Now it seemed my problem was solved, but I was down to only a single line.

Later that day, I called my friend, the phone guru, and asked for his advice. "You've probably pushed in the conference button," he suggested. "What conference button?" I asked myself.

So, finally, I turned to the operations manual. Right there, in black and white, was a simple drawing explaining the workings of my set. The phone did indeed have a conference button, cryptically labeled CONF, that I had never noticed. How did it get pushed in?

As I retraced the events leading up to my phone's Jekyll-and-Hyde behavior, I recalled an incident involving my cat, Winston. Always insanely jealous of the time I spend on the phone, Winston had jumped on it the previous day and evidently landed on the CONF button, linking the two lines together. (How did he know?) My problem was permanently solved when I pushed the CONF button again to break the connection.

The moral of this story: Read your phone manual. It contains information that can definitely save you troubleshooting time. Or, I suppose I could kick the cats out of the office. Nah!

HEADSETS

If you spend several hours a day on the phone or suffer from headaches and neck cramps caused by scrunching the phone between ear and shoulder, it's time to get a headset. Headsets let you take calls and work comfortably hands-free, and they come in both corded and cordless models.

More and more professionals are using headsets—stockbrokers, technical support engineers, travel agents, journalists, pharmacists, marketing and sales personnel, as well as dispatchers, telemarketers, and customer service agents. Depending on the features and reception quality of the set, prices range from a low of $50 up to around $300.

Using a headset reduces neck and back strain, adds ergonomic comfort to your workspace, and decreases both stress and job turnover. Industry studies show that headset use will increase productivity by at least 11 percent. In once case, productivity improved as much as 43 percent. If you're on the phone two hours a day, headset use can save you approximately an hour a week.

Productivity increase based on headset use

Time spent on phone calls per day	Hours saved per day	Additional calls possible per day
25%	.22	4
50%	.44	8
75%	.66	12

(Source: "Do Headsets Save Money? You Bet!" *TeleProfessional*, October, 1993)

Connecting a Headset

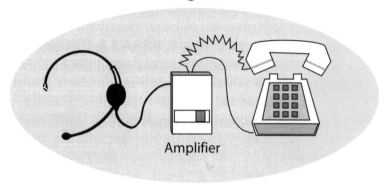

Amplifier

Headsets replace your handset. They use a modular plug that connects to an amplifier plugged into your phone base. Your handset is connected to the amplifier as well. Headsets usually have a flexible boom featuring a tiny microphone at the end to pick up your voice.

HEADSET FEATURES

Amplifier
Your headset connects to an amplifier, and the amplifier connects to the phone. Good amps can increase the volume of the call up to 30 percent.

Compatibility with your telephone
Headsets are compatible with most business telephones. Check with your headset vendor to make sure.

Cordless capability
Some headsets are cord free and let you roam as far as 50 to 100 feet from the phone base.

Earpiece(s)
Headsets are available with either one or two earpieces. The single earpiece allows you to hear what's going on around you. However, if you suffer from hearing problems or work in a noisy or distracting environment, you'll want to get a headset with two earpieces.

Headband or over the ear?

Some models hang over your ear, while others fit on a headband. You can adjust some headbands more than others, so check them out to find your preference.

Headset/phone combinations

If you're in the market for a new phone, consider buying a phone with headset compatibility built in. Several manufacturers offer these combos, including Vtech, Uniden, IBM, Hello Direct, and Plantronics. These phones come with a belt clip, so you can "wear" them anywhere. Plug in a headset, pop it on your head, wander anywhere in the office or nearby outdoors, and still stay connected. Great for answering the door while on a call!

Microphone

Make sure the microphone has the capability to cancel noise. Otherwise, your callers may hear extraneous background noises.

Microphone boom

A telescoping boom allows you to position the mike as close to your mouth as possible. Some headsets have a boom that swivels, so you can wear the mike on either your right or left side.

Mute

You'll definitely want mute control. This way, your mike is cancelled out, but you can continue to hear the caller. Some headsets put mute control in the microphone boom—up position for MUTE and down for TALK. Others place the mute control in the amplifier.

Operating range

If you choose a corded model, make sure the headset cord is long enough for you to reach a file or turn around without pulling up short. You don't want the feeling of being tethered to your phone. For cordless models, find out how far you can roam before static interferes. Some cordless headsets allow travel up to 1000 feet.

Quick disconnect

Look for a headset that features an easy method for disconnecting from the amp or phone. When you want to get up and walk around, it's more convenient to simply disconnect rather than take your headset off.

Voice recognition capability

If you plan to use your headset with a software voice recognition program, such as Dragon NaturallySpeaking (www.dragonsys.com) or IBM ViaVoice (www.ibm.com), you'll want a compatible headset. Most require a 3.5 mm jack to plug into your computer.

Y-adapter

These adapters allow another person to plug in to your phone line. They are useful for monitoring and training purposes.

Weight

When it comes to headsets, the lighter the better. However, lightweight sets may have fewer built-in features.

☎ In my office

I love my headset phone, which is a hands-free cordless model from Hello Direct (800-444-3556 or www.hellodirect.com). The Office Rover (as it's called) comes with a lightweight remote pack that I carry in my pocket or clip on my belt. The headset is an over-the-ear model, the SOLO II, also from Hello Direct. This setup lets me roam around the house or yard and answer calls with a single touch.

In addition, I hooked up Hello Direct's ReadiLine remote handset lifter to my office phone. This device lifts the phone's handset whenever I activate my headset, so I don't have to rush back to my telephone to pick up when an incoming call. When the call is over, ReadiLine hangs up for me. I use the headset frequently at my desk, especially when I'm conducting interviews. It's great to be able to type comfortably with no neck cramps.

Earphone

Maybe you don't like wearing a headset, but you still want cordless convenience without the hassle of a handset. If so, look into the Jabra EarSet (www.jabra.com or 800-327-2230). This is a tiny, thimble-sized device that fits comfortably in your outer ear and replaces your telephone handset. It contains a miniature microphone that picks up only the sound of your voice.

The earphone is connected by a cord to a clip-on unit that contains mute and volume controls. The control unit plugs into the handset jack on your phone. In addition to making an earphone that works with several different cellular phones, Jabra also offers a model that can turn your computer into a smart phone.

Using a headset

Headsets are a bit like eyeglasses—they take getting used to. It's best to wear your headset for short intervals at first. Then gradually increase the wear time each day until you are handset free. This process should only take two to three weeks.

In most situations, headsets can take the place of handsets. However, unless you buy a special phone designed to work only with a headset or have a LINE or SPEAKERPHONE button, you'll need to lift the receiver in order to get dial tone. Also, the receiver must remain off-hook during the call and be placed back on-hook before you can receive the next call. To simplify things, you can get an off-hook device that attaches to your phone base, such as the Touch-N-Talk handset lifter from Hello Direct. When you want to make a call, pressing a lever on this device lifts the handset. At the end of the call, just lower the lever.

When you're wearing a headset, it's not always easy for your coworkers to tell whether you're on the phone or not. To reduce interruptions, you might install a busy light, which is an add-on device that lights up when you're on the line.

PHONE ACCESSORIES

AMPLIFIED PHONES AND HANDSETS

If you suffer from a hearing loss or the inability to hear high-frequency sounds, you might consider investing in an amplified phone. You can get one from Hello Direct or Lucent Technologies. These phones do more than simply adjust the volume on the earpiece. Special circuitry improves the clarity of the sound by selectively increasing the volume of only high-frequency sounds. Controls for tone and volume settings are usually found in the handset.

Another alternative is to get a handset amplifier. There are several varieties. One type plugs in between your handset cord and your handset. The volume on this type is modified with a control dial. Another type replaces your regular handset with a special handset that has volume control built in.

RECORDING DEVICES

Writers, attorneys, real estate agents, and many others who want to keep accurate records of their calls find that phone recording is a useful tool. Recording eliminates the need to scribble copious notes while on a call.

Some people believe you must use a device that generates an annoying beep tone every 15 seconds or so while recording. This is not required. According to the FCC (Rule 6, subpart E), you may legally record a phone conversation as long as you inform the other party that you are recording. As an extra safeguard, be sure to record the notification at the beginning of your conversation.

If you need to record a telephone conversation, you can get a voice-activated recording adapter. It has a modular jack on one end to plug into your phone line (though some plug in between the base and the handset) and a plug on the other end to connect to your tape recorder. Just turn on the device to tape a call. The recorder will pause when there's no voice on the line.

☎ In my office

I use an Olympus Pearlcorder L100. It's a tiny recorder that uses microcasette tapes, each capable of recording an hour's conversation. That's plenty for my needs. When I'm ready to listen to my recording, I plug in a tiny earpiece to play back the tape silently.

I attach the recorder to my phone via Hello Direct's Universal Telephone Recorder interface, which records everything I hear over the phone as well as my end of the conversation. While I'm recording, I usually make a few quick notes and jot down the time of segments I especially want to use. Afterwards, I can quickly find the sections that I noted.

CALL SIGNALERS

Are you unable to hear the phone ring over the sounds in your workspace? Do you need to hear the phone ring from great distances? Do you want to know if the phone is ringing, but don't want to hear it? There are call signaling devices available to solve these and any other phone ringer issues you can think of.

You'll want to shop around, because there are so many options to choose from. You can get an adapter that turns off your ringer and activates a strobe light; or one that augments your ringer with a loud horn, warble, or tweet; and even one that makes your desk lamp flash when a call comes in.

CONFERENCE PHONES

If you frequently need to conference several people on a call, you should consider a conferencing system. It consists of a quality speakerphone possessing the following features: several built-in microphones for 360 degree sound pickup; digital signal processors to cancel out voice echoes; and automatic gain control so that quiet speakers can be heard. These speakerphones are full duplex, meaning you and your called party can talk at the same time without experiencing the clipping and one-way conversations of standard speakerphones.

Quality speakerphones and conference phones are rated for the number of people they're designed to support. They also come in a variety of configurations to accommodate various room sizes. A triangular-shaped phone with mikes in each angle will normally handle up to ten people in a room up to 20 by 24 feet. Larger spaces will require a speakerphone with extension mikes.

To set up a conference phone, all you need is an analog line and a power outlet. If you have only digital phone lines in your office, you'll need a digital-to-analog adapter.

TELECONFERENCING

Teleconferencing is a powerful tool. It can be used for product launches, distance training, media briefings, problem-solving meetings, information-sharing events, team get-togethers, and status sessions.

Compared to the cost of business travel, teleconferences are an attractive alternative. According to a 2000 survey of business travel by Runzheimer International, a domestic three-day business trip averages $970, and the cost of an average seven-day international trip is $3,455. In contrast, a dozen participants located all across the country can meet for a one-hour teleconference for about $200. If they all flew in just for the meeting, that same meeting would cost around $6,000.

TYPES OF TELECONFERENCE SERVICES

Conferencing services offer a variety of conference-calling options. Here are some of the most common:

Meet-me number

Conference participants call a preassigned telephone number and pay for their own long-distance charges. There are no on-call operators or automated announcements. Meet-me calls take a bit of getting used to—if you're the first person to call in, you hear nothing until someone else joins you on the line. If participants are not briefed, they may hang up as I did the first time I encountered one of these lines. So be sure to inform all parties on how it works, and insist on promptness. This type of service works best for small meetings.

Automated service

Participants in automated service conference calls also pay for their own long-distance charges. After dialing the preassigned number, they are greeted by an automated voice and prompted to announce themselves. At this point, they are automatically placed into the conference call. Operator assistance is available, often by pressing zero. This type of call is recommended for smaller groups where people know each other.

Operator-assisted call

After dialing a toll-free number, which is answered by a human being, conference participants are placed in a hold queue until the conference begins. The operator/assistant might also take roll, control the question and answer session, or help with offline technical questions. When the call is over, you can arrange for a tape or transcript of the call—very handy if you need to keep comprehensive notes or minutes. This type of service works best for calls with large numbers of participants, and especially for calls where everyone is not already acquainted.

Advanced services

Conferencing companies are adding lots of special services to enhance these calls, such as the ability to upload and display PowerPoint slides on a website, electronic whiteboarding services, or document collaboration services.

To locate a teleconferencing services company, call your local telephone company or look in the yellow pages under *Teleconference Services*. Major national companies include:

- AT&T   800-232-1234
- The Conference Center   800-825-2578
- Confertech   800-525-8244
- networkMCI   800-475-5000
- Sprint   800-366-2663

To set up a call, specify the number of ports or phone lines you need, the date and time of the call, and the services you will require. Then send your agenda to everyone who will participate in sufficient time so they'll all know how to use the service you've selected. Send an e-mail or fax with the most important particulars: the phone number to dial, the time and date of the call, the call duration, conference name, host name, and, if required, password. If conferees are in different time zones, list the correct time for each or specify the host time zone.

TIPS FOR BETTER TELECONFERENCING

A good leader can maximize the effectiveness of a teleconference. Here are some tips to help you make yours the best:

- Send all participants an agenda. If possible, get it to them a few days in advance so they can prepare. If you're going to be discussing written material, email it to everyone in advance.

- Inform everyone of the objective of the meeting at the beginning of the call. If someone starts to wander, interrupt and guide the discussion back to the topic.

- You'll save money if some of your members gather around a speakerphone and share a port. Just make sure that they're equipped with a good speakerphone designed for the size of the group.

- Be a stickler for timeliness. Keep to your time limit.

TELETIQUETTE

Even Miss Manners has a section in her new book, *Miss Manners' Basic Training: Communication*, on how to behave when participating in a conference call. Here are Langhoff's tips:

- Don't be late to a call—it's rude. Call a couple of minutes prior to the scheduled call time. If others are habitually late on regular calls, speak up about it. They're wasting everyone's time and costing the company money.

- Limit distractions. Close the door to your office and post a sign that you are not to be disturbed. If you have call waiting, turn it off before dialing in.

- Identify yourself when speaking. Don't assume that people will recognize your voice when you speak.

- Don't hog the limelight. Say your piece, then stay quiet so that others can contribute.

- Beware of cheap speakerphones. It's OK to use your speakerphone for listening to the call, but be sure to use the handset when you want to speak. Otherwise, your audience will have difficulty hearing you. (Not to mention that you'll come off sounding like the voice of the Wizard of Oz.)

COMPUTER PHONE

Take a computer, plug in a telephone line, add some software, a microphone, and maybe an internal card, and you get a very smart telephone. Computer telephones save valuable desktop real estate and provide greater functionality than other phones.

Computer software can run on Macs, UNIX, or in Windows, and it fulfills many communications functions. Such software lets you make or take a phone call, manage your phone lists, store an unlimited phone directory, autodial a number by picking it from a list on the screen, and automatically log calls. You may also have answering machine, fax-on-demand, or paging capability.

If you recently purchased a computer, most likely you already have everything you need to start phoning from your desktop. Many new models are prepackaged with computer telephony products, including voice mail, answering machine capability, fax-on-demand, and data modeming.

Using your computer as your telephone is not the solution for everyone. You may have to leave your PC on all the time. If you have too few resources, such as memory and drive space, your computer may slow to an irritating crawl when you receive a call. Plus you'll need a goodly amount of hard disk space to store voice messages. Even compressed, a minute of voice can take up to 1.3 megabytes of disk space.

For more information on computer telephones, see *Internet Calling* in Chapter 3. Computer telephony is a fast-changing field. To stay current, look into these publications:

Computer Telephony Magazine
1265 Industrial Highway
Southampton, PA 18966
215-355-2866
www.computertelephony.com

Internet Telephony
One Technology Plaza
Norwalk, CT 06854
203-852-6800
www.itmag.com

Communications Solutions
(same as above)
www.tmcnet.com

RESOURCES

Product comparisons
Consumer Reports publishes a survey of both cordless and corded telephones every few years. Check your library, or, if you have access to CompuServe, go to the *Consumer Reports* section (Go CSR) and look under electronics.

Books
Internet Telephony for Dummies
by Daniel D. Briere, Patrick J. Hurley, IDG Books, 1996

Websites
The Phone Source
www.thephonesource.com

Looking for a novelty phone gift? Maybe you'd like to give someone the Marilyn Monroe phone—when the phone rings, she sings, "I wanna be loved by you"—or a replica of the phone used in Casablanca.

Hello Direct
www.hellodirect.com

This is the best business telecom site on the Web. The online store offers loads of top-quality telecom products, plus a complete information center with tutorials, news, reviews, and buyers' guides. There's even an online Web board, where you can post questions about products and read comments and recommendations from other users.

Radio Shack
www.radioshack.com

You'll find a large catalog of phone stuff at this site, including hard-to-find items, such as alligator clips, terminal connectors, and cables of all kinds. The site also provides comprehensive online manuals for the products they carry.

Catalog of Unique Telecom & Cable Installation Products
www.sandman.com

Mike Sandman, Chicago's telecom expert, offers his personal choices in a number of categories, including problem-solving tools, test equipment, telephone repair parts, and training videos. My favorite is the Ringing Telephone Magnet. It attaches to your phone's handset and actually rings like a real phone when you press the start button. Whoops, my other line is ringing! Gotta go.

Phone Systems

. . . .

AT SOME POINT, YOUR BUSINESS may outgrow the stand-alone phones you've been using. Once your needs exceed the capabilities of two- or three-line phone sets and a bunch of extensions, you'll need an integrated phone system. This usually happens around the six-user mark, but it could happen sooner, especially if you expect to grow fast.

Phone systems allow you to maximize your line usage, transfer calls, and have intercom capability between extensions. You can take advantage of line-sharing capabilities to get along with fewer lines, thus saving money on monthly line service costs. Four lines can easily support eight stations in an organization that does not have telephone-intensive applications.

You may also save money on outgoing calls by using toll-call restriction and least-cost routing, features available on most phone systems.

Phone systems are available in six broad categories:

- Key system
- KSU-less system
- PBX
- Hybrid system
- Wireless
- Centrex

KEY SYSTEM

Key systems were first introduced in the 1920s; they were the marvel of the modern office. Since then, they've become electronic, smaller in size, and easier to operate. Key systems are still very common in offices today, though they are losing ground to hybrid systems.

You can spot a key system by the multiple lighted buttons that allow each user to select an outgoing line or answer an incoming one. Instead of having six phones on your desk, each with its own line, you could install a six-button key system that lets you select a line. Having a key system is like having a miniature phone switch in your workplace. The keys or switches let you share lines with others in your facility, thus reducing the number of lines needed.

Key Phone System

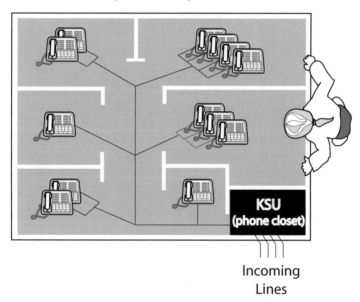

KSU
(phone closet)

Incoming
Lines

The key system allows your phone system to carry additional signals that reveal line status. These signals might tell the system to light up line lights on some phones or lock out a particular line. Key systems are good for three to one hundred users, depending on the individual system. They come with standard features, such as hold and conferencing, and optional features, such as loudspeaker paging, intercom, call restriction, and music-on-hold. The overall expense of a key system ranges from $175 to $500 per phone. The features you select, plus installation charges, will determine your final cost.

Modern key phone systems have several components:

- **Key service unit (KSU)**
  This box houses the power supply, switches, the central processing unit (to run the system), and a bunch of feature-control cards.

- **Telephones**
  Key set telephones are proprietary and are not interchangeable.

- **Add-on features**
  Often, circuit boards or electronic units provide special features, such as intercom, music-on-hold, or paging.

You cannot use your current telephones in a key system; nor can you add off-the-shelf telephone hardware, such as a cordless phone, in the future. Also, adding a modem or answering machine usually requires an expensive adapter or a block. If you have series wiring, you'll need to rewire because key systems require star (parallel) wiring. See *Connections* in Chapter 2 for more information.

Key systems do not require a centralized attendant or receptionist to field calls. Any extension user can answer an incoming call on any line by pushing the corresponding button. Therefore, these systems are best suited for smaller offices where anyone who answers the phone can take a message or track down the called party.

Focus on a key user

Tom Fox operates the FoxBerry Group, a computer consulting service based in Monroe, Michigan. He uses a Starplus 616 from Vodavi and "loves it." He and his staff of five currently use seven of the sixteen stations available. He has four voice lines; the other three lines are dedicated for data purposes—a modem line, a fax line, and a fax-on-demand line.

One of Tom's favorite features is the music-on-hold device. It plays a customized advertising message whenever a caller is waiting on the line. "Many of our customers comment positively on it," says Tom. He also likes the visual nature of a key system, because the lights let you know at a glance what lines are available and whether or not a call is on hold.

The Starplus system has single-line compatibility, so Tom was able to attach a modem and fax machine with no difficulty. If his company eventually outgrows this system's capacity, Tom can still use the same station sets with larger Starplus systems. He paid $1,500 for this starter Starplus system, which consists of a controller box and five phones. That works out to about $300 per station. Also, FoxBerry was able to keep costs down because parts of the system were pre-owned.

Tom chose a key system because "a PBX was really more than we needed." The only disadvantage he sees is that the system has no voice mail port, so it won't be easy to implement voice mail.

KSU-LESS SYSTEM

This is an introductory phone system suitable for two to four lines and four to eight extensions. Instead of having a phone cabinet (KSU), the smart electronics are built into each individual phone set. These systems are relatively inexpensive, but not as flexible as key systems. Because all the controls are built into the phone itself, you cannot use your current telephones in a KSU-less system.

There's no difficulty involved with installing KSU-less systems. You simply plug the new phones into your existing phone jacks (RJ-11 or RJ-14) using standard two-pair wire, and plug the electrical jack into an outlet. You can purchase a KSU-less system at your local electronics store (or via mail order) and have it installed in less than an hour. These systems work with series or star wiring—there is no need to rewire. Costs per telephone set will range anywhere from $100 to $300.

Southwestern Bell makes both a three- and a four-line KSU-less phone system. Each system comes with a built-in intercom for hands-free conferencing, line status lights, and a speakerphone. Standard features include one-button speed dialing, hold, transfer, and three-way calling. An LCD display shows the number dialed, the duration of the call, plus the time and date. The cost per phone is about $250 for the three-line system and $300 for the four-line system. If you installed a three-line system with five extensions, it would run you around $1,250.

Focus on a KSU-less user

Charlie Swanson runs Edgewater Productions, a film, video, and multimedia production house in San Francisco. He recently upgraded his two-line phones to four-line KSU-less sets made by GE. These phones provide a two-way intercom, a speakerphone, and three-party conferencing, plus do-not-disturb mode, line selection, and status indicators.

The phones require no special wiring. They plug into the power and phone jacks the same way regular that single-line phones do. Each phone cost about $150, so the total investment was just $1,200. Swanson picked the GE four-line phones because they were "cheaper than a phone system, easier to install, and don't need any special support."

The Southwestern Bell systems are remarkably easy to install. For example, to get the three-line system up and running, you plug one line cord into a RJ-14 (two-line) jack to access lines 1 and 2, then plug another line cord into a RJ-11 (one-line) jack for the third line. Plug the phone into a wall outlet for electrical power, and that's it!

PBX (PRIVATE BRANCH EXCHANGE)

It used to be that you had to have at least 50 users before a PBX was cost justified. That distinction is blurring, however, as more manufacturers are offering mini-PBXs at competitive prices. You can usually spot a PBX because you have to dial "9" before making an outgoing call. The "9" takes the place of the plug system operator in older PBXs. You may see systems called PABX (the "A" stands for automatic) or EPABX (the "E" means electronic), but PBX is most commonly used.

A PBX is more flexible than a key system. In addition to smoothly integrating phone, fax, and modem lines, you can tailor your PBX stations (the telephone extensions) with features such as paging, voice mail, and call pickup. Regular, off-the-shelf single-line phone sets can be used with these systems, or you can also install proprietary feature phones sold by the PBX vendor. PBXs require star (parallel) wiring, and costs per station for smaller systems amount to about $300 to $450 installed.

Perhaps the best reason for getting a PBX is the control it gives you over phone costs. You can easily generate reports on who calls where and for how long. PBXs also excel at saving you money on your long-distance charges by the use of least-cost routing.

Least-cost routing employs algorithms to search for the most economical line for an outgoing call. You or your vendor must program the least-cost rules and update them as prices change. If your organization is a heavy long-distance user and subscribes to several long-distance services, a PBX could save you up to 20 percent on your monthly long-distance bills.

Using a PBX will also allow you to improve your trunk (phone line)-to-station ratio. Larger PBXs can often get along with one trunk for each ten users. Unfortunately for small businesses, those economies of scale don't work in the reverse. Smaller PBXs often have a trunk-to-station ratio of about 1:3, which is still pretty good.

PBX users compete for a limited number of lines. If all lines are in use, the next outgoing call is blocked and incoming calls receive a busy signal. Because of this call blocking, you don't have to pay for excess phone lines that you seldom use. The tradeoff, of course, is that sometimes your customers will receive a busy signal during the busiest times of the day, and your staff may have to wait for an outgoing line.

To avoid the need for a full-time receptionist, you can program a mini-PBX to ring certain phones in sequence. This process is similar to a hunt group. For example, you might first have the phone ring twice at a secretary's station. If no one answers, the call will ring a few times more at the office manager's phone. Then, if still no answer, the phone in your office rings. You'll need a receptionist to handle the attendant console that is required for larger PBXs.

HYBRID SYSTEM

Hybrid phone systems combine key and PBX technology. Unlike regular key systems, hybrids allow you to install your current single-line phones on some extensions. Hybrids can also offer you more flexibility by virtue of a nice feature known as non-squared design. Essentially, non-squared design means you don't have to have every phone line appear on every phone set as key systems do. Hybrids require star (parallel) wiring. Some systems require an attendant; others don't. The price for hybrids ranges from $300 to $550 per station.

Lucent Technology's Partner Communications System is a hybrid system. The Partner is a modular system, which works well for small businesses with plans to grow. Although you may start with only one or two employees, the Partner lets you grow gracefully.

The initial setup provides a two-line, six-extension system. As business warrants, you can purchase an expansion unit that will allow you to accept up to four lines and twelve extensions. The system can easily expand up to 16 lines and 48 extensions by adding more modules. To install the Partner, you simply mount a small box on the wall, plug your lines and phones into the box, and you're in business.

The Partner can connect standard off-the-shelf telephone equipment, such as single-line phones, faxes, modems, cordless phones, or answering devices. It comes with a bunch of built-in and programmable features that include privacy, recall, last number redial, intercom, hands-free announce, intercom page, toll restriction, transfer, conference, and, of course, hold.

WIRELESS

There's a wide range of telephone systems that rely on wireless technology. Some are based on cordless technologies; others are true wireless phones, using radio waves to send signals.

CORDLESS SYSTEM

Cordless phone systems are relatively inexpensive. For example, a Siemens Gigaset is a cordless multiuser system that can support up to nine extension telephones using one wall jack servicing two phone lines. The initial setup costs about $400, and each additional phone set is about $150. The phones are lightweight, cordless, and can clip to your belt. They also have intercom capability, so you can talk to fellow workers without tying up a phone line.

Focus on a cordless user

Margaret and Fred Robinson run two separate businesses from their home in St. Louis, Missouri. Margaret operates The Wordstation, a business support services company. She shares her office space with FNR Designs, her husband's store planning and design firm. Together, they use a Siemens Gigaset 2420 with three remote units.

Though the system was difficult to set up, Margaret says it works well now. "Retrieving remote messages is excellent," she says. "You can get just the new messages and not have to listen to all the old ones."

WIRELESS SYSTEM

If you need a larger system, you might consider a wireless phone system. Most operate from radio base stations that may be installed in the building's ceiling or mounted on the wall. Wireless systems usually work in conjunction with traditional phone systems, such as a PBX or key system. Centrex also supports a wireless product. Often, companies keep a few wireless sets in a pool, checking them out to employees as needed. Companies that especially benefit from wireless systems include health care facilities, schools, construction firms, car dealers, restaurants, real estate offices, and other service businesses.

WHAT'S BEST, WIRELESS OR CORDLESS?

According to Sondra Jordan, author of *How to Buy the Best Phone System*, wireless phones provide superior quality, but they are far more expensive than cordless systems. If you have five or fewer employees, lots of fluorescent lighting, a low budget, and need the phones mostly for internal use, cordless is a good choice.

On the other hand, wireless is a better choice if security is important, you tend to have lengthy conversations, and if your budget can handle it.

CENTREX

Centrex is a service that you can lease on a month-to-month basis from your local telco. Centrex gives you phone-system control without having to buy any special equipment. You can select from a broad range of PBX-like services, such as conference calling, intercom, call forwarding, flexible route selection, automatic call back, caller ID, call pickup, and call transfer.

The features you select are up to you. You can even decide which station sets get which features. For example, you might give managers do-not-disturb and hotline ability, but restrict warehouse phones to local dialing only.

Centrex is the most flexible of your phone system choices. Because Centrex can accommodate anything from two lines to 20,000 lines or more, your growth potential is virtually unlimited. You pay only for the lines and features you need, and it's easy to add or remove features. You can also expand or downsize as necessary. Centrex works with your current equipment, so you don't have to purchase proprietary phone sets or adapters to hook up single-line phones.

Because calls come in directly, you don't need an attendant, assuming that all your callers know the direct number they need to dial. If you need some kind of directory or receptionist, you can add on an attendant console or set up an auto attendant system. If you want to add features to your Centrex system, work with your local telco to be sure you get compatible equipment.

If your company has more than one location, Centrex may be your best choice. Centrex can connect multiple sites and provide them with the same features and capabilities as those on your main premises. For example, you can dial your warehouse down the street without having to place an outside call, thus saving the per-call charge. All you have to do is key in the last four or five digits of the phone number. However, your various locations must all share the same central office for this to work.

Because there isn't any switching equipment on your site, you don't need to worry about housing, maintenance, repair, software upgrades, or obsolescence. Centrex is housed in the telco's central office and is tended by 24-hour on-site personnel.

Focus on a Centrex user

Precision Navigation in Mountain View, California, manufactures digital automobile compasses. The company started with five people and two phone lines, but in less than a year it expanded to 30 employees. According to office manager Christine Sherer, "Our Centrex system is currently at seventeen lines and can grow right along with us."

When Precision Navigation moved its manufacturing operation down the street, the relocated group was able to stay in the same Centrex system. Sherer likes the convenience of being able to dial only four digits to reach them, and "it's not an outside call." This way, the company saves money on each call made to manufacturing.

In addition, Centrex works with your current wiring, so there's no need to rewire. This fact was a "godsend" to Father Paul Martin of Mission San Juan Capistrano. The mission needed a new phone system to connect the convent, school, and parish, but the phone system installers wanted to dig up the grounds in order to run new cable. Unwilling to damage the historic mission grounds, Father Martin opted for a Centrex system that was installed without digging a single hole.

If you live in an area that experiences power outages or is prone to disaster, such as earthquakes, Centrex has a decided advantage over premises-based phone systems. That advantage is its power backup system. Centrex service is rarely interrupted by a commercial power failure because most central offices are built to withstand just about anything Mother Nature can hurl at them.

On the downside, Centrex will probably cost you more than a PBX in the long run. Industry experts estimate that a PBX will start to save you money over Centrex after about five years. Then again, considering the speed of telco technological development, that same PBX may be desperately out of date in five years.

If you like the control of moving phones and changing lines whenever you wish, Centrex will slow you down. Usually, you have to call your phone company to reprogram before you can make a change. You can sign up for an optional control package that lets you make changes, but it comes with a price.

Centrex prices vary considerably, depending on which company provides your local phone service. In Pacific Bell territory, Centrex starts at $15.65 a month per line, plus installation costs of $75 per line and a start-up fee of $200. When comparing costs, be sure to note that Centrex service replaces your current business lines and includes a group of features that you would have to pay for separately on a business line.

SELECTING A PHONE SYSTEM

Here are some issues to consider when thinking about a phone system:

CAPACITY

According to the researchers at Telecom Library Inc., "Buying too small is the biggest and most expensive mistake most buyers make."

When evaluating sizing needs, you need to know the maximum capacity of the system. Fortunately, this is easy to determine. Almost all key system manufacturers (plus many KSU-less and hybrid companies) follow the convention of listing capacity numbers as part of the product name. Armed with this knowledge, we can decipher that a Lucent Technology Merlin Plus 410 will provide for four trunks (phone lines) and ten stations (extensions), and an Executone 4 x 8 accommodates four lines and eight stations. A Code-A-Phone 616 can handle six lines and 16 stations. Easy, huh?

In case it's not obvious, maximum capacity means just that. If you get a 6 x 12 system, for example, you can only add 12 goodies on that system. If you need a thirteenth device (phone, fax, or whatever), you're out of luck. On the other hand, Centrex offers nearly unlimited capacity. You won't outgrow it until you need more than 100,000 lines!

Determining the number of lines you'll need depends on the type of business you're in and the number of people requiring phone access. According to the U.S. Small Business Administration, companies should add one line for each employee who spends a third or more of his time on the phone. Though there are no universal rules regarding lines-to-people ratios, many organizations find that one line for each three stations is adequate. Here are some examples that might help you sort it out:

- A florist or pharmacist may only need two lines—one for voice orders; one shared between fax orders and credit card authorizations.

- A real estate office might need one line for every two or three agents. After all, they're out of the office a lot, or they should be.

- A travel agency might need two or even three lines for every agent—one for incoming calls, another for modeming to online ticket services, and a third for outgoing calls.

- A motel may need a lot of stations, but few outgoing lines. Each room would need one phone, but only one line could accommodate twenty rooms.

Years ago, a friend of mine, recently graduated from medical school, set up a solo practice. She hired only a receptionist, but she spent almost all her first month's receipts on (what seemed to me at the time) a whopping, big 6 x 16 PBX. Sixteen stations for two people?

It sounded crazy, but she was right. Her practice grew and the system grew with her. That same phone system worked for ten years. Only now does she need to replace it with a larger one. Remember, it makes sense to buy more capacity than you currently need.

SUGGESTIONS FOR DETERMINING YOUR ORGANIZATION'S NEEDS

✔ Contact your local phone company and ask your rep for a busy line study. This is a statistical printout of the number and frequency of incoming calls that receive busy signals. (Be sure to ask for the cost of the study before ordering.)

✔ Check with your professional association or Chamber of Commerce. They may keep statistics on members' telephone setups and typical costs. Other good information sources are online forums, such as the Working From Home forum on CompuServe.

✔ Ask your staff to keep a phone log for a couple of weeks. Divide the log into incoming and outgoing calls, and have your staff write down the beginning and ending time of each call. Look for patterns of usage. Do all your customers seem to call right before lunch?

✔ Analyze your current phone use. Do all members of your staff need access to incoming and outgoing lines? Do some people need more than one incoming line at their desk? Does every employee need a phone on his or her desk?

✔ The U.S. Small Business Administration suggests that you allocate a line for each employee that spends at least a third of his day on the phone.

Lines to People Ratio

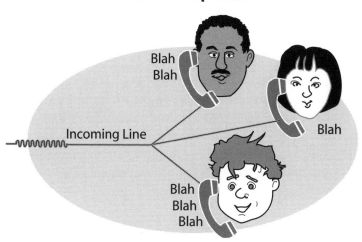

Be sure to allow for extra phone lines to accommodate fax machines, modems, credit card authorization terminals, and answering machines. Some organizations install a phone outside the entrance for safe after-hours entry. You may also need a phone in the reception area, in the copy room, or back in the warehouse.

Decide whether you want to hardwire certain peripherals, such as credit card or check authorization lines, or run them through your phone system. Depending on your business, it probably makes sense to have dedicated circuits for certain lines. After all, you might not want customers paying by check or credit card to wait while your cashier queues for an outside line.

COMPATIBILITY

Phone systems sound like a great idea—until you try to add a modem or a cordless phone made by another manufacturer to your communications system. Unfortunately, there is little industry-wide standardization.

Each key system manufacturer handles signaling a little differently. The net result is that you probably can't use another telco manufacturer's device in your system and are limited to your vendor's proprietary equipment. This situation could be serious and expensive. Just adding a modem may require separate wiring or the purchase of some kind of converter.

Things are beginning to change, though. Look for systems that advertise Open Application Interface (OAI). The operant word here is "open." If your system is designed with OAI, you can use your computer to customize your telephone switch, integrate call processing with computer databases, and mix and match equipment from various manufacturers. Standards are still being settled, however. So, shop with care and ask a lot of questions.

MIGRATION PATH

Many key system and PBX manufacturers offer modular systems that can grow with you. You begin with a small starter set and gradually upgrade to larger systems. All the original hardware, including phone sets and control units, can be used for each system. You'll recall that the Lucent Technology Partner phone system described earlier in this chapter can be purchased in modules. By adding modules, you can expand from a two-line, six-station system to four lines and twelve stations, and ultimately to a 16/48 configuration.

Combining phone systems may be another interesting option. You'll find companies offering combinations of Centrex with a PBX or a key system running "behind" a PBX. This arrangement is sometimes called "piggybacking." Here's how it works: You have a PBX, but you want a particular department or group to be more accessible to outside callers. The solution is to install a key system (or Centrex) in that department. Now callers will be able to dial in direct via the piggyback system rather than calling your main number and getting the receptionist.

DIGITAL OR ANALOG?

All modern PBXs and hybrid systems, as well as higher-end key systems, are digital. This means that the electronics that run the system use digital rather than analog signaling. Having a digital phone system will give you cleaner sound and more "intelligence." For example, a digital phone set is "smart" enough to display the station number or even the name of the person calling from within your system. Often, the buttons on a digital set can be programmed for easy one-button access to frequently used features or dialing codes.

Don't confuse digital phone systems with digital lines. Most digital phone systems today are designed to work only with analog lines. To work with digital lines such as ISDN, DSL, or T1, you'll need a phone system that is compatible. For more information on phone lines, see Chapter 4.

COST

How much will a phone system set you back? It depends. (Don't you hate that answer?) But in the phone system world, you don't often find price lists. A major portion of the price may be the charge for the installation itself. Other variables also come into play, such as the features you select and the type of station sets you choose. If you call for a quick quote, often you'll get nothing more than a vague answer or, at best, a range.

Phone systems are usually quoted on a cost-per-station basis. This quote is derived from simply adding up all the costs of hardware, installation, warranty, and other extraneous charges, then dividing it by the number of extensions. Thus a 4x8 Executone key system quoted at $1,799 would cost out at $450 per station. Thinking in terms of cost per station makes it somewhat easier to compare prices.

Although we all want to save money, buying a phone system based solely on price considerations is a false economy. Harry Newton, author of *Newton's Telecom Dictionary*, gives three reasons why it's unwise to shop price exclusively:

1. The people who answer your phone cost a great deal more than your new telephone system. If they hate the system, they'll do a lousy job of answering the phone.

2. Ninety percent of a customer's contacts with your organization take place initially over the telephone. You want that first impression to be as positive as possible.

3. A phone call is much less costly than other types of communications, especially when you factor in employee time.

If you need to save money, consider buying a used or refurbished system. Savings from 30 to 50 percent are common. You can locate used equipment at a business auction or by calling a local installer. You might also contact the North American Association of Telecommunications Dealers (NATD) at 561-266-9440. They can provide you with the names of NATD-certified secondhand equipment dealers in your area.

FEATURES

Phone systems usually come with loads of features—probably more than you need and maybe more than you want. I've listed some of the most useful below. You won't find all these features in every phone system. The feature set depends on the price and the technology, whether key, Centrex, or others. I have also included some features that are more appropriate for larger organizations. After all, you're going to grow.

ACD (automatic call distribution)

This feature allows you to program routes for incoming calls to a designated group of stations. Which station gets the call is based on which agent has been idle the longest. If all stations are busy, calls are queued and processed on a first-in/first-out priority. ACDs are more common in larger phone systems. They can provide useful management reports, such as which agents were idle the longest, the number of calls abandoned in queue, and the number of callers waiting.

ADP (analog device port)

These ports are used for plugging in modems, fax machines, answering machines, cordless phones, and credit card verification devices.

Alarm signals

Alarm systems—smoke detectors, fire alarms, doorbells, intruder alerts, and the like—can be connected to your phone system. When an alarm condition is detected, you will be alerted by a ringing phone, a horn over the loudspeaker, etc.

Automated attendant

An automated attendant is a program that answers your phone, plays a prerecorded greeting, and prompts the caller to choose a route for his or her call. There may have one or many levels that branch out to provide choices. The automated attendant will prompt the caller to choose the specific extension number of the party desired, such as "0" for operator. It can also deliver helpful messages to the caller.

Automatic call back

This feature allows office mates to select automatic redial if a dialed station set was busy. It can also be used as a message reminder.

Call accounting codes

These codes, often several digits long, are used to charge a call to a department or project number rather than the calling station. It is especially useful when you need to bill specific projects or clients for your time. Usually, you can set up the system to force the code, force the code and verify that it is entered on your list, or accept an optional code. Forced and verified codes have the additional benefit of curtailing unauthorized access to your telecom system. See *SMDR* later in this chapter.

Caller ID display

Also known as automatic number identification (ANI), this feature displays the phone number and the name of the calling party, if available. You need to get caller ID service from your telephone company for this feature to work. Some phones also have a memory capable of storing a running list of incoming caller's numbers. The memory feature even records the phone numbers of callers who hang up before you answer.

Call forwarding

You can direct your incoming calls to another station by using the call forwarding feature. It is similar to the phone company's call forwarding, but, of course, you can only forward to other stations within your phone system. Some systems reroute calls when the intended station is busy or doesn't answer after a specified number of rings. The system itself may have call forwarding as well. System-wide call forwarding allows you to forward all your after-hours calls to an answering service or to voice mail, for example.

Call park

Call park is often used by systems that have a limited number of holding paths. You place a call in a waiting condition, page a third party, and have that party pick up the parked call from any station in the system.

Call pickup

Programming call pickup groups enables you to retrieve a call directed to another station in the same group. For example, if the phone in the next office is part of your pickup group, you can transfer the call to your phone and answer it, thus saving steps.

Call queuing

This feature is a simplified version of automatic call distribution. It keeps a running queue of all incoming calls and delivers them to the call answering staff in the order received. See *ACD*.

Call screening

Using a headset or a speakerphone, you can monitor calls that have been sent to your voice mailbox. While the person is leaving a voice message, you can decide if you want to pick up.

Call transfer

This is the feature used to transfer a call to another station. The call will ring and light up a LINE key only at the station that was called. Because there's no need to wait for a reply from the party being called, the person transferring the call, such as a receptionist, can process calls faster.

Camp on busy

If you're dialing an extension within your office and the line is busy, you can push the CAMP ON button (or dial a code) to let the called party know there's an internal call waiting. Your phone will ring you back automatically when the called party is off the line. This feature is also called call waiting on intercom.

Conference

The conference feature lets you add other persons to an existing conversation. It is especially useful for professionals who often need three-way conversations.

Data privacy

A user can specify that no interrupt tones, line signals, or pauses are allowed to interrupt a call. This safeguard eliminates the danger of inadvertently transferring a call to a line being used for data transmission via a modem.

DID (direct inward dialing)

Used by PBXs and Centrex, this feature allows the caller to bypass the receptionist. The call is passed straight through to the dialed extension, which saves call handling time. In effect, each station user gets an exclusive telephone number for incoming calls.

DISA (direct inward system access)

DISA allows you to designate a line or group of lines that may be accessed from a remote location. The incoming caller can then use the phone system's features or special circuits. For example, you could call the office from home and charge the call to your office line by dialing the appropriate code. This way, you can take advantage of your office's long-distance dialing plan discounts.

However, DISA has a big disadvantage. It is not secure. There-fore, phone hackers could get into your system and ring up an enormous phone bill that you are responsible for—$50,000 in one weekend is not unusual. The telephone industry reports that DISA phone fraud costs businesses over $1 billion per year.

Beware: Hackers especially like to prey on small businesses be-cause smaller organizations usually don't have phone fraud de-tection equipment.

If you still think you need DISA, you'll want to create complex hard-to-hack codes. Don't use birthdays, anniversaries, your name, or dates. Also, be sure to change codes often, and always change codes whenever an employee leaves.

Distinctive ringing
Calls ring differently depending on whether they originate in-ternally or externally. Distinctive ringing lets you distinguish between an intercom call and a client call, for example.

"Do not disturb" mode
If you invoke this mode, your station appears busy to incom-ing telephone and intercom calls. Some systems give the caller a distinctive tone that alerts him that you are in, but not avail-able. This is a great feature if you need to get a project done and can't afford interruptions. It's also useful when you're on the phone and do not want to be disturbed by the intercom.

DSS/BLF stations
Direct station selection/busy lamp field stations are telephone sets that allow you to visually recognize busy line status. By pressing a key on the phone, you can select a line or station.

Exclusive private line
A line reserved for the exclusive use of one station is often an executive privilege. It allows the user to receive confidential calls that bypass the receptionist. Also, it ensures the availability

of an outgoing line even at the busiest of times. You rarely see this feature in smaller phone systems.

Executive barge-in

Also called executive override, this feature is programmed to allow a certain person (or persons) the ability to listen in on a call or override privacy features, such as do-not-disturb mode. Depending on the design of this feature, the employee whose conversation is being overheard may or may not hear a beep tone. Managers often use executive override to observe a worker's telephone performance, and it can be a useful training tool. It can also be a major intrusion and seriously harm morale.

Fax detection

Incoming fax calls are automatically routed to the extension where your fax machine resides. Fax detection eliminates the need for a separate fax number.

Flexible line assignment

You can program your phone system so that certain departments or individuals have groups of outside lines assigned solely for their use. For example, to ensure that your sales force doesn't have to wait for an outgoing line, you would assign them exclusive lines.

Group intercom

This feature establishes a private intercom line between members of a preselected group. You then have the ability to reach anyone in your group fast without having to dial an extension number.

Hands-free off-hook announce

With this option, you gain the ability to page (and respond to internal paging) through the station speaker without having to pick up the handset. For example, your secretary pushes a button to notify you of a call or an onsite visitor. You could then respond to your secretary and ask him to take a message. It's much nicer than just hearing a buzz to alert you to a call or visitor, but there's a downside, too. Unless you have a privacy button and use it, anyone can interrupt you at any time. Even worse, anyone can listen in to whatever goes on in your office without your knowledge—sort of a reverse bugging.

Hot line

You can program the phone to dial the same number or extension number whenever you pick up the handset or punch a designated key. The hot line feature is a timesaver if you frequently call a specific number.

Intercom paths

The number of possible simultaneous internal conversations (intercom paths) will not necessarily be the same as the number of outside lines available. Some systems support only one or two intercom paths. If you use or plan to use intercom widely, be sure to check this out.

Intercom

An internal communications system lets you communicate with other phones in your office either by dialing an extension or pushing a button that buzzes a particular extension. The dialed or buzzed party then picks up the phone to carry on a conversation with you. See also *Paging*.

ISDN compatibility

ISDN technology gives you the option of converting a normal twisted-pair copper phone line into three digital channels (virtual phone lines). If you combine two of the lines, you can use ISDN to provide a broadband channel for bulky information transfer. Because you may want to add ISDN in the future, stay flexible and look for a phone system that can work with ISDN—about half of them do. For more information on ISDN, see Chapter 4.

Integrated voice mail

Some phone systems come with a built-in or optional private-labeled voice mail system. However, it may cost you less to get an add-on device than to purchase voice mail as a phone system option.

Least-cost routing

You can predetermine routing for your calls based on the least expensive routing available at the time the call is placed. You or your phone system vendor program choice rules for selecting phone lines for outgoing calls. Organizations using least-cost routing schemes report savings on toll charges of 20 to 30 percent. This feature is appropriate for companies that use a combination of dialing options, such as multiple carriers, DDD (direct distance dialing), foreign exchange, and tie lines. Least-cost routing is also known as automatic route selection.

Message waiting

The attendant can activate a lamp on a station set to indicate that information, such as a message, is waiting. This is especially useful in a busy office and reduces the frequency of lost or forgotten messages.

Music/message on hold

You can give your callers on hold something to listen to by hooking up to a local radio station, playing a classical tape, or running advertising or informational messages. Many callers like knowing that they are still connected. Some key systems contain a music synthesizer that plays music-like sounds. I don't know about you, but I'd rather listen to pounding heavy metal or country corn—anything but elevator music.

Tip: If you use local radio, be sure to listen to it yourself. Make sure your callers won't be irritated by rude or loud announcers, soppy music, or, worst of all, commercials from your competitors. It's happened before.

Night service

When there is no attendant to answer and transfer an incoming call at night, the night service option can help you. You can program the night bell to ring at a specific station, such as the security guard, or at a specific department that regularly works late. This service is most often found in PBX systems and some hybrids. See *TAFAS*.

OPX (off-premises extension)
An OPX may be a person's home or another building. This feature connects the OPX to the office telephone system.

Paging
This kind of paging has nothing to do with dialing a pocket pager or beeper. In the phone system world, paging refers to announcement features, such as:

- **Internal paging**—You can make simultaneous announcements to all stations via an internal speaker located in each station set.

- **External paging**—This type of paging is most useful in warehouses, construction yards, or large open spaces where a telephone or internal paging would not be practical. You can make amplified announcements over speakers or paging horns. Recall those speakers you hear when shopping for a used car? "Frank, you have a phone call on line four."

- **Zone paging**—Whether internal or external, zone paging lets you make announcements to specific areas within an office or facility.

PC programming interface
This interface allows you to program your phone system using software running on a personal computer. It greatly simplifies maintenance and updates.

Peripheral adjunct
This option connects peripherals—answering machine, fax machine, modem, security system, credit verification or other POS

(point of sale) terminal, cordless phone, or headset—to the phone system or to a station set by using an adapter.

Pooled access

Telephone sets with direct line appearance, which is a light for every outgoing line, can be expensive. Pooled access lets you share outgoing lines, thus eliminating the need for more expensive sets. To dial out, you just press a group access key or dial a specific code.

Power failure protection

Phone systems need electrical power in order to operate. Unlike ordinary phones that get their ringing power from the telephone line itself, telephone systems get their ringing power from an electrical outlet. If there's a power outage, your phones won't ring. This situation is unacceptable to most businesses, so telephone system designers install backup battery packs or a bypass system. If power is out, at least a few of your phones will ring.

Recall from hold

Sometimes it's easy to forget that you have a call on hold. To alleviate this problem, you can program your phone to remind you that a call is on hold. After a predetermined length of time has passed, the phone will ring or flash as if a new call is arriving.

RS-232 jack

Some digital telephone station sets include an RS-232 jack that can be connected to a like RS-232 port on a personal computer, fax, modem, or printer. This arrangement is known as dual port design, and it allows you to have a computer terminal at the same location as a telephone set without the need for a separate dedicated data line.

Single-line telephones allowed

This feature lets you attach non-proprietary off-the-shelf telephones to your telephone system.

SMDR (station message detail recording)

Frequent reviews of SMDR reports can significantly reduce your local and long-distance bills. They provide you with a chronological record of all outgoing calls and include information such as the station ID number, the date and time of call, the duration of the call, the number called, and the trunk (telephone line) used. You can then use these reports to bill calls back to departments or tenants, check for unauthorized call use, and spot lengthy calls.

Speed dial/redial

This feature works just the same as the speed dial/redial feature of a stand-alone phone—frequently called numbers are assigned a one-, two-, or three-button code for dialing. Redial (or last number redial) automatically dials the last number you dialed.

Station-to-station messaging

Within an organization, members can create and send brief alphanumeric messages that will either appear on the display of a coworker's telephone set or illuminate a light indicating that a message is waiting. This is a convenient way to inform others that you're OTL (out to lunch) or GFD (gone for the day.) You're not limited to these abbreviations, however. You can spell out anything you want.

TAFAS (trunk answer from any station)

This type of night service (also called night answer mode) activates a ring or other signal (bell or gong) when a call comes in. To answer the call, you pick up the handset and dial a special code.

Tenant service

Tenant service is useful in office buildings shared by more than one business. Certain phone systems will allow you to create system subsets, so each tenant can have his own attendant console and, possibly, his own telephone lines. This arrangement reduces the overall cost of communication services.

Toll restriction

To save money on your long-distance bill, you can restrict certain stations' access to long-distance or specified toll calls. Restrictions can apply to one or more area codes or even specific area code and prefix combinations.

Trunk queuing

If each member of your organization does not have her own line, she may have to "get in line" for an outgoing trunk (phone line). When an outside line becomes free, the system rings the next station user in the queue.

Trunk-to-trunk transfer

This feature allows you to transfer an incoming call to a number outside your phone system, such as a voice mail service.

UCD (uniform call distribution)

Both ACD and UCD permit a group of incoming lines to be answered by a group of stations. However, UCD uses a round-robin or top-to-bottom distribution scheme rather than ACD's "most idle" scheme.

Voice mail

This feature gives you the built-in capability to set up and maintain multiple voice mailboxes.

WHICH WAY TO GO?

Choosing the right phone system for your business is not easy, so here's a checklist to assist you:

✔ Project your estimated growth for the next five years, then double it. You'll need to get a system that can gracefully grow to that size. Plan on a five- to eight-year life span for the equipment you purchase.

✔ What do you currently pay for monthly phone service? Will a phone system allow you to cut back on the number of lines coming in? Will it reduce the number of phone company features, such as three-way calling, that you may be paying for? If so, how much will that save you now? Over the next five years?

✔ Read the features section in this chapter and then make three lists: must have, like to have, nice to have. Can you get those same features in stand-alone phones?

✔ Can you use your current equipment (phones, accessories) with this system, or do you have to buy all new stuff—and only from the vendor?

✔ Will you have to rewire? If so, figure that cost in.

✔ Is your business cyclical? Campaign organizations, seasonal businesses, and the like need to downsize at times and grow rapidly at other times. If you have major ups and downs, you don't want excessive hardware, Centrex may make the most sense.

✔ Are capital funds limited or difficult to spend? Many schools, government agencies, and charitable groups opt for Centrex service because it's easier to fund.

✔ Watch out for long feature lists. Just because a phone comes with "57 labor-saving features" doesn't guarantee that you or your staff can use them. How often have you heard someone say, "if I lose you," as the preface to transferring a call? What does that tell you?

One final note: While doing research for this book, I talked with lots of businesspeople. Some were content with their phone system; many were not. Pick a system that can grow with you. Otherwise, you'll end up with an expensive mistake. Consider this comment from Pacifica real estate broker John Doyle, who recently purchased a system. He warns, "As soon as you buy it, it's out of date."

RESOURCES

Books and magazines
How to Buy the Best Phone System:
Getting Maximum Value Without Spending a Fortune
by Sondra Liburd Jordan
Aegis Publishing Group, 1998

Introduction to Telephony:
Understanding Telephone Systems and Services
by Jane Laino
Telecom Library, 1999

Which Phone System Should I Buy?
The Guide to PBXs and Key Systems, tenth edition
by Lyle Deixler
Telecom Library, 1998

Teleconnect magazine
Published monthly by Telecom Library
800-677-3435
www.teleconnect.com

Chapter

7

Mobile Phones

DOES YOUR BUSINESS TAKE YOU OUT of the office a lot? Do you need to keep in touch with your customers at least as often as they need to call you? Are you always on call, or do you spend a lot of time in your car or at a field site where a phone is not readily available? If so, think wireless. With a wireless phone, you can conduct business almost anywhere—restaurants, ballparks, parking lots, grocery stores, building sites, and roadways, to name a few. Mobile phone service can add extra hours to your working day, and it can provide a ready link to emergency services. According to the Wireless Telecommunications Industry Association, there were more than 94 million wireless users in the United States as of June 2000. Maybe you should be one of them.

This chapter is about all kinds of mobile phones, including portable, transportable, and car phones. I've added advice on selecting a wireless carrier, plus information to help you keep your mobile phone bills under control. I've also included information to help you decide whether analog, digital, or PCS (Personal Communications Services) is best for you. (*Note*: Cordless phones rely on a different technology than mobile phones. They are covered in Chapter 6.)

A BRIEF HISTORY OF MOBILE SERVICES
Wireless service has its roots in the radiotelephone service used by oceangoing vessels. In the 1920s, a few urban police departments experimented with installing radiophones in their police cars, but the technology worked poorly on land. There were

too many obstacles. During World War II, however, the technology was given a huge boost when engineers developed two-way radio systems, such as the FM Handie-Talkie and Walkie-Talkie from Motorola.

In 1973, Motorola's Martin Cooper demonstrated a viable wireless phone. It was still a far cry from modern phones—it weighed 2½ pounds! Then, in 1979, the first commercial cell phone network was inaugurated in Tokyo, Japan.

The Federal Communications Commission (FCC) oversees the licensing of wireless service in the U.S. In 1983, it granted the first commercial service license to AT&T in Chicago. Today, the FCC is also responsible for establishing how many channels are available.

Until recently, the FCC divided the country into 305 metropolitan areas and 428 rural service areas, but they allowed no more than two wireless carriers to compete in each area. This situation changed in 1996 when the FCC auctioned off a group of licenses that allowed communications companies to sell a new generation of mobile phone service.

Called Personal Communications Services (PCS), this new technology offered expanded services, better sound quality, and lower prices. A PCS phone operates on a different frequency than a cell phone, and it can operate with less power. The result is longer battery life and lighter phones. Now, instead of just two wireless providers in an area, there can be as many as eight PCS service providers in a given market.

That's the good news. The bad news is that there will be a number of incompatible transmission standards until a clear winner appears in the fight for wireless buyer loyalty. If you buy the wrong kind of phone, you may be out of luck. To decide which mobile technology to go for, you're going to need to learn how to decipher wireless acronyms and plow through competing claims. This chapter will help you through it.

HOW WIRELESS WORKS

Wireless phones are basically two-way radios that operate on certain airwave frequencies. Unlike typical two-way radio communication, however, a wireless system can connect you to the wired telephone network. Also, unlike two-way systems, wireless systems are full duplex. Both parties in a conversation can talk and listen simultaneously, just as they would on a normal telephone line.

A wireless system is made up of hundreds of miniature radio communication transmitters and receivers, each situated a few miles from the adjacent station. Each of these stations is called a cell. As a wireless user moves through the service area, the call is electronically switched from one station to the next, thus allowing calls to continue without interruption.

How Cellular Phones Work

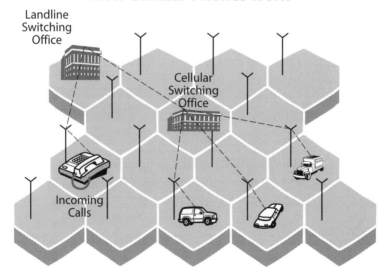

None of this activity is apparent to the user. You place your calls in a manner similar to using a land phone, except there's no dial tone and you press the SEND key after dialing in the number. When you want to hang up the phone, you press the

END key. Once your phone is off, you can't make or receive calls. People who call you will hear a message telling them that your phone is not available. If you want to receive calls, you place the phone in standby mode. Then, to answer a call, you press the SEND key.

Wireless isn't perfect. Because radio waves bounce off walls and are diminished by trees and other greenery, they can get distorted. You may get disconnected, have calls fade in and out, or even hear cross talk (someone else's conversation on your frequency or channel). You'll also experience great difficulty attempting to make or receive calls in tunnels or canyons.

COMPETING TECHNOLOGIES

Unfortunately, wireless phones come in different incompatible flavors. Several technologies exist, each with its own transmission standards. In many cases, your choice of phone will lock you into a particular service provider. These are the choices available:

- **AMPS (Advanced Mobile Phone Service)**
  AMPS is the standard 800 MHz wireless band where all analog cellular systems operate. It is widely available.

- **NAMPS (Narrowband Advanced Mobile Phone Service)**
  This technology operates at the same frequencies as AMPS, but provides a hybrid service capable of switching between digital and analog technology.

- **CDMA (Code division multiple access)**
  This type of digital phone also shares the same 800 MHz wireless band as analog cellular.

- **TDMA (Time division multiple access)**
  TDMA service also operates in the same 800-MHz band as analog cellular, but it is more widely available than CDMA.

- **PACS (Personal Access Communications Systems)**
  Cordless phone capabilities are combined with wireless phone features in this hybrid system.

- **PCS (Personal Communications Services)**
  These digital phones operate at 1900 MHz and use one of four different transmission standards—TDMA, PACS, CDMA, and GSM.

- **GSM (Global System for Mobile communications)**
  Also known as PCS 1900, this system is the digital standard throughout Europe. However, it operates on a different frequency, so your American model GSM phone probably won't work in Europe.

- **Nextel**
  A unique digital wireless service, Nextel provides two-way radio capabilities and paging functions, as well as digital mobile phone service, wireless Internet access, and one-number service worldwide.

Bottom Line

Analog user
Analog cell phones all use the same technology. Roaming capabilities will allow you to use your phone wherever you are.

Digital phone user
The varying standards won't be such a headache if you use your wireless phone only within your own service area. If you plan to travel with your phone, however, you'll need to know what works where. Alternatively, leave your phone at home and rent one at your destination.

Is any one format better than another?
Not in any way that the normal user would notice. Industry insiders note that because GSM has been out longer, it has

undergone more testing than other formats. Also, some phones are equipped to handle multiple technologies. Nextel is a particularly good choice for businesspeople who need two-way communications or travel abroad frequently.

WIRELESS CHARGES

In addition to a one-time setup fee, you will face three types of monthly charges: a monthly subscription cost, a charge for any landline services provided (directory assistance, for example), and an airtime charge, which is the actual time you spent using your wireless phone. The first two charges are fixed. It's the airtime charge that can get you.

Unlike land-based phone service, the wireless subscriber pays for both incoming and outgoing calls. You pay per-minute charges for the time you spend on the system plus your monthly access charge. To reduce your charges, shop for promotions, discounts, and packaged regional service plans. Many carriers are offering plans featuring "buckets of minutes." These plans provide a specified number of prepaid minutes each month at low bulk-rate prices. Bucket plans are often a good deal, especially if you can accurately anticipate your usage.

The average wireless owner uses 155 minutes a month, according to a February 2000 survey conducted by *Consumer Reports*. Heavy users, those using 20 to 30 minutes per day, should look for a big bucket plan—1,000 minutes or more. It's a good idea to shop carefully because the price for these plans can vary widely.

The best way to cut your costs is to give your wireless number to only your best clients. Or you could combine wireless with a numeric paging service. Arrange for your voice mail or paging service to beep your pager and display the number of the caller. Depending on who the caller is, you can dial out on your mobile phone or call later from a less expensive landline. Dave Steele, a maintenance management consultant in Mill Creek, Washington, uses this method. He explains that using a pager saves him $20 to $30 a month in wireless charges because he only checks his voice mail box when the pager alerts him. "Working from a wireless phone," he says, "I hate to spend the 45 to 90 cents a minute just to find out I have no new messages."

Your carrier charges for calls you place the moment they are connected to the cell site. For this reason, you may get charged for calls that never went through. Long distance adds up fast because you pay two charges—airtime and normal long-distance charges.

Carriers offer a variety of pricing plans that cater to light, medium, and heavy phone users. You can sometimes find plans that offer inexpensive off-peak evening and weekend service for as low as 1 or 2 cents a minute. The lowest monthly rates are often called "emergency" plans. You get a cheap rate for after-hours calls, but calls made during business hours may be billed at a much higher rate, up to 45 cents per minute.

Bottom line: Although the average monthly wireless phone bill in 2000 was $41.24, plan on spending quite a bit more if you use the phone as a business tool.

ROAMING—USING YOUR PHONE OUTSIDE YOUR SERVICE AREA

When you sign up for a mobile service, you're allowed to make and receive calls within your calling area. If you travel to another city and want to use your wireless phone, you'll be operating in another calling area. This situation is called roaming.

Roaming calls are charged at the rate of the host carrier, and they could end up being quite a bit more expensive that your budget allows. Some carriers charge a roaming fee that can run as high as $3 a day and $1 a minute. Fortunately, the trend is toward the elimination of roaming fees.

If you plan to roam a lot, consider installing more than one NAM (numeric assignment module) in your phone. A NAM is a chip installed by the dealer that contains your unique mobile phone number. Most phones come with room for two NAMs; some allow up to six. If you have multiple NAMs, you can register your phone with several different wireless providers. Another option is to choose a wireless provider that offers same-as-home rates. If your provider has a regional network, this plan will charge the same rates anywhere within the region as those in your home area.

Roaming costs add up even faster when you receive incoming calls. This is because you are charged long-distance forwarding charges for the connection between your home wireless service and the current location.

For example, imagine you have signed up for service near your office in Dayton, Ohio. While on a business trip to New York City, you set your wireless phone on roam. One of your clients, Anne, is supposed to meet you for dinner, but she calls from Grand Central Station to tell you she is running late. Anne will have to pay for the long-distance charges to forward her call from New York to Dayton, but you will be charged for the call forwarding costs from Dayton back to New York. Worse yet, the calls are often charged at daytime rates, regardless of the time of day.

One way to avoid long-distance surprises is to use your calling card for outgoing calls. For incoming calls, your best bet is to leave your roaming access number only with those people who may need to reach you in an emergency. You could also sign up for caller notification service with your carrier. This service will play a message for your callers and give them the roamer access number.

GLOBAL ROAMING

As more and more businesspeople work across borders, the need for international roaming is growing. If you tend to travel abroad frequently, check into a world phone program, such as GlobalRoam from GTE or Nextel Worldwide.

PREPAID WIRELESS

Some mobile phones can be purchased with a prepaid number of minutes. Once your minutes are used up, you can buy another bunch of minutes or even change carriers. These phones are handy for emergency use, and they're useful if you travel to different areas and don't want to fuss with roaming charges. Prepaid wireless phones have also become popular as gifts.

Warning: Prepaid phone plans are costly—65 to 75 cents a minute. There are no monthly service charges, so a prepaid phone can be a smart solution for a backup emergency phone, but a poor choice for a power user. Be sure to do the math.

PRIVACY

Although wireless calls are not as leaky as cordless phone calls, electronic eavesdropping is still possible. Conversations can be overhead by some types of radio receivers and scanners. If your business requires you to make calls that are sensitive and must be secure, avoid wireless phones.

For the same reason, you might not want to give out your credit card numbers over mobile phones. You could buy a scrambler, but the person on the other end would need a matching descrambler. Or you could buy a high-end phone with voice encryption. Digital cell phones are much more difficult to tap than analog wireless phones (more on this later).

WIRELESS PHONE FEATURES

Here's a sampling of the more common features available:

A/B switching

This feature allows you to switch easily between carriers, but you must have a dual-NAM phone to use it. A/B switching is particularly useful when roaming.

Alphanumeric memory

You can type in names to go with the numbers you have stored in your phone's memory, but this process isn't as simple as it sounds. Because there are only eight buttons on your phone to correlate with all the letters of the alphabet, you have to employ a weird coding scheme. For example, for the letter *C*, press the 2 key 3 times; for the letter *U*, press the 8 key twice; and so on.

Any key answer

This option permits you to answer the phone by hitting any key. It's especially helpful if you're driving and your pocket phone rings.

Automatic credit card dialing

If you make a lot of long-distance calls over your wireless phone, this feature can save you money. It gives you quick access to your choice of long-distance carriers.

Automatic NAM selection

With this feature, your phone will detect which call area you are in and set the correct NAM for you. Doing so ensures that you won't incur roaming charges. You also save time because you don't have to figure out which NAM you need.

Battery level meter

Try to get a phone with one of these gauges. They are graphical displays of battery strength, and you will know exactly how much power you've got left. Earlier and cheaper models use a low-battery light for the same purpose.

Battery life

Battery life is usually described by two numbers: the amount of talk (air) time and the amount of standby time (waiting mode). Low-end phones give you about 60 minutes of talk time, while high-end phones go up to 2.5 hours. Standby time ranges from 12 to 72 hours.

Built-in pager

This useful feature saves you from having to carry two devices.

Call restriction

This option prevents specifically designated calls from being connected without an entry code. For example, you can restrict calls from numbers outside your immediate service area. Call restriction helps you keep your phone bills under control by curtailing more expensive calls.

Call screening

The phone number of an incoming call is displayed if you opt for this feature. Also, if your phone has alphanumeric data capability, the name of the caller will be displayed. Based on this information, you can then decide whether you want to pick up the call.

Call timer

Many phones have more than one call timer option, such as call-in-progress timer, resettable cumulative timer, and last-call timer. The one-minute alarm is a handy feature. It beeps you, but not the caller.

Data port

If you want to send a fax or download a file remotely, you'll want to link your wireless phone to a notebook computer or portable fax. For more information, see *Wireless fax* later in this chapter.

DTMF

This acronym stands for dual-tone multifrequency. That's a fancy phrase for Touch-Tone. If you plan to use your mobile phone to check your bank balance, transfer funds, call into voice mail, or effect other automatic call processes, be sure your phone can send valid Touch-Tone signals. To be absolutely certain, get a phone with extended DTMF.

Dual mode

This feature allows you to switch your phone back and forth between analog and digital technologies.

Dual NAM

If your phone has dual NAM capability, you can save on roaming charges by registering for home service in two cities.

Electronic volume controls

These separate settings control the volume for the earpiece, ringer, and keypad of your phone.

Internet access

If you opt for Internet access, you can surf selected sites over a wireless phone enabled by WAP (Wireless Internet Protocol).

Note: To make this work, you'll also have to subscribe to a wireless Internet service provider, such as Sprint PCS Wireless Web. See Chapter 11 for more information.

Lock

To prevent unauthorized use of your phone, you can use the lock feature to disable transmit and receive functions.

Memory

You'll definitely want your mobile phone to have memory dialing. How many numbers do you want to store? Thirty is standard, but many phones can handle 100 or more. For those rare human beings that can remember more than 100 phone codes, a few phones store up to 300 codes.

Missed call counter

When your phone is in standby mode, this feature will register all unanswered calls that are received. It's especially helpful if you have voice mail.

Multiple NAM capability

A NAM is a chip installed by the wireless dealer that contains your unique mobile phone number. If you have multiple NAMs, you can register your phone with several different wireless providers. Some advanced phones offer anywhere from three to eight NAMs.

Numeric answering mode

This setting answers incoming calls and instructs the caller to enter a callback number that waits in temporary storage until you pick it up.

PCS compatibility

A few high-end analog cellular phones will operate with PCS at 1900 MHz as well as analog AMPS at 800 MHz. These phones are also known as dual band.

Remote control

Use this feature to call your wireless phone from another phone when you want to power down or lock up the device.

Ring tone selection

When you're in a crowd, how do you know whose mobile phone is ringing? One way is to use the ringer selection feature—just select the ring of your choice. An even better choice is no ring at all. You can now get a phone that vibrates as a call comes in.

Scratchpad

With this feature, you can type a number into your phone's temporary memory while on a call. Silent scratchpads are best.

Secret memory

If others use your phone, you may want to prevent them from accessing sensitive phone numbers, names, or information. To do this, you can program your phone to require a passcode for retrieving certain names or phone numbers stored in its memory.

Signal level meter

The strength of your wireless signal is displayed on this meter. It's sometimes useful to know that you're moving into an area with a weak signal.

Tri-mode

These phones provide both dual-mode and dual-band access. They operate on digital networks at 1900 MHz and 800 MHz.

When you move out of range of your digital service, the phone switches to an analog network at 800 MHz.

Voice-message waiting indicator

This indicator eliminates the need to check with your service for voice messages. You are alerted when a message is waiting. If you're out in the field and get frequent voice messages, this feature could be handy.

TYPES OF WIRELESS PHONES

There are three basic types of wireless phones:

- Portable phone
- Car phone
- Transportable phone

PORTABLE PHONE

These are the smallest types of mobile phones. Called portables, or pocket phones, they run on rechargeable batteries. The heavier batteries last longer between charges and that means longer talk time for you. Portables may weigh anywhere from three to eighteen ounces. However, price is inversely related to weight—the lighter the phone, the "heavier" the cost.

The maximum power level available for portables is 0.6 watts, which is plenty for normal urban or suburban use. If you often travel to rural areas, suburban fringes, or concrete canyons, you might need the greater power that is available with transportables and mobile phones. Of course, if you take your phone with you everywhere, you'll probably want a portable.

BATTERY BASICS

Batteries are a big deal with portables, so the choices are wide. Some models let you recharge your battery while you're on a call; some models come with an extra battery. If an extra battery is not standard with your model, you'll want to buy one anyway. Otherwise, you'll be kicking yourself when you run out of power during that all-important deal-maker call.

Battery chargers range from small portable trickle chargers to desktop-sized rapid chargers. If your model uses nickel cadmium batteries, get a charger that has a discharge button so you can fully cycle, or discharge, the battery. Otherwise, your battery life will get shorter every time you charge, a phenomenon known as memory effect.

Memory effect occurs when batteries are only partially discharged and then recharged. For example, your battery may be only 80 percent used, but after recharging it, you think it is 100 percent charged. Not so. If you recharge the battery again after only 80 percent use, you have recharged 80 percent of 80 percent—that's only 64 percent. In this way, the battery gradually loses its power.

Nickel metal hydride (NiMH) and lithium ion (LiSB) batteries are much better at resisting memory effect than nickel cadmium batteries. Lithium ion batteries are also free of heavy metals, a bonus for the environment.

Digital phones provide much longer battery life than analog phones. According to tests administered by *Consumer Reports*, batteries in digital phones lasted about 80 percent longer than did those in analog phones.

Tip: Keep your mobile phone away from direct sunlight. Temperatures over 105° F. can fry your battery.

If you're having trouble finding a replacement battery or if your particular model is no longer being produced, contact iGo.com (www.igo.com). This discount mail order company specializes in batteries for notebooks, laptops, cell phones, and the like.

CAR PHONE

Car phones are permanently installed in your vehicle. They are powered by the car's battery, so you never have to think about battery life or where you can recharge your phone.

Of the three types of mobile phones, car phones are known to have the best reception. This is largely because the car itself serves as part of the antenna. In addition, car phones operate with more power. They transmit with 3 watts of power, whereas many portables have only 0.6 watts.

Car phones are harder to steal than other phones. Usually, the transceiver is installed in a hidden area, and the handset can be removed or camouflaged. However, this arrangement poses a major disadvantage as well because the minute you leave your car, you've left your phone behind, too. There are optional transportable kits available, though, that allow you to carry the handset with you. They are equipped with a battery, an antenna, and a bag. There's also a transmobile kit that permits you to easily move the car phone from one car to another.

CAR PHONE FEATURES

Common features available on car phones include:

Automatic volume controls

If you connect your phone to the car radio, the radio will automatically turn off when you receive or place a call.

Call summons

You can also hook up the phone to your car horn. If the phone rings while you're out of the car, your horn honks. Fortunately for your neighbor's nerves, you can switch this feature on and off at will.

Hands-free answering

After a predetermined number of rings, this option answers the phone call and switches to your speaker. Any key answer is a similar feature that allows you to answer the phone by punching any key on the handset. Either of these features is certainly safer than taking your eyes from the road and hunting for the SEND key.

Hands-free dialing

Voice recognition technology enables you to program your phone with a list of commonly called numbers and give each number a code name, such as "home" or "office."

Hands-free operation

This important safety feature is similar to the speakerphone feature on a land phone. It permits you to talk on the phone while leaving both hands on the steering wheel. Hands-free employs a small microphone that clips to your windshield trim, plus a speaker. A good installer will hide all the wires behind the car's trim and upholstery.

Multiple NAMs

If you regularly drive long distances, you should purchase a car phone with multiple NAMs. This way, you can register your car phone with several different wireless providers.

RJ-11 jack

If you travel with a computer, you'll find this feature handy. It lets you plug into a modem or portable fax machine using a modular phone plug.

Theft alarm

Once the phone is powered up, an alarm prompts the user to enter a secret code within a specified time. If the code is not entered, a call is silently placed to a security number, and the called party is notified that the phone has been started without the code.

Voice recognition

Some of the more expensive wireless phones can be operated by a set of voice commands. You set your phone into a speaking mode, and the phone "reads back" each number as you press it. It's a great way to confirm that you're dialing correctly.

ANTENNA CHOICES

If you opt for a car phone, you'll need to purchase an exterior antenna. There are several choices:

- Glass mounted
- Roof mounted
- Trunk mounted
- Removable

A glass-mounted antenna consists of two parts—one part is glued outside your rear window, and the other is glued inside and connected to the phone by a cable. This type of antenna is nice because you don't have to drill a hole in your car to install it. It's also less obtrusive. On the downside, some users report that the windshield defroster causes interference.

A roof-mounted antenna provides the most powerful reception, mainly because the antenna is higher. Roof mounts are not very popular, however, because they need to be lowered before entering most garages. Also, because the installer has to drill through the roof and the ceiling lining, the installation is a bit more expensive.

Trunk-mounted antennas are the most popular today. The wireless transceiver is usually installed in the trunk of the car, so signal loss is kept to a minimum.

Removable antennas are designed for particular mounts—your trunk, roof, or even a side window of your car. They attach with powerful magnets, a clip, or a suction cup. The advantage? You can move the antenna from vehicle to vehicle. These antennas works with convertibles, rental cars, tractors, and even baby strollers. If you sometimes have to park in areas that suffer from vandalism, just detach the antenna and lock it in your trunk.

In addition to the location of the antenna, you can opt for a cordless or corded antenna. Transportable phones or car phones require a corded antenna; portable phones require a cordless clip-on or glass-mounted antenna.

You'll also have to select the antenna power. Basically, you have three choices:

- **Quarter wave antenna** (unity gain antenna)
  This is the type of antenna that originally came with every mobile wireless phone.

- **3 dB gain antenna**
  This type of antenna is the most popular choice today. It is designed for metropolitan areas where wireless sites are numerous.

- **5 dB gain antenna**
  These antennas are best suited to rural areas and open spaces where wireless sites are less frequent. They reach across greater distances than the 3 dB antennas. The 5 dB antenna is also an appropriate choice if you're using a mobile phone in a truck cab or other tall vehicle.

TRANSPORTABLE PHONE

Transportable phones run on portable batteries, weigh between two and six pounds, and are more powerful than portables. Up to three watts of power helps these phones maintain the signal when reception is weak.

You'll often find transportables phones packaged as "bag phones." A bag phone comes with a separate handset, transceiver, and battery pack, plus a sack to lug it around with you. A sleeker alternative builds the phone right into a special briefcase for that James Bond look.

Transportable kits are also available that allow you to take your car phone with you. A variation on this theme is the transmobile or car-to-car kit. It consists of a bag, a cigarette lighter adapter, and, often, an antenna. With this kit, you can move the phone from one car to another without messing with a lot of wiring.

CHOOSING A CARRIER

First, consider how often you intend to use your mobile phone, as well as where and when you'll use it. Wireless carriers and resellers of airtime offer different rate packages depending on how and when clients are most likely to use their service. Your carrier will offer several rate packages, ranging from emergency phone use only to heavy business use.

Look in your local yellow pages under *Wireless Telephone Service* for carriers that offer service in your area. Your wireless phone dealer should also have information about the rates and coverage of the carriers available in your area. Some dealers work only with one carrier; others contract with several. You are not restricted to the carrier your dealer suggests, however. Sometimes the dealer's recommendation is based on which carrier pays the heftiest sales commission. That's important for the dealer, but it's no use to you. Ask around and find out which carriers your friends, customers, and coworkers are using.

Once you locate the carriers in your area, ask for information on the rate plans they offer. Be sure to compare the charges carefully. You can find rate plan comparisons on the Web that will help you with this task. For example, Point.com (www.point.com) provides information on all service plans sold in your city—all you do is enter your zip code. Another source is *Wireless Week* magazine (www.wirelessweek.com). It tracks airtime prices in 50 major U.S. markets and publishes the results on its website.

Many wireless carriers charge on a per-minute basis. The problem with this rate structure is that a 61-second call is billed as a two-minute call. If you have a choice, it makes sense to go for the carrier that charges at smaller intervals, such as six seconds.

Check to see if the carrier has send-to-end billing. With this billing method, charges for all calls (even busy or unanswered calls)are based on the elapsed time between pressing the SEND button and pressing the END button on your cell phone. Pick the carrier that does *not* bill send-to-end.

Ask what roaming charges apply if you want to use your phone outside your service area. Roaming fees range from 60 cents to $1 per minute. In addition, you'll be charged at long-distance rates—anywhere from 10 cents to 35 cents a minute.

Tip: If you travel outside your service area frequently, look for a plan that does not charge roaming fees.

Be sure to read the small print on your contract. You may find that your current low rate is available for only three months and then climbs rapidly. Sometimes dealers offer really cheap phones, but the usage charges are higher. Airtime adds up quickly, so beware. There may also be hidden extras, such as installation or an antenna, that are not included in the advertised price.

Ask what it will cost to get service started. Plans with fewer minutes often have higher activation fees. Also, be sure to check the disconnect clause in the service agreement, because some wireless dealers impose a whopping penalty for disconnecting early.

Carriers sometimes offer perks to differentiate their service. Some offer statewide or area-wide paging services, warranties, or special rates for the disabled or elderly. Roadside assistance services are popular, too. You might sign up for a lost-driver service that will give you directions over the phone, or a roadside rescue service that furnishes jump starts, locksmith service, or emergency gasoline.

ACCESSORIES FOR YOUR MOBILE PHONE

Once you have your basic phone, you may want to accessorize it. You can add face plates to make it prettier, get faster battery charges, enable hands-free use, or shut off the sound.

Quick charge

Are you tired of waiting while your wireless phone battery re-charges? You can purchase a quick charger and battery condi-tioner that will have your NiCd batteries ready for use within an hour. Conventional chargers can take up to ten hours. ORA Electronics (818-772-2700 or www.orausa.com) makes such an item.

Vibrating phone

ORA also makes a battery that silently vibrates when a call comes in to your cell phone. All you have to do is replace your standard battery with the VibraRing. It's great for those times when you need to be unobtrusive, but available.

Face plate

For the fashion conscious among you, you can buy a face plate that changes the color of your phone. Some even come with Disney characters.

Call alert pen

Fox makes a sensor pen that detects incoming signals from mobile phones. When your phone number is dialed, the pen lights up. You can find these beauties at Everything Wireless (www.everythingwireless.com).

Headset

For hands-free operation and increased safety, you can't beat a headset. They are available in several styles: over-the-head, over-the-ear, and earbuds, which place both the microphone and the receiver inside or near the ear. Cell phone headsets are available through Plantronics and Hello Direct. Jabra makes earbuds.

Tip: Make sure the headset you're considering will work with your phone. Some mobile phones have nonstandard headset jacks that require special equipment.

Cigarette lighter adapter

This handy device plugs into the cigarette lighter receptacle of your auto, van, or boat. Your phone battery is bypassed, and you get power directly from your vehicle's battery, thus conserving phone power. Several companies sell these items, including Belkin, Everything Wireless, and Hello Direct. Hello Direct also sells a device that turns your cigarette lighter into a four-socket extension outlet. This way, you can power three more 12-volt accessories, such as your fax modem, battery charger, and portable computer.

WIRELESS FRAUD

Wireless carriers report that they lost $182 million in 1998, which represents the most recent data available. One of the most common types of wireless fraud is cellular cloning. Cloners pose as legitimate users, but, in actuality, they have stolen the ID and serial numbers programmed into cellular phones. The stolen numbers are then installed into another wireless phone, and all subsequent calls made on the cloned phone are billed to the legitimate customer. Often, the customer doesn't know that his number has been cloned until a huge phone bill arrives.

Cloners lurk at airports, business centers, and other public places. Using radio wave scanners, they lift phone numbers and ID numbers off the air. They also buy phone IDs from dishonest service personnel, such as car washers, valet parking attendants, and the like. However, cloning is a problem only for analog phones manufactured before 1995, so it is gradually becoming less common.

HOW CAN YOU TELL IF YOUR PHONE HAS BEEN CLONED?

Do you experience frequent interrupted or dropped calls? If so, you may be bumping into the person who has your cloned number. When you and the cloner attempt to make or receive calls at the same time, the calls "collide," and the later call knocks the earlier one off the air. This is because both calls are using the same channel. Don't just assume that bad equipment or an overloaded system is the cause of these dropped calls. You should report them to your wireless company, which is very interested in stopping fraud.

Carriers are fighting back by installing sophisticated clone detection systems. Some systems monitor each subscriber's calling patterns and investigate if a significant change is detected. Others pay extra attention to international calls and limit international dialing to those customers who request it. One clever method being used by Bell Atlantic Mobile pinpoints cloned transmissions down to a particular apartment, car, or office. Then, just send in the cops, and it's goodbye to that cloner.

SAFEGUARDING YOUR MOBILE PHONE

☎ If you frequently experience interrupted calls, terminated calls, wrong number calls, or hang-ups, you should report them to your carrier.

☎ Avoid using your phone in or near airports, business centers, and other areas where wireless usage is high.

☎ Don't publish your mobile phone number on company phone lists or print it on your business card. If someone needs it, write it for him.

☎ Don't allow access to your car phone by people you don't know. When using a valet service or getting your car washed, take your phone with you or lock it away.

☎ Carefully review your bill every month. Even if you have to pay more for an itemized bill, it may be worth it. A clever phone cloner will be subtle in his use, so additional charges may not be noticeable.

MOBILE PHONES AND YOUR HEALTH

The wireless industry awoke to health and safety issues in 1993 when David Reynard, appearing on the *Larry King Live* show, alleged that cell phone use caused his wife's terminal brain cancer. As proof, he showed X-rays of her tumor that eerily matched the shadow of a cell phone antenna. This story created quite a stir and led the cell phone industry to pledge millions for health research.

In addition to the cancer scare, there have been reports of headaches, changes in blood pressure, changes in sleeping patterns, long-term memory loss, genetic mutations, and kidney damage. According to Dr. George Carlo, chairman of the Health Risk Management Group in Washington, D.C., and former director of Wireless Technology Research, wireless phones send electromagnetic waves into users' brains. The amount of radiation a user is exposed to is determined by the proximity of the phone antenna to his head. In adults, the antenna radiation plume penetrates two to three inches into the brain, but in children, it penetrates the entire brain.

ABC's *20/20* commissioned independent tests on the radiation emissions of five popular cell phones. The results were aired on the program in October of 1999. Four of the five phones exceeded the FCC safety standards in at least one antenna position. The only phone that was within the allowable range was Motorola's Star Tac—its design positions the antenna away from the head.

Research into the long-term effects of wireless phone use is continuing. In the meantime, concerned users can follow these guidelines from the Food and Drug Administration's Center for Devices and Radiological Health:

- Time is a key factor in how much radiation a user is exposed to. Therefore, if you spend long periods of time talking on your handheld mobile phone, you should consider holding lengthy conversations on a conventional phone. Reserve the handheld models for shorter conversations or for situations where other types of phones are not available.

- It's a good idea to mount the antenna for your car's mobile phone outside. However, this arrangement requires you to permanently install some components, such as a power booster, a speaker, and a microphone. You'll most likely need a professional installer to do the work. A faster, cheaper solution is to purchase a device that plugs into your cigarette lighter and provides an external speaker and microphone. Ask your cell phone vendor for advice on finding the one that works with your equipment.

WIRELESS ALOFT

It's almost impossible to use your mobile phone in the air. Though technically feasible, the Federal Communication Commission has made it illegal to use a wireless phone while airborne due to fears that wireless usage will interfere with vital air-to-ground communications. The FCC does allow wireless phone use while a plane is parked. However, FAA regulations permit individual airlines to ban wireless use on the ground, and most do. Someday, these regulations should change. In the meantime, you'll need to use the airline's phones to make a call in the air.

If you have a private plane, you can set up an air-to-ground cell phone using service provided by AirCell, Inc (www.aircell.com). It's pretty pricey, though. At last look, the mobile phone cost $4,000 and airtime was $1.75 a minute.

WIRELESS AT SEA

Can you use a wireless phone on a boat or a cruise? It depends on where you're going. If you're cruising in the Caribbean, contact Caribbean Wireless (www.caribcell.com) or BoatPhone (800-BOATFON).

When cruising inland waterways within your service area, you can use your handheld mobile phone. However, if you move too far from land, your portable won't have the broadcast power to send your signal to the next cell. You'll need a full-powered installed phone if you range far at sea. If you do decide to install a mobile phone on a boat, be sure to get a special marine-quality antenna.

For distant cruises, there are mobile satellite phone services. Contact Comsat (800-685-7898 or www.comsat.com) or Stratos Marine Services (888-766-1313 or www.stratos.ca).

WIRELESS FAX

Yes, you can send or receive a fax over your wireless phone service. One way to fax remotely is to plug your portable fax machine or modem into the RJ-11 phone jack of your mobile phone. Then, just dial the desired fax number. Or, you can get a phone with fax and modem capabilities built in.

A third option is to buy a wireless fax modem. This credit card size device uses a built-in interface to connect to your wireless or landline phone. It lets you send and receive faxes from your computer to virtually anywhere.

Caution: If you're attempting to use wireless fax in a mobile phone, don't drive anywhere. You need a strong, clear signal to maintain the fax transmission. Analog wireless communications are often electronically noisy, and radio interference and weather conditions can also mess up your fax transmissions. The newer wireless fax modems feature error correction and data compression formats that improve your odds of getting good fax.

WIRELESS DATA

Currently, wireless data transfer is slow, topping out at around 14.4 kbps, but that is scheduled to change. Industry experts predict speeds approaching 364 kbps by 2001, and up to 2 megabits per second by the end of 2002 when third-generation wireless technologies come online.

Meanwhile, if you don't have a phone connection, but want to send and receive email or hitch up to the Internet, there are several technologies that will let you connect:

- **ARDIS**
  Advanced Radio Data Information Services is a packet-switched data network service that provides email, wireless fax, and operator-assisted messaging. Pricing is based on the size of the file (number of kilobytes) you send and/or receive. For more information, check www.motient.com.

- **CDPD**
  Cellular digital packet data services send packets of data over the analog wireless network at speeds of up to 19.2 kbps. CDPD is available through your local wireless carriers. It works via a wireless PC card, complete with tiny antenna. You can use this service to connect to office networks and the Internet, as well as email services.

- **Cellular**
  This type of connection employs your normal cellular service and a cell phone equipped with a modem interface. Like wireless fax, analog cellular data transmission is prone to error and costly. If you establish a data connection, you must stay put until the data has been transmitted. Otherwise, should you move from one cell to another, your connection will be lost and you'll have to retransmit.

- **RAM Mobile Data**
  This service relies on transmitting stations to send and receive data. It is limited to text-based data, such as email and fax, and, like ARDIS, pricing is based on the number of

kilobytes you send and receive. For information, contact www.mda-mobiledata.org.

- **Ricochet**
  The Ricochet Wireless Network from Metricom (www.metricom.com) is an affordable wireless service that you can use for Internet browsing, as well as email access and other standard data services. You pay a flat rate for unlimited access, but you'll also need to buy a special Ricochet modem.

RESOURCES

Books
The Cell Phone Handbook:
Everything You Wanted to Know About Wireless Telephony (But Didn't Know Who or What to Ask)
by Penelope Stetz
Aegis Publishing Group, 1999

This book provides a solid understanding of wireless technologies that will help you to make informed purchase decisions.

How to Shop For A Cell Phone:
One Quick, Easy Read Could Save You Thousands
by Curt Lenart
Black Forest Press, 1999

Magazines
Wireless Buyer's Guide
Mobile Computing & Communications Magazine
470 Park Avenue South
New York, NY 10016

Subscription department
P. O. Box 52406
Boulder, CO 80323-2406

Cahners Online Wireless Week magazine
www.wirelessweek.com

Rent a mobile phone—nationwide
In Touch USA
www.intouchusa.com
703-222-7161

Rent a mobile phone—global
IMC WorldCell
www.worldcell.com
888-967-5323
301-652-2075

CellHire
www.cellhire.com
888-GSM-RENT

SmartComs
www.smartcoms.com
888-880 0082

Associations
Wireless Telecommunications Industry Association
Suite 800
1250 Connecticut Avenue, NW
Washington, DC 20036
www.wow-com.com
202-785-0081

Products
Hello Direct
www.hellodirect.com
800-444-3556

Mobile Planet
www.mobileplanet.com
800-675-2638

Chapter

8

Voice Messaging

ONE OF THE MOST SIGNIFICANT problems business people face, especially those with small or solo businesses, is fielding phone calls. How many times have you been deeply involved with one customer, whether over the phone or in person, and had to leave that customer to answer another line? And, unfortunately, sometimes ended up losing both?

What you need is a dedicated, efficient, cheerful assistant who works around the clock and never takes coffee breaks. As that option is unlikely, how about some kind of automated message taker—either voice mail or an answering machine? This chapter discusses voice mail and answering machines, and then compares the two. We'll touch briefly on answering services as well.

VOICE MAIL

Unless you've been living on a desert island, you've come in contact with voice mail. Though there are many variations, voice mail is basically a computerized messaging system that routes incoming calls to private voice mailboxes. Depending on the setup, callers may listen to an announcement, leave a message, transfer to a live operator, or request that you be paged.

Callers usually interact with voice mail via the Touch-Tone keypad on their phones. There are two overall voice mail options: (1) installing voice mail equipment on your premises, and (2) using an off-premise service provided by a phone company or a service bureau.

A survey conducted by the Voice Messaging Educational Committee concluded that a majority of callers prefer to leave a voice mail message rather than leave a message with a receptionist or operator. Voice mail systems were rated second only to the telephone as an invaluable communications system. They beat out fax, memos, letters, and email. Nearly 80 percent of voice mail subscribers feel that voice mail improves their productivity on the job.

The above survey also reported that only 22 percent of callers who reach voice mail hang up, and the remaining 78 percent leave a message. This fact can save your company money. The Association of Telemessage Services International reports that phone tag costs a business anywhere from $50 to $150 per employee each month.

A major benefit of voice mail is convenience. Because many voice mail services pick up calls automatically after a certain number of rings, you don't have to remember to turn your voice mail system on. Also, voice mail prompts callers to leave detailed messages, so telephone tag is greatly reduced. In fact, the editors of *Teleconnect* magazine estimate that voice mail technology cuts callbacks by 50 percent.

WAYS TO USE VOICE MAIL

Businesses of all sorts employ voice mail as a useful communications tool for after-hours messaging, 24-hour order entry, market research, salesperson check-ins, product information hotlines, prescription renewals, and real estate listings. Many newspapers have added voice classified ads to their services; restaurants use voice mail as a backup for reservation call overflow; and the list goes on.

VOICE MAIL TYPES

You have several voice mail options. You can purchase and install a voice mail card or voice modem in your computer, or you can buy a dedicated voice mail system. Alternatively, voice mail is a popular service that is offered by most local telephone

companies, paging services, and outside service bureaus. Charges
are added to your monthly bill.

COMPUTER-BASED VOICE MAIL

If you have a spare slot in your computer, you can install a
voice mail card. You then connect your phone line to it and
load the associated voice messaging software. Voice mail will
run on your computer either in the foreground or the background. You can record a standard greeting, or you can record
a series of branching greetings to give your callers choices.

Callers can leave messages in one or several mailboxes. The
messages are digitized and stored on your hard disk until you
retrieve them. Most of the time, you're notified via your screen
that you have a message, but some voice mail software has the
ability to page you or dial another number and deliver the
message. Obviously, you must leave your computer on during
the times you want to receive voice mail.

Voice modems and cards are quite inexpensive, but they give
you complete control over your system. Cards come with single-
or multiple-line capabilities, and many have built-in fax modem, audiotext, and auto-attendant capabilities. Mailbox capacity is determined by the amount of disk space you have
available.

On the downside, unless you love tinkering with computer
hardware, you might not enjoy being responsible for installation, fine-tuning, and maintenance chores. Voice processing
uses a lot of computer power—a digitized message requires about
10 kbps. Therefore, most users suggest that you run voice mail
on a separate computer. You'll also need to allocate a lot of disk
space to store your voice messages. One hundred megabytes
for an afternoon's worth of calls is not unusual.

If you plan to work at the computer and run voice mail at the
same time, be aware that voice quality may be affected. Remember, too, that phone messages are transmitted via your

modem, so your callers will get a busy signal if you go online or send and receive faxes. Power outages and brownouts constitute a further disadvantage to computer-based voice mail, because, of course, they will take your system down.

All kinds of companies make computer-based voice mail systems for Windows, Linux, and Macintosh computers. Just visit your local computer store or favorite telephone website and browse the modem section.

DEDICATED VOICE MAIL SYSTEM

These systems are designed to work with PBXs and some key phone systems. They offer plug-ready voice messaging plus other voice technologies that can run on stand-alone computers.

To use a dedicated voice mail system, all you have to do is plug it in, attach your phone lines, and then record your outgoing messages—you're in business! However, because these systems are proprietary, you may have difficulty integrating dedicated voice mail with the rest of your communications system.

Many dedicated voice mail systems are too costly for a small organization to consider. Nevertheless, if your voice messaging needs are complex, or you need to support two or more lines, you might look into one of the following:

- Repartee (Active Voice)
  206-441-4700
  www.activevoice.com

- Infinite Whisper (Vodavi)
  800-843-4863
  www.vodavi.com

- Resound (Digitcom)
  310-584-0750
  www.digitcom.com

Voice mail service

According to a recent AT&T study, almost 75 percent of business calls go unanswered. Why? There are a variety of reasons. Perhaps the person called is either on the phone, not there, or unavailable. Whatever the reason, it is clear that a small operation could be losing a significant amount of potential business.

A voice mail service provided by a phone company or service bureau can answer any number of calls simultaneously. Therefore, a higher volume of messages are able to get through, resulting in improved customer service and increased sales. This is probably the most significant reason for choosing voice mail service over other voice mail options.

If you choose voice mail service, your phone will be answered automatically even when all your lines are busy. Using standard phone company call forwarding services, your overflow calls are directed to the voice mail computer located at your service provider's premises. You determine when voice mail should pick up your calls, such as after a specified number of rings or when your line(s) are busy. Messages are then stored on the voice mail machine. To pick up messages, voice mail subscribers call a special phone number from any Touch-Tone phone and key in a password.

Voice mail service firms offer a wealth of built-in features that can make your voice mail system sound as professional as that used by major corporations and other large-scale users. Optional features include paging, out-call notification, transfer to attendant, and the ability to send calls from two different numbers to the same voice mailbox. Usually, there is a limit to the number of messages and the length of a message that can be stored. However, these limits can be increased for a higher monthly fee.

The Bell operating companies, as well as many smaller companies in your area, offer voice mail. Prices average $20 a month for a business line and $4 to $8 per month for a residential line. If you have paging service, ask your paging company whether it provides voice mail service. Many do. You might find this to be a cost-efficient alternative to the telco service.

A budgetary note: Depending on your particular type of phone service, you may be billed for calls forwarded to your voice mailbox as well as for calls you make to pick up messages. These charges can add up quickly. Also, if your assigned voice mail machine is not located within your local (low-cost) calling area, you will rack up toll charges every time a call is forwarded to voice mail.

There are two main service options:

- **A separate voice mail number**
  Also known as stand-alone voice mail, this service uses a completely separate phone number for voice messaging that never rings at your location. Your customers can dial the direct voice mail phone number, or you can forward your calls to voice mail for after-hours (or lunch time) coverage via the phone company's standard call forwarding service.

  Calls are answered promptly, usually before the first ring. Your callers will hear your outgoing message and then have the opportunity to leave a message. Message waiting indicators—either special tones on the line or a light on your phone—are not activated by new messages. You either dial in to check for messages or specify that you want to be paged.

- **Voice mail added to your phone line**
  This service adds voice mail capability directly to your phone line. When your line is busy or if you don't answer within a specified number of rings, your calls are forwarded automatically to the desired mailbox. There, callers hear your outgoing message and are prompted to leave a message. If

you receive a message, you are notified by a light on your phone set or a special beeping dial tone on your phone.

West Virginia-based Intra-State Insurance opted for voice mail after its phone system went down during an electrical storm. "We lost power, and our answering machine was out of commission," explains Allan Hawkins, the company's owner. He chose Bell Atlantic's Answer Call service. The company is now available to customers twenty-four hours a day. In addition, salespeople can now retrieve their messages even when they're out of the office.

FREE VOICE MAIL

A bunch of companies now offer free voice mail. WebVoice (www.webvoice.com), eVoice (www.evoicelcom), and myTalk (www.mytalk.com), among others, allow you to access voice mail over the phone or the Internet. Sounds great, right? After all, who can argue with free?

But there's a downside. First, you have to listen to or view ads whenever you pick up your voice messages. Secondly, unlike phone company voice mail attached to your phone number, free voice mail cannot answer more than one call at a time. Finally, most of these accounts require that you give your callers a new number. You can't answer this number yourself, and it may be located in an area code that is a long-distance call for yourself and your callers.

Though free voice mail may be handy for some, it's not a good choice for a business. Basically, you get what you pay for.

☎ In my office

I've had voice mail service for years. I pay the residential rate, which in California is less than $7 per month. Because I have a special rate plan that allows unlimited calls in my local calling area, I pay nothing extra for forwarding calls to voice mail. Also, as long as I call from a local phone, there is no extra charge for accessing my messages. Although the monthly fee is cheap, it has added up over the years. However, I'm quite happy with my choice because I enjoy virtually unlimited incoming message service.

Frequently, I get messages in bursts—three or four may come in at the same time on Monday morning, and then there's another flurry right before lunch. Unless I had several lines or several ports, my callers would reach a busy signal, and they may or may not decide to call back. Outside voice mail service ensures that callers will never get a busy signal. I also like the messaging function. It allows me to exchange messages (send and receive) with voice mail subscribers throughout California, but I never have to place a phone call.

I know one workaholic editor who used to call me at 5:30 A.M. As I work out of my home, these calls were quite an intrusion. Now she can leave a message in my voice mailbox, which I access when I wake up at a more civilized hour.

VOICE MAIL AND CALL WAITING

If your voice mail system picks up calls when your line is busy, the tones generated by call waiting notification can play havoc with the setup. That's because call waiting and busy call forwarding will then be in conflict. The first feature (call waiting) tells your phone switch to alert you when a call comes in, but the second feature (busy call forwarding) instructs your phone switch to bypass you and send the call to the forwarded number.

Phone systems employ decision trees that tell them which function takes precedence if and when there are conflicting instructions. In this case, call waiting will override the busy call forwarding feature. The result is that none of your overflow calls will reach voice mail when you're on the line.

Note: Phone companies are addressing this problem and are in the process of developing technology to correct it. Also, you can check with your voice mail provider for additional suggestions on how to solve this problem.

In the meantime, you can handle the conflict between call waiting and busy call forwarding in one of the following three ways:

- **Cancel call waiting before every outgoing call**
  Temporarily turn off call waiting before making an outbound call. Most central office switches allow you to do this by dialing *70. Call waiting is then canceled for the duration of that one outgoing call, and your incoming calls will forward to voice mail.

  The *70 method will take care of calls that come in while you're making an outgoing call, but it still won't help you when you've answered an incoming call and second call comes in.

- **Remove call waiting**
  Call your phone company and tell them to remove call waiting from your line. You don't really need it now that you have the ability to get a message from every incoming caller. You will save money, too.

- **Remove busy call forwarding**
  If you can't part with call waiting, ask your phone company to remove the busy call forwarding feature. The call waiting feature prevents you from taking advantage of it anyway. Also, depending on how the pricing is bundled, you might save some money.

ADDING MESSAGE WAITING NOTIFICATION

Most voice mail services feature a tone to alert you a message is waiting. If you dislike picking up the telephone handset and listening for the message-waiting tone, there are alternatives. MessageAlert is a device that clips directly onto your phone line and notifies you that messages are waiting. It is available from Hello Direct (800-444-3556 or www.hello-direct.com). In addition, there are many phone sets that include built-in message-waiting lamps.

SCREENING INCOMING CALLS

To screen your incoming calls, the folks at SoloPoint (408-364-8850 or www.solopoint.com) have come up with a device called SmartScreen. It's easy to set up—you simply plug your telephone line into a jack on the back of SmartScreen, and then plug the line from SmartScreen into your telephone set.

You'll need to sign up for both three-way calling service and voice mail from your phone company. Once these services are in place, you can listen to your incoming call before deciding whether to pick it up or let it go to voice mail. Your caller never knows you're listening in. This clever device also includes a message-waiting indicator, and it even has the ability to route your voice mail and fax calls.

BASIC VOICE MAIL FEATURES

Voice mail systems and equipment do not all come with the same feature set. Here are some of the more common features:

Caller message controls

These controls allow messages to be reviewed and even rerecorded before they are sent. Callers can compose, play back, erase, repeat, and edit messages.

Date/time stamp

Each message is automatically stamped with the date and time it was sent.

Future delivery

You can use this feature to send yourself a reminder for an important meeting or other event. Although these messages won't show up in your mailbox until the date you specify, be aware that they *do* take up disk space. If your message capacity is limited, use this feature sparingly.

Group broadcast

This is a useful aid for notifying a workgroup about the time and/or location of a meeting. The same message can be sent to one or several mailboxes simultaneously, which is a real time-saver. This feature is sometimes called a group list or distribution list.

Guest mailbox

This option allows mailbox owners to set up temporary mail-boxes for guests, such as important visiting clients, temporary workgroups, and so on.

Mailbox extensions

When different departments or individuals must share a single line, this function allows them to create one or more separate extension mailboxes. Calls can then be routed to the appropriate private mailbox. Each extension can also have its own outgoing message.

Mailbox security

The privacy of mailbox messages can be protected with a personal password. Some voice mail systems also provide additional security against hackers by locking your mailbox shut after a series of unsuccessful passwords have been attempted.

Messaging

This feature is often available with off-premises voice mail systems. It allows you to record a message when you call in for your own messages, and then send it to any other mailbox within your system. Depending on the reach of your system, your entire service area or even your entire state might be included. Besides saving on possible toll charges, you get a jump on your workday by responding to messages when it's convenient for you.

Message annotation

With this feature, you can add voice notes to a message and save them along with the message. You could also forward the message with your attached comments to one or several people who share the same voice mail system.

Message capacity
This refers to both the maximum number of messages that can be stored and the total message length.

Message copy and forward
You can copy a message that you receive, add comments to it, and then send it on to one person or a group.

Message playback controls
These controls eliminate the need for you to furiously copy down messages at the speed of actual speech. You determine the pace at which your message is received by using the pause control, skipping forward or backward, skipping to a new type of message (such as new saved or erased), repeating the date and time stamp, backing up to the beginning of a message (or the beginning of all messages), jumping ahead, and so on.

If you are using an off-premises voice mail system, you can control the message playback by entering one- or two-digit commands from your telephone keypad. On-premises systems often control message playback via commands typed on a computer keyboard.

Message reply
This function enables you to reply immediately to a message.

Message retention period
This refers to the length of time a system will retain stored messages before they are automatically purged.

Message reviewing options
These options allow you to quickly scan all messages and listen to urgent messages first. Messages may then be saved, erased, replied to directly, or forwarded with or without comments.

Message scanning

You can use message scanning to quickly skim through a stack of voice mail by listening to an "envelope" description that details who sent the message and when.

Message sending options

You may choose to mark certain messages as urgent or private. You can also choose whether they are routed for normal or future delivery.

Message waiting notification

When you pick up your phone, some off-premises systems use a special "stutter" dial tone to alert you that a message is waiting. Others systems light up a lamp on your phone, beep you, or display an icon on your computer screen.

Multiple greetings

You can compose and store different outgoing greetings based on the time of day or the day of the week. You then specify when the appropriate greeting should be played.

Outgoing greeting length

This refers to the maximum length of your initial greeting.

Out-call notification

You can specify whether you want your system to page you for every message received or only for messages marked urgent. Some systems will automatically dial a predesignated number and deliver the voice message to you.

Training/tutorials

New users can familiarize themselves with mailbox usage skills by using these self-tutorials or help-prompts.

Urgent message handling

If a caller marks a voice mail message "urgent," this function will place it first on your message stack. You can also specify that urgent messages prompt out-call notification or paging.

ADVANCED FEATURES

Audiotext
This service provides prerecorded information to your callers. They can control the flow of information via their Touch-Tone keypad. It may also be used in conjunction with a voice choice tree. (See *Automated attendant* below.)

Automated attendant
These programs answer your phone and play a prerecorded greeting that prompts the caller to choose a route for her call. There may be one or many levels that branch for further choices. For example: Press 2 for sales inquiries; 3 for technical support, and so on. This feature is also known as a voice menu, a voice choice, or a menu tree.

Call screening
Call screening requires callers to record their names before being transferred to an extension. The recorded name is played to the recipient, who then has the option of accepting the call or not. If the call is rejected, it is forwarded to your voice mailbox. *Note*: Callers aren't wild about this feature.

Delivery notification
If you choose, you can be notified when a recipient picks up your message. An alert message is automatically generated and sent to your mailbox. Alternatively, you can be notified that a message was not picked up within a specified time limit, thus eliminating the "I never got your message" excuse.

"Do not disturb" mode
When enabled, this feature sends your call directly to your voice mailbox without even ringing your phone.

Multilingual greetings and system prompts
Both users and callers are offered a choice of language. This is a useful feature if your customer base includes a minority population, or if you have frequent international communications.

Names directory

An automated attendant feature that provides a directory of all the people and departments in your company. Assists callers to find the correct extension and then rings them through or sends them to voice mail. Often this requires only a partial spelling of the last name using the touchtone keypad.

Night mode

A different set of caller instructions can be programmed for after-business hours. Messages may or may not be taken.

Number of ports

In this context, ports are basically the same as phone lines. Each time a caller leaves a voice message or you call in to pick up a message, a port is involved. Therefore, the number of ports your system has dictates the maximum number of people who can access the system at the same time. Voice mail systems come in various port sizes—anywhere from two to 9,600 ports. Voice mail boards usually handle only one or two ports. As a general rule, you should plan one port for each four employees.

Outside number messaging

To send a message to a person who is not a member of your voice mail system, you can employ this feature. You simply record the message, and the system places the call and delivers it. If the line is busy or unanswered, the system tries until the message is delivered or until a specified number of retry attempts has been made.

Rotary access

This option enables callers with rotary phones to access voice mail and leave messages.

Transfer to attendant

If your caller needs to speak to a receptionist or assistant, this option transfers him out of voice mail to a "live" person.

Caution: If you include this option, make sure that someone is available at all times to answer calls. You don't want to dump your callers into "voice mail jail." Their only recourse would be to hang up or leave a message for you in the wrong mailbox— the mailbox belonging to the receptionist or assistant.

Voice recognition

With this feature, you activate mailbox controls by speaking common word commands, such as play, save, repeat, erase, forward, yes, or no.

Voice status announcements

These announcements provide your callers with a status message regarding each call's progress. For example: "I'm transferring you to extension two," or "Extension three is on the phone, would you like to leave a voice message?"

WHICH VOICE MAIL OPTION IS BEST?

When comparing the virtues of voice mail service to those of purchasing your own voice mail system, there are many issues to consider. One significant advantage of voice mail service is that there are few up-front costs and, consequently, much less commitment required. You pay only an initial setup fee and a monthly usage fee thereafter. This way, you can try out voice mail for a minimal cost and see how it works for your business. If you subsequently decide to use voice mail for the long haul (and the dollars work out), you'll feel more confident about investing in voice mail hardware.

Voice mail service is easier to set up than voice mail hardware. As you already have a phone line, all you need to do is add a call forwarding feature or two. Also, because voice messaging technology changes so rapidly, you avoid the possibility of shelling out precious dollars for a system that may be obsolete within a year.

Stand-alone voice mail systems are an attractive option for some businesses, such as seasonal businesses or organizations that want to establish a presence in another market without actually setting up an office there. This option gives them a separate phone number that does not ring anywhere except at the voice mail switch. (Technically, it doesn't ring there either!)

The ability to receive multiple calls simultaneously is probably the most important advantage that voice mail service has over do-it-yourself voice mail. When using a phone company service, your phone will be answered automatically even if all your lines are busy. In addition, overflow calls are forwarded (via standard phone company call forwarding services) to the voice mail machine located at your service provider's premises.

On the other hand, voice boards and voice mail systems provide you with all the control you'll ever want. You're not limited to a set number of messages or a predetermined number of mailboxes. You can customize the system to meet your unique needs. If you want seven mailboxes with outgoing messages of six minutes apiece, so be it.

When you later decide to add five more mailboxes, page your technician for urgent calls, and reduce outgoing messages to two minutes, all you have to do is program the changes. Though you pay more up front for a voice mail system of your own, it will eventually pay for itself.

As I mentioned earlier, voice mail services limit the number and length of your messages. Also, if you require additional mailboxes, it will cost you extra—anywhere from $3 a month for residential service to $20 a month for business service.

There are other disadvantages as well. It's not easy to save a message permanently, because voice mail services employ built-in delete timers, and users must call the service to make any changes. Often, any kind of change, such as varying the number of rings before voice mail answers, triggers an administration fee. Finally, of course, the bill comes month after month.

Voice mail technology continues to change at a rapid pace. If you don't own a system, you can enjoy all the latest upgrades as your vendor institutes them. If you buy, however, your system may quickly become too limited for your future needs. Unless you have a number of phone lines or a communications-intensive application, such a major capital outlay may not be cost justified.

PURCHASING A VOICE MAIL SYSTEM

Be aware that buying a voice mail system also means you are responsible for maintaining it. This may be easy or difficult, depending on your technical ability and the design of the system. You have to house it somewhere, and it must be kept clean, dry, and cool. If you're adding ports, you may need to rewire.

Should you happen to be shopping for a phone system at the same time, be sure to check out its voice mail functions. Many PBX and key systems include optional voice mail capabilities.

Compatibility with your existing key system or PBX can be tricky. The phone companies have done a good job of making Centrex compatible with their voice mail. However, if you have a phone system already installed and want to add a voice mail board or stand-alone system, it's a good idea to contact your phone system vendor and check on compatibility before making your decision.

An important first step is to figure out how many ports you'll need. Remember, the number of ports available dictates how many people can access their mailboxes at the same time. A typical voice mailbox is used only a fraction of the time, though, so a four-port system can easily be used by 50 to 100 people.

Signing up for voice mail service with the phone company on a trial basis is a good way to find out what your call demands and patterns are. Their systems are enormous—with hundreds of ports—so callers rarely run into busy signals or other types of contention problems. Then, note the frequency of calls coming in at the same time and keep a record to analyze later.

Depending on the type of business you're in and how you use voice mail, you'll probably find that you can get by with one or two ports. If you're still unsure, check with your vendor—there are guidelines and tables to help you determine your needs.

BEYOND VOICE MAIL

Virtual assistant software provides you with an automated secretarial service that also functions as an efficient personal assistant. Much more than a voice mail system, virtual assistants can return calls to people who leave messages, keep track of your whereabouts, and even interrupt a call to whisper the name of an incoming caller. You can then decide whether to take the call or send it to voice mail. There are several virtual assistant software programs, including Portico (www.general-magic.com), Webley (www.webley.com), and Wildfire (www.wildfire.com).

When you call into Wildfire, a pleasant voice cheerily greets you. At any time during a phone call, you can bring Wildfire onto the line and instruct it to place a call for you, create a reminder message, or add the caller's number to your database. If you have given your callers a special password or code, Wildfire will greet them with "Oh, hi!" and play back a message that you've left just for them.

Wildfire works with a series of voice prompts. This feature is especially useful if you are calling from a car phone, because your hands can stay on the steering wheel while placing calls or looking up numbers.

Service fees for Wildfire can be somewhat hefty. Basic service costs about $40 a month, but you will also pay usage charges of around 19 cents a minute. For heavy usage, there are discount plans, and 800 numbers are available.

Though an average user will rack up charges of $150 to $200 a month, compare that cost to the expense of a dedicated secretary or receptionist. Wildfire is a deal. This service is particularly well-suited for the consulting architect whose office location varies daily, the contractor who works in the field far from the office, or anyone who spends much time on the road.

Large businesses can buy their own Wildfire server for about $50,000 to start. For the rest of us, there are several companies that offer Wildfire service on a subscription basis. To find out what's available in your area, contact Wildfire (800-WILDFIRE).

Profile of a Wildfire user

Rick Smolan belongs to a new breed of entrepreneur—the itinerant executive. He is a photojournalist who has been responsible for several *A Day in the Life* books. His projects often involve complex coordination with writers and photographers in up to 150 locations around the world. To handle it all, Smolan relies on Wildfire, his electronic assistant.

Smolan is also president of Against All Odds Productions, which is based in Sausalito, California. He coordinates his forces from his office-of-the-moment—plane, automobile, hotel room, telephone booth, home, or—his office.

While working in Vietnam, Smolan scheduled his electronic assistant to call him each morning. Once connected, he could handle all his calls at U.S. phone rates, thus avoiding overseas hotel charges of about $10 per call. By using Wildfire, Smolan also avoids the $15-per-call fee charged for airline phone access.

"I once spent four and a half hours on one phone call," Smolan explains. "I made many, many calls through Wildfire, but never hung up. I finished half a day's work on my way to New York." Though his phone bills have gone up, "so has my efficiency, so that's a pretty good trade," he says.

TIPS FOR USER-FRIENDLY VOICE MAIL

The ideal voice mail system is effective, easy to use, and caller friendly. The key to designing such a system is to always keep your caller in mind.

Do you remember how you felt when encountering a new voice messaging system for the first time? Was it helpful or infuriating? Did you appreciate the convenience of a logical system, or did you feel as though you had just entered an electronic twilight zone? Were you confident that the mailbox owner checked in and picked up messages often? Or did it seem that the owner used voice mail as a shield to keep callers at a distance?

If you're new to the voice mail game, or just want to brush up on your skills, the tips on the following pages will help you tune up your voice communications.

✔ **Encourage callers to leave details**

A message consisting of only a name and number doesn't do much good. You'll have to call back just to find out what the caller needs. Suggest that your callers ask their questions now and, if they have one-way information, to leave it. A friend of mine adds this as a tag end to his message:

> If you leave me a detailed message, I'll be able to get back to you with the information you need.

✔ **Replace your regular greeting with an alternate greeting for after-business hours and on weekends**

Many voice mail services allow you to record and store an optional greeting. Changing from one to the other is a simple matter of a few keystrokes. Explain your regular business hours, give instructions on how to leave a message, and, if possible, provide emergency contact information.

> This is Power Plumbers. Our normal business hours are 8
> A.M. to 5 P.M., Monday through Saturday. After the tone, please
> leave your name, number, and the nature of your call, and
> we'll call you back in the morning.

✔ Change your greeting frequently

Your greeting should let callers know whether you are just
briefly away from the phone or gone all week. Some people
even put the day's date in their greeting. Such a message
serves a twofold purpose:

1. You're giving the caller an idea of how soon you'll return his call (two hours, end of the day, next week).
2. Your frequent caller will know that you use voice mail
actively.

> You've reached Brenda Copeland at Acme Engineering. It's
> Tuesday, August 14th. I'll be in meetings this morning, but
> will be checking for messages. This afternoon, I'll be in the
> office.

✔ Keep your greeting short and businesslike

Although some people may enjoy a good joke or your comments about the latest ball game, the majority of your callers will resent your attempts at joviality.

✔ Provide instructions for emergencies

If your business survives on prompt service and your callers
need help fast, be sure to give them options. For example,
to label a call urgent, the caller could press a special key
combination that would ring your pager, or you could provide the caller with an alternate number to dial.

This is the Computer Clinic. I'm out on an emergency right now. Please leave your name, number, and a detailed message. I'll get back to you as quickly as I can. If you need help immediately, press the "4" key after you leave your message, and I will be paged.

✔ Speak in a natural tone

When recording, never read your greeting message. You'll sound nervous or remote. It's a good idea to rehearse your outgoing message until you sound relaxed and upbeat. You might want to send yourself messages periodically to check how you sound.

✔ Pay close attention to the audio

Somehow, my neighbor's dog always knows when I'm getting ready to change my voice mail greeting. I guess he wants to be included in the outgoing message. If you have potentially distracting background sounds, close the door or change the greeting at a time when it's quiet. Such a moment can be hard to find in a busy garage or machine shop, but your callers will definitely appreciate it. Whatever you do, don't use a speakerphone when recording your greeting—unless you want to sound imperious and distant.

✔ Provide shortcut tips for regular callers

I really appreciate voice mail greetings that recognize frequent callers may hear the same informational message over and over and over again. So, tell your callers how to skip your greeting and get right to the message-leaving part.

If you would like to skip this message and leave a message for me, press the pound sign now.

✔ **Check in often**

Besides simplifying the task of returning calls, checking voice mail frequently allows you to respond quickly to important or urgent calls. Be sure to avoid all possibility of appearing to hide behind your voice mail.

CREATING A SUCCESSFUL VOICE MAIL MENU

A poorly designed voice menu can drive your callers away in droves. If you set up a menu tree for callers, you might want to consider these suggestions to avoid "torture by telephone."

- **Limit the number of menus and options**
  According to industry experts, callers can't remember more than four choices at a time. Try to reduce the number of levels your callers must wade through before reaching the information or mailbox they need.

> This is the City Planning and Development Division. For planning, press two. For zoning information, press three. For engineering, press four. For all other calls, press five.

- **Keep greetings and instructions short**
  Fifteen seconds or less is about right for each instructional message.

- **Use a consistent form for instructions**
  It is helpful to offer the desired option first and then say which key to press.

  For example, rather than saying: "For sales, press two. Press three for service," you should say: "For sales, press two. For service, press three." Always say "zero" instead of "oh." Otherwise, your callers may think you mean the letter *O* and press six, the corresponding key.

- **Provide the most important or most frequently requested information first**
  If the bulk of your callers want to know your hours of operation, give them that information first before going into your menu of options.

- **Provide an escape valve**
  Don't run your callers through a long list of options or announcements with no chance for escape. Early on, give them instructions such as, "If you've already heard this message, you may skip it by pressing the pound key," or "If you know the extension of the person you're calling, you may press it at any time." If possible, provide the capability to transfer to an attendant so that the caller can speak to a live person.

- **Be kind to rotary phone callers**
  Develop a plan that provides instructions for callers who use rotary phones. According to AT&T, 38.5 percent of American households are still using rotary telephones. The heaviest concentration of rotary users is in older, urban households.

ANSWERING MACHINES

"Dave, this is Hal, your answering machine. Can we talk?" If your answering machine could speak for itself, it could probably tell you a lot: "We've had the same old message since 1994," or "I'm on my last legs; don't you think it's finally time to retire me?"

If you purchased your last answering machine several years ago and are getting ready to shop for a new one, you're in for some nice surprises. The new crop of telephone answering devices have been reengineered to avoid most of the old bugaboos, such as hanging up on a long-winded caller in midsentence or continuing to answer your calls even though the message tape is full.

Today's answering machine is also smaller, using microcassettes and memory chips to reduce its footprint. That's an attractive benefit for those of us with limited desktop space. Some even mount on the wall to get out of your way.

Many modern answering machines include full-featured business telephones and useful functions, such as caller ID displays and paging capability. Last, but not least, they are available in all colors and varieties, from simple stand-alone one-line devices to multifunction office assistants.

ANSWERING MACHINE OPTIONS

There are a number of types to choose from:

- **Tape-based answering machine**
  If your answering needs are basic, you can probably get along with an inexpensive tape-based device. Steer clear of machines that use a single tape for both greeting and incoming messages, however. These machines force your caller to wait while the tape shuttles back to the appropriate section for leaving a message.

- **Digital answering device**
  Digital machines offer better message quality and faster message access. Because you don't have to wait for the cassette tape to rewind or fast forward, you save up to 15 seconds on each message.

- **Phone plus answering device**
  Many manufacturers will package a telephone and answering machine together. Look for a cordless receiver with a built-in answering device. These models allow you to screen calls from anywhere without having to be near the base unit.

- **Computer-based answering**

  If your computer has a voice/fax/modem card, you can use your computer to manage your messages. Many of the latest computers include preloaded computer phone-answering software. Some will also work when your computer is off.

- **Portable answering machine**

  There are even a few portable answering machines. Motorola makes one that operates like a pager, but it sends complete voice messages from your callers.

ANSWERING DEVICE FEATURES

Announcement only

Some models have a switch that allows you to set the machine to play a greeting or an announcement, but not take a message. This can be handy if you're on an extended vacation or don't want to take messages on weekends.

Auto attendant

At the touch of a button, callers have the option of receiving information, leaving a message, or speaking to someone.

Automatic cutoff

This feature turns the answering machine off as soon as any handset on the line is picked up.

Tip: If you have an older machine that doesn't cut off, you can get an interrupt device for about $10. You plug it into the wall jack and then plug the answering device into it. The second you pick up the handset of any phone on the same line, your recorded outgoing greeting is blocked. You can then take the call without shouting over your greeting.

Automatic reset

After playing your messages, the unit will automatically reset itself, ready to take the next call.

Call screening

Also called call monitor, this feature allows you to listen to the incoming message by turning up the volume. If you want to talk to the caller, you just pick up the handset.

Caller ID

The name and/or number of the person who is calling is displayed, which is very useful for call screening. To get caller ID service, you need to sign up with your telephone company.

Change outgoing message by time of day

You can program your answering device to play different outgoing messages for various times of the day. For example: Out to lunch, gone for the day, and so on.

Tip: If your current machine only supports a single outgoing message, try recording several outgoing messages, each on a different cassette. Label them appropriately—"gone for the day," "in a meeting," "closed until Monday." Then, simply pop in the correct tape, and you're outta there.

Confidential message for caller

When you want to leave a specific message for a particular caller, you can use your caller ID service to recognize a particular phone number or numbers. You then program your phone to play a special message for these numbers. Alternatively, some answering machines have a function that lets you give out a special PIN code to certain callers. When they key in their PIN, they hear the special message. Such a capability might be valuable for important customers or vendors.

Dictation

This feature gives your answering machine the capabilities of a dictation device.

Distinctive ring mode

If you subscribe to a distinctive ring service from your local phone company (see Chapter 3), you can program a switch to play a different message for up to four different ring modes. Doing so will give your organization the appearance of having multiple lines—all for the cost of one line plus the monthly distinctive ring service fee.

Earphone jack
This appliance allows you to listen to your messages privately.

Greeting bypass
You can give your frequent or impatient callers the option of skipping your outgoing message by pressing a Touch-Tone command. You'll have to include instructions on using this command, such as pressing the asterisk key, in your outgoing greeting. Your frequent callers will love you for this.

Greeting length
Some devices require your greeting be a specific length, say 30 seconds. If you don't use up all the time in your outgoing message, your callers are subjected to a few seconds of silence before they can leave a message or hang up in disgust. Be sure your device lets you record an outgoing message of any length.

Mailboxes
Separate greetings and mailboxes can be created for various departments or staff members. Callers select the appropriate mailbox after listening to an announcement that instructs them to: "Press one for sales; press two for service," and so forth.

Message forwarding
This feature allows you to program your answering device to call another number and play back your message(s) automatically. A security code is usually required.

Memo
This function can serve as an electronic notepad. You can leave messages for others in your office who use the same answering device without having to place a call.

Message counter

The digital readout will usually let you know how many new messages are waiting. Some devices have two counters—one tells you the number of messages; the other tells you the total number of calls, both messages and hangups.

Message only

If you have this feature, your machine counts only those messages that have voice on them. Hangups are not saved or counted.

Message playback controls

Fast forward, rewind, repeat, pause, skip, erase, save—you should be able to access these control functions remotely as well. Digital answering devices offer even more functions, such as instant repeat, play new messages only, and selective save.

Message-waiting indicator

This indicator may be a flashing light or an LCD display. It alerts you that a new message is waiting. If you have more than one mailbox, each mailbox may have its own lamp. Some machines use a voice alert: "Dave, you have a message waiting."

Multiple line coverage

Though you pay more, you can now purchase devices that handle two lines. Be sure to check whether these devices can actually take a message for two lines at once. Most of them can only ask the caller to "please wait a moment" until the first message has been recorded.

New message playback only

Selecting this function tells your machine to play only those messages that haven't been accessed before. If you tend to save messages or share a machine with others, this feature could come in handy.

Paging

When you receive a message, this option dials your pager to alert you.

Power failure protection

A small backup battery device will save your time/day setting, remote password setting, message count, greeting(s), and any messages in the event of a power failure. If you need this capability, be sure to replace the batteries periodically. Some models also come with a battery condition indicator.

Priority codes

An alternative to call screening is to give select callers a special two-digit code. After the answering machine picks up, your caller enters her code and the machine then alerts you that a priority call is coming in.

Programmable hours of operation

You can program your machine to automatically turn itself on. In this way, you avoid the problem of remembering to turn the machine on before leaving the office.

Remote controls

Almost all machines allow you to retrieve your messages remotely from a Touch-Tone phone. Some devices will also let you turn on the machine from afar (by letting it ring 10 or 12 times) and update your greeting. If you live or travel in the land of rotary phones, you might also want to have remote capability for rotary phones or carry a tone generator with you.

Security

Answering machines are not famous for security—all you have to do is punch the play button and they tell all. You can usually obtain a bit of security remotely, however. Most machines have a choice of at least 99 security codes, and some have 999. In my opinion, the more the better. Be sure to get a machine that lets you change your password, and then change it frequently.

Warning: Don't take security for granted. Clever phone fraud experts have been known to call an unattended answering machine, crack the PIN code, and record the following greeting:

"Operator, I'll accept the charges." They then proceed to charge calls to your phone number. You don't find out about the switch until your humongous phone bill arrives.

Tape full

When the recording tape fills up, some answering machines can play an alternate greeting to your callers advising them that they can't leave a message. Hopefully, you pick up your messages often enough so that you don't encounter this problem.

Other machines simply stop answering the phone when the tape is full—definitely a bad design. If you have one of these models, you can't clear the messages remotely because the blankety-blank thing won't answer the phone. Replace it.

Time and date stamp

Using digitized voice, the machine will tell you the time and date that the call came in.

Toll saver

This is a setting that instructs the phone to ring longer if there are no messages on the machine (usually four rings), but to answer more promptly if you have messages (one or two rings).

When calling in from a remote location for your messages, you can simply hang up after the second ring because you know there are no messages. In this way, you avoid paying for a toll call just to find out that you don't have a message.

Two-line capability

This convenient feature lets you take messages for two phone lines on the same machine.

Two-way recording

When you need a recorded copy of a telephone conversation, this function allows you to record both sides. Be sure to get your caller's permission, however.

Variable answering setting

This setting allows you to determine when the machine will answer—on the first ring, second ring, or whatever ring you choose. Some machines have fewer settings; some have more.

Variable maximum message length

You might want the ability to specify the maximum length of a caller's message, whether 30 seconds, 5 minutes, or even 30 minutes. Doing so will protect your machine from being filled up by one or two talkaholics. On the other hand, you may run the risk of hanging up on an important client, who just happened to need to leave a long message. Good-bye, client.

Voice activation (VOX)

This technology enables your answering machine to detect when a caller has hung up, and thus when to stop recording. Consequently, tape space, or chip space, is conserved, and those long blank spots at the end of messages are eliminated. Unfortunately, some machines may interpret a short pause or a soft-voiced caller as the end of the message. Be sure to test out this feature in the store.

Voice-assisted operation

A series of voice prompts will confirm that your commands have been implemented: "Dave, I saved that message for you." This function is especially useful when accessing your machine remotely.

Volume controls

These controls increase or reduce the volume of your recorded messages.

A MENU OF MESSAGES

Do you wish your answering machine had an elegant voice or spoke with a British accent? Now you can download a message as a wave file via the Internet. You'll find a menu of messages at www.answeringmachine.co.uk, including serious, humorous, Hollywood, musical, and so on.

For example, you could select: "At this time, we are unable to answer your call," spoken in a top-drawer British accent. Do your callers enjoy humor? You could experiment with one of these messages:

- **Mission Impossible**
  "Hello, caller. Your mission, should you choose to accept it, is to leave your name, number and a brief message."

- **Star Trek**
  "We are the Borg. You are to leave a message now or you will be assimilated."

- **A singing message—to the tune of "Heartbreak Hotel"**
  "Well since my baby left me, there's just no one left at home. No one to take your call except my answering machine."

Caution: Such messages could be risky, as not everyone shares the same idea of what's humorous.

WHAT'S BEST FOR YOU?

One thing we know for sure—you definitely need some kind of messaging capability. Thankfully, most people have finally gotten over the phobia of leaving a message with a machine. Now, what kind of service or device should you get?

Telephone answering devices are very flexible because you are in control of the programming. You can see at a glance that you have messages waiting, and you don't have to place a phone call to pick them up. If you buy a digital answering machine, you eliminate all worries about snarled tapes or scratchy outgoing messages.

There are many other advantages to answering machines. Usually, they are far less expensive than voice mail. You can monitor your incoming calls, which is a big help if you need to get work done while waiting for that all-important call. Also, if you need to keep audio records, it's a simple thing to archive your messages, though you might get sick of a filing cabinet overflowing with tapes.

Answering machines are not the most reliable devices, however. In a *Consumer Reports* survey conducted in November of 1991, 40 percent of the respondents reported some kind of answering machine malfunction. Most importantly, if security is a concern, voice mail is the best choice hands down.

Voice mail's biggest advantage is that callers can leave messages even when you're on the phone. Clients, customers, vendors, and friends will never encounter a busy signal. Message handling with voice mail is also much more functional. The broadcasting and messaging capabilities are especially useful. A message on an answering device is just that—you can listen to it, save it, or erase it, but you can't send it to another user, add comments, or export it to your PC for later reference.

Finally, if you need to speak to your callers in real time the first time they call, voice mail is no better than an answering machine. Your best bet is a cellular phone or a follow-me-anywhere phone number.

VOICE MAIL OR ANSWERING MACHINE

Take this quick survey. If you find yourself agreeing with two or more statements, you need voice mail (or an answering device with multiple mailboxes).

▶▶ Your callers complain that you are difficult to reach
▶▶ You spend lots of time on the phone providing the same information to many callers
▶▶ You want to add services, but you don't have the personnel to handle the phones
▶▶ Your callers could most likely place an order once they've heard an informational message
▶▶ You engage in more than one business
▶▶ Your messages need to be kept completely private from others in your organization or household

SHARING A LINE

Many business phone lines have to do double duty. If yours must handle a variety of tasks—fax, voice, and answering machine—read on. (Also, refer to Chapter 13 for more detailed information on line-sharing for fax machines.)

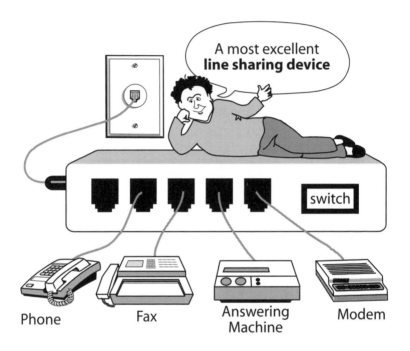

Phone   Fax   Answering Machine   Modem

DAISY-CHAINING

If you need to plug a number of devices into the same phone line, you can daisy-chain them. Here's what to do:

On the back of your answering machine you will find two phone jacks. One is labeled LINE, and one is labeled PHONE. Plug your answering machine into the wall jack using the LINE port. To attach the next device, plug another phone line cord into the PHONE port on the back of the machine. Continuing in this way, you can string up to four additional devices onto the same phone line.

Switching

Depending on what devices you are connecting, you may need to add a switch so that fax calls are directed to the fax machine and voice calls are directed to your answering machine. Some line-sharing switches work with distinctive ringing. This service is supplied by the telephone company, and it permits up to four different phone numbers to ring on one line (see Chapter 3). You specify which phone number rings at each jack. Simpler switches only distinguish between modem and fax calls.

The least inexpensive solution is a manual switch. You simply turn a knob to switch between two devices on a single line. Of course, you have to know what type of call is coming in—no easy feat, unless you're psychic!

ANSWERING SERVICES

Some users still need the human touch that an answering service can provide. Answering services are invaluable if you need someone other than the caller to make an on-the-spot decision or if you need immediate follow-up when you're not available.

An efficient, well-organized answering service can make your small business appear larger and more professional. Three basic options are available:

- You can rent a phone number from the service.

- You can hardwire your phone line to the answering service. Then, if you don't answer within a certain number of rings, the service picks up the call.

- You can forward your calls to the service via the telephone company's call forwarding feature.

The call forwarding approach is the preferred method for most business situations. It's simple, inexpensive, and easy to change. You can retrieve your messages in a variety of ways. The service can fax messages to you, send them by modem to your PC, or you can call in to pick them up.

Answering bureaus provide a wide range of useful services for small businesses that include:

- Alpha and digital paging
- Audiotext services
- Wireless dispatching to on-call personnel
- Fax broadcasting
- Credit card/order processing
- Brochure requests
- Dealer locator services
- Hotline handling
- Mail service
- Cellular alert
- Wake-up services
- Personalized toll-free 800 numbers
- Voice mail
- Reservations

Answering services are often willing to handle more complex tasks than simple message-taking. For example, they may take orders, which is an involved task for any voice mail system. Also, many people do not like to give their credit card number to a machine, but they are used to giving that information to a live operator. Ask your local answering bureau for a list of other services it may provide.

TIPS FOR LEAVING AN EFFECTIVE MESSAGE

Seventy-five percent of the nation's largest firms employ a voice mail system, and almost all the rest use some sort of telephone answering device. So, the chances that you will one day need to leave a message with a machine have risen dramatically. Even if you hate talking to a machine, you're going to have to do it. To that end, I am including some tips to help you leave voice messages that reduce phone tag and get your calls returned.

✔ **Organize your thoughts before calling**

Be brief, get to the point, and skip the small talk. If necessary, make notes or even rehearse before you call. When you need a response, be sure to mention what the best time for reaching you is and where.

✔ **Say your name in the first ten seconds**

Most voice mail systems and some answering machines offer a scanning feature. If the recipient is scanning her messages, she will play only the first few seconds of each message. You want her to know who's calling.

✔ **Start your message with a "headline"**

Explain the subject of your message. Doing so helps the recipient decide whether to listen to the message now or save it for later.

✔ **Always provide your phone number**

Unless you are absolutely sure that the recipient knows your phone number by heart, say it again. If the recipient doesn't have to look up your number, your chances of a callback are greatly increased.

✔ **Leave your phone number at the end of the message**

Most voice systems allow users to skip to the last ten seconds of the message because the majority of callers leave their phone number last.

✔ **Speak slowly when leaving numbers or technical information**

Doesn't it drive you nuts when someone leaves you a perfectly clear message and then races through the phone number at the very end? Though you may be bored with repeating your phone number, resist the temptation to hurry through this part.

RESOURCES

Books, magazines, and newsletters
1-800 Courtesy:
Connecting With A Winning Telephone Image
by Terry Wildermann
Aegis Publishing, 1999

Not just another telephone etiquette book—this one offers useful tips on managing your phone and working effectively from home.

Escape From Voicemail Hell/Boost Your Productivity by Making Voicemail Work For You
by Paul LeBon
ParLeau Publishing, 1999

Teleconnect
12 West 21st Street
New York, NY 10010
800-677-3435
www.teleconnect.com

This publication is packed with product reviews and stories concerning voice messaging and general office telephony. Look for the annual voice mail buyers' guide.

Shopping suggestions
Consumer Reports publishes a survey on answering machines every few years. You can find it in your library or search it online for a fee (www.consumereports.org).

Chapter

9

Paging

HOME-BASED BUSINESSES and small organizations are faced with a catch-22 situation. Often, their personnel must be out of the office to perform business tasks, but at the same time they need to be in the office to field calls and maintain customer contact. Too many tasks? Too few hands? One way to handle these conflicting responsibilities is to take advantage of wireless communications.

Industry studies indicate that initial business calls have an average completion rate of less than 20 percent. Utilizing a pager or other wireless communication device increases the probability of call completion to 90 percent. Those figures can translate into more business for you, and they free you from waiting by the phone or playing endless telephone tag.

Wireless communications devices are classified by transmission technology and/or frequency. There are several categories:

- **Cellular**
  A wired telephone network connects you to a system of transmitters and receivers

- **Paging**
  Messages are broadcast over a wide area

- **Wireless data networks**
  A radio modem is used to transmit information

Even though cordless phones use wireless technology to handle connections from the base to the handset, they are not technically classified as wireless communications. Information on cordless phones can be found in Chapter 5, and Chapter 7 discusses mobile phones. This chapter will focus on paging, the most useful and affordable wireless technology.

Pagers have come a long way from the intrusive beepers of yesteryear. Today, you can get a pager that vibrates silently, plays a melody, or quietly winks to let you know a page has come in.

There are a variety of styles available that include credit card size pagers, belt clip pagers, and ankle clip models for athletes and joggers. Some pagers hang from a lanyard around your neck; others double as fountain pens or wristwatches. They even come in jazzed-up colors such as hot pink, grape, and glow-in-the-dark green.

Numeric pagers show the telephone number of the party trying to reach you. Alphanumeric pagers display short messages, often saving you the time and expense of having to make a call to get much-needed information. Two-way pagers give you the option of sending an answer. Voice pagers go one step further and actually speak to you.

Today, pagers are frequently used to notify you of more than just a message. They deliver email, voice mail, and even provide information services, such as news feeds, weather, and hourly stock quotes. Some PDAs (personal digital assistants), handhelds, and laptop computers also have built-in paging capabilities. In addition, pagers could come in handy if you get lost. There are services available that will send you detailed directions to help you get where you're going.

You see all sorts of people using pagers, and a study conducted by BIS Strategic Decisions reported that nearly one out of three cellular subscribers also carries a pager. You probably know some of the folks who use pagers today:

- Lawyers use a silent two-way pager while in court to communicate with members of their team

- Real estate agents carry alpha pagers to receive listing information on the fly

- A nurse has a silent beeper that alerts him when a patient needs assistance

- Reporters tote a PDA with paging capability to get heads-up information on late-breaking leads

- Field service agents carry numeric pagers to stay in touch with the office

- A sales manager downloads the latest price list and then broadcasts it to her sales force in the field

A painting contractor in my area uses alpha paging to keep in touch with his customers. Because most of the job sites he works on have no phones and he doesn't carry a mobile phone, answering a page can be difficult. If potential clients need him to drop by for a quote, they can leave the address with a service that types the message and sends it to him. The system pages him, displays the message, and he can check out the client's job without having to call back to get the details. This way, he doesn't miss out on opportunities to bid on jobs, and he avoids the hassle of constantly checking for messages.

Internet America, a Dallas-based Internet service provider, replaced a bunch of its cell phones with two-way pagers from Research in Motion (www.rim.net). The company connected their pagers to a network-monitoring system, and the pagers automatically alert field service support if there's trouble with the Internet system. Because the RIM pagers feature automatic message notification, the company knows exactly when a page is received. Doug Davis, chief operating officer, notes that trouble is handled 25 percent faster than it was when his field service relied on mobile phones. The company has also experienced a 40 percent savings in communications costs.

Paging can be used in very creative ways. For example, restaurants give a loaner pager to patrons waiting for a table so they can roam as far away as two miles. While waiting, they can shop at a nearby mall, go for a walk, or hang out in a noisy bar. When a table becomes available, the pager alerts them. In California, an enterprising windsurfer offers a paging service that monitors wind speed and direction, and then beeps you when the wind conditions are right for a wild ride.

You can also link your car to your pager, using a service such as CommandLink (www.pagecar.com). In the event that you lose your car keys or lock them inside, the service will unlock the door. Travelocity, a web-based travel company, offers a paging service that alerts busy travelers to last-minute flight and boarding gate changes. There are even paging services that send wireless messages to electronic signs, updating them all with a single page.

A SHORT HISTORY OF PAGING

Paging was first used by the United States military during World War II. Al Gross, an electrical engineer from Cleveland's Case School of Applied Sciences, was invited by the Office of Strategic Services to develop radio communications for the war effort. One of his inventions involved a safer system for blowing up train bridges. First, a receiver was attached to the explosive material and placed under the target bridge. Then, a plane flying nearby would send a signal to trigger the blast. This was the first paging system.

In 1949, the Federal Communication Commission allocated a group of radio frequencies that could be used for radio communications. Motorola introduced its first paging system, designed for medical use, in 1956, and its first consumer pager, Pageboy I, came out in 1974. Pageboy I had no display, could not store messages, and simply beeped the wearer when a message was received. Because pagers had a minimal range, paging was restricted to on-site situations, such as within a hospital.

By 1980, there were 3.2 million pager users worldwide. It wasn't until the 1990s, when wide-area paging was introduced, that paging became popular for personal use. By 1990, over 22 million pagers were in use. According to the Personal Communication Industry Association, approximately 70 million Americans carry pagers today.

HOW IT WORKS

To receive pages, you'll need both a paging device and a paging service. When you sign up with your paging service, you must specify the geographic area where you want to receive pages. This area can be as small as a portion of a city or as wide as several nations.

At the same time, you will also sign up for the type of paging you want—numeric, which sends you the telephone number of the calling party; alphanumeric, which can send a short message; or two-way. In addition to a service contract, of course, you'll need to purchase a pager or a multifunction device equipped as a paging receiver.

How Paging Works

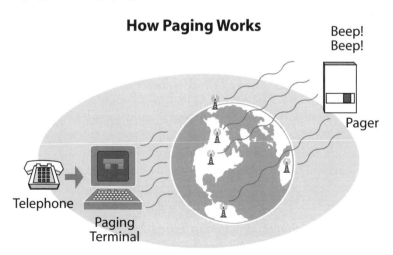

Beep!
Beep!

Pager

Telephone

Paging
Terminal

Callers can leave messages for you via a paging operator, voice mail, or other system. The paging information is first entered into the system's computer. Then, the data, whether a telephone number or a message, is broadcast over every part of the covered territory using radio towers and/or satellites to deliver the signal. If your pager is on, it "catches" the broadcast and your pager alerts you.

Once you have been alerted, you can call in to your paging or voice mail service to pick up your message. If your pager has word display capabilities, you simply read the message on your screen. A security code is necessary for picking up messages, so only you or someone who knows your code can access your messages. All other pagers within your area are locked out from the data being sent to your pager address.

RELIABILITY

Pagers are very reliable communications devices. Because they were originally designed for doctors and others requiring emergency communications, pagers were developed with reliability in mind. They use redundant and overlapping broadcast systems, plus a powerful signal that ensures the message gets through. Pagers can run for over a month on a single set of batteries. Also, due to the broadcast nature of the signal, they can reach spots other systems can't, such as the interiors of steel office buildings, tunnels, and subways.

Pagers did experience a spectacular failure in May 1998. An onboard computer failed on a paging satellite, thus knocking out 90 percent of the nation's paging calls. Only one nationwide company, SkyTel, continued to function. Unlike the other paging services, SkyTel had a backup plan and was able to switch to another satellite provider within minutes of the mishap. Other providers weren't so fortunate, and many paging customers went without service for several days. According to John Beletic, PageMart CEO, "This is the first time in 35 years pagers have gone silent."

SECURITY CONCERNS

Now that many pagers have messaging capabilities, they are being targeted by hackers who change the security codes and take over mailboxes. If this happens to you, your security code won't work and you'll be unable to pick up messages.

You'll need to contact your paging company and have the code changed for you. To reduce the odds of being a victim, change your password frequently and don't use easy-to-crack passwords, such as your name or birth date.

Paging companies are fighting back against fraud and airwave theft. If you send critical information over a paging network, ask your paging service how it can help protect your data. For highly sensitive information, use more secure communications.

TYPES OF PAGERS

Pagers come in several varieties:

- **Numeric pager**
  These models display the phone number of the person paging you. If your paging service is connected to voice mail, the number displayed will be your voice mail access number. For callers paging you directly, the number displayed will be the number they keyed in on their Touch-Tone phone.

  > 212-555-5873

- **Alphanumeric pager** (also called a word pager)

  > PLEASE BRING MORRISON FILE
  > WITH YOU TO THE 2PM STAFF
  > MEETING TODAY

  Word pagers display a message or coded information, such as a sender code. These messages could also include a phone number. Callers can send you a word message over the Internet from a computer equipped with a modem or by calling a live operator. This type of pager reduces the number of return calls you have to make.

- **Two-way pager**
  Two-way pagers allow you to send and receive both wireless email and wireless instant messaging, plus receive information on demand.

- **Voice pager**
  This pager works with your voice mail to collect, store, and play back voice messages. You could carry a voice pager as a portable answering machine.

PAGER FEATURES

Alarm clock
You can use your pager as a travel alarm. The alarm rings with a different tone than the regular message alert tone.

Automatic message lighting
When a page comes in, the message is automatically illuminated to insure readability, even in the dark.

Display size
If you have alpha or numeric paging service, you'll need a pager with a display to see the message. Some pagers display just one line of the message at a time, while others can display two or four lines. Although the size of the pager may be affected by display size, larger displays are handy because you can read a longer message at one glance.

Loss protection
You may be interested in this type of insurance policy. It covers pagers that are lost, stolen, or damaged beyond repair.

Message lock

With message lock, you can store a special message or two in a secure area that can't be erased. Even if the pager memory fills up or the pager is turned off, you won't lose these messages.

Number of message memory slots

This feature controls how many messages you can store. Sixteen is the standard number.

On/off programmability

To maximize the life of your batteries, you can program the pager to turn itself on every morning and shut itself down every evening at preset times. It's a great feature for those of us who forget to turn the darn things on or off.

Out-of-range notification

When you are outside your call-receiving range, your pager will notify you by displaying a code or out-of-range message.

Preprogrammed reply

If you have a two-way pager, you can save time by selecting a reply from a menu of typical answers. Such a menu might include "yes," "no," "will call later," and "thanks."

Priority override

This optional feature will notify you of an incoming page, even though you've turned off the tone or vibration mode.

Selectable alert modes

You can control how you want your pager to alert you— whether tone, vibration, or light. Some pagers offer a choice of several different melodies.

Time and date stamping

This feature keeps a precise record of when each page was sent from the paging service.

Total memory

Total memory controls the number of phone numbers and messages you may store. Memory is usually stated as a number of characters and indicates the actual storage space available. On average, there are about 1,000 characters per typewritten page.

SHOPPING ADVICE

When determining the type of pager you need, consider how you plan to use it. Here are some tips to help you make your decision:

- **Alpha or numeric?**
  Will an alphanumeric pager save you money? Or just add to your communications costs? To answer that question, determine how much you would save in phone calls each month if your pages contained messages, not just numbers. According to the editors of *Mobile Computing & Communications* magazine, you should go with the alpha pager if you estimate a savings of $15 or more.

- **Do you need a two-way pager?**
  Two-way pagers are not cheap. The average cost of these devices is $350, plus up to $50 per month for service. However, a two-way pager lets you send a quick note to any email address in the world and get just the facts. If you need rapid communications and cost is not a major factor, two-way may be the answer for you.

SELECTING A PAGING SERVICE

There are hundreds of companies that sell paging services. Many are resellers that provide services supplied by one of the major pager manufacturers. Often, the reseller's price is as good or better than that of a well-known service, so it makes sense to comparison shop. Many paging services advertise in the sports section of the newspaper. You can also find pagers listed in your yellow pages under *Paging and Signaling Equipment*.

Because paging services offer a bewildering number of service plans and options, price comparisons are often difficult. Don't automatically pay the listed price, though. Pager prices and paging service charges are often negotiable. To help you analyze your options, I've included many of the most common coverage plans and features below.

SERVICE COSTS

Costs vary greatly based on your usage, coverage plan, and the services you select. Standard fees include a one-time activation fee, a monthly service charge, and over-call charges if you exceed your monthly page allotment. A few paging services offer fixed-cost plans, which may be attractive if you receive lots of pages.

COVERAGE

When you choose a paging company, you must choose a paging plan based on the geographic area of coverage:

Local

Though local coverage is the least expensive, it is adequate for most needs. Usually, you have the option of adding one or more neighboring cities to a local plan. Monthly service fees range from $8 to $10 for numeric service.

Statewide

If you are responsible for a specific sales territory, for example, you can purchase a plan that includes your entire state. Costs are 25 to 35 percent more than local service.

Regional

A regional plan will cover your state and surrounding states. For example, SkyTel's plans align with Eastern, Central, and Western time zones, with the Western zone combining Mountain and Pacific time zones. The cost is approximately 25 percent more than statewide service.

National

If you travel widely and often, a national plan may be best for you. National paging plans cost two to three times more than regional plans.

International

Paging plans are not yet global, but you can get service in many nations: the United States, Canada, Mexico, Argentina, Brazil, Bermuda, Hong Kong, Indonesia, Malaysia, Australia, and Singapore. More countries are being added as the networks build out and alliances are made.

Roaming

A less expensive alternative to a national or international plan is to purchase a plan that lets you roam. Whenever you arrive in a new area, you simply notify your paging company, and the system will automatically forward your messages to you. In effect, you can get national coverage at regional prices.

PAGING SERVICE FEATURES

Alpha message length

Depending on the type of service you have, your message length may be restricted. Some services break long messages into shorter segments for broadcasting. Usually, you get a message allowance for each month and pay a premium for messages exceeding that allowance.

Automatic message notification

When a message is picked up, this service will send a reply message immediately. Organizations that need message confirmation find this feature especially useful.

Broadcast paging

You can send the same email or alpha page message to a group of people via your pager. For example, a financial consultant could send stock market advice to a select group of clients.

Follow-me roaming service

With this feature, your paging service will transfer your pages automatically to a specified city, region, or country outside your normal paging area. Messages will be broadcast simultaneously in your home area as well as your destination area for the period of time you specify.

Follow-me roaming is much less expensive than nationwide or international paging service, and it is very useful if your travel plans include more than one foreign country.

Information services

Two-way paging services offer a number of information-on-demand services, such as news, weather, sports, stock alerts, driving directions, and airline arrival and departure status.

Message receipt notification

Your paging service can notify you when a message you sent was received. You can also specify that you want to be notified if a message was not received by an assigned deadline.

Multiple language capability

If you deal with a lot of international callers or callers from specific ethnic groups, you might want to specify the language the paging system uses when playing system prompts. Spanish, English, Japanese, and Cantonese are among the languages supported.

Number of paging attempts

You can choose the number of times the paging system will attempt to reach you for each message. The standard is two, which is usually sufficient.

Over-call charges

Some paging services will bill you extra for calls exceeding the monthly allowance. Try to pick a plan with no per-call charges or with a high paging limit, so you won't be nickel-and-dimed to death.

Page recall

This feature allows you to dial into your pager system and retrieve stored messages. These could be messages you have never received or messages that you stored for later retrieval. Page recall is convenient if you were outside your paging coverage area or your pager was turned off for a time.

Personalized greeting

Some paging systems provide the option of creating a digitized greeting in your own voice. When callers dial your pager number, your greeting is played. You can use this feature to update others on your travel plans and business developments, or give instructions on how to access you.

Personal 800 number

For a small monthly fee, your paging company can supply you with your own toll-free number. Callers can dial this number to leave you a message, and you can use it to pick up messages.

Personal identification number (PIN)

Unless you have a personal 800 number that is forwarded to your pager, your callers may need to know your PIN code in order to have you paged.

Personal security code (password)

You must enter your password in order to pick up your messages. Try to get a paging service that allows long passwords. Many paging companies allow only four-digit passwords. In my opinion, four digits are too few for adequate security.

Priority paging

This is an optional service that will attempt to deliver a single message more times than normal paging would. The standard is only two attempts. If you need to be sure that urgent messages get through to you, this is a useful service.

Sequential page numbering

Pages are numbered in the order sent, and this feature lets you see the number of each message on your pager display. If the unit was turned off or out of range, this handy option will help you determine whether you missed any messages.

Simulcast service

You can specify that all page attempts be broadcast both in the United States and the country listed in your international paging plan. This service is most useful if you frequently travel between two countries and don't want to be bothered with setting up special paging arrangements for each trip.

Time-of-day paging

This feature allows your callers to send time-sensitive messages for future delivery, thus making it easy to communicate across time zones.

Usage security code

You can control who can leave messages for you by requiring callers to enter a special security code. No code, no message. This feature helps you control costs and avoid unnecessary pages.

Voice mail option

Voice mail service is often available through your paging service at a reasonable cost.

Voice page copy and forward

You can electronically copy a voice mail page, add comments, and forward the message to another person.

For example: A real estate agent receives a voice message containing a property offer, copies the message, adds voice notes about a counteroffer, and forwards the message to the seller's agent.

DO YOU NEED A PAGER?

Take a moment to complete this survey. If you answer yes to three or more statements, paging would benefit your business.

▸ Are you losing business to your competitors because you aren't able to speedily return calls?

▸ Do you want to be able to respond to callers more quickly, but need an economical method?

▸ Are you out of the office a lot, but not near a phone?

▸ Do you need to keep abreast of late-breaking developments?

▸ Do you need to be in touch, but don't require two-way communication?

▸ Do you run a service business, such as computer repair, automobile towing, plumbing, or delivery?

▸ Do you worry about not being reachable in an emergency?

▸ Do you waste time (and phone change) constantly checking in?

▸ Do customers, coworkers, and clients need to contact you at a moment's notice regardless of where you are?

PAGING TIPS

• When paging numeric pagers, press the "#" key after you've entered your callback number. That way, the recipient will know you've finished the phone number.

• Invent numeric codes that you can tack onto the end of your numeric message. Since most numeric pagers allow

20 digits, you have room at the end of your message. Here are some common codes:

86	I'm leaving now
411	Where are you?
911	Emergency, contact me at once

- If you have an alphanumeric pager, check with your paging service to find out how to use an Internet messaging service. One warning, though—don't use Internet paging for urgent messages. You can't always count on speedy delivery, especially during peak usage hours.

- Use alkaline batteries to maximize battery life. You'll also extend battery power if you respond to pages quickly by interrupting the incoming call alert tone.

RESOURCES

Nationwide paging companies
Arch Communications
888-534-1397
www.arch.com

PageMart
800-864-4357 (numeric)
800-381-4357 (alpha)
www.pagemart.com

PageNet
800-PAGENET
www.pagenet.com

SkyTel
800-456-3333
www.skytel.com

Verizon Wireless
888-466-4646
www.verizon.com

Websites

Pagers Unlimited
www.pagersunlimited.com

Personal Communications Industry Association
703-739-0300
www.pcia.com

Chapter

10

Email

EMAIL IS SIMPLY AN ELECTRONIC method for moving information—whether text, graphics, video, or sound—from one person to another over a computerized connection. However, it is more than just a substitute for a fax transmission or regular postal service (dubbed snail mail by online humorists). Once a message is computerized, you can copy it, store it, or forward it to someone else for handling. You can even get an electronic return receipt to let you know when your mail has been opened.

Another advantage of email is that it eases communications across time zones. For example, sending an e-message to trading partners in the Far East is much easier than getting up in the middle of the night to place a phone call. It's less expensive, too.

Electronic mail is especially useful for small businesses. When you're doing business electronically, there's really no way to tell whether yours is a tiny start-up or a large firm. Email helps to level the playing field and allows you to compete with the big guys. Thanks to your email address, you are as accessible as anyone else.

A BRIEF HISTORY OF EMAIL

Email has its origins in the academic community. The first reported use was in 1960 when students at Smith and Dartmouth exchanged an electronic message using the same computer. In 1971, the first e-message between two different computers was achieved. Then, in 1976, the International Telephony and Telegraphy Association developed a computer networking protocol (X.25) that could support electronic messaging traffic.

Email usage began to grow when the U.S. Department of Defense developed ARPANET, the forerunner of the Internet. The first ARPANET network email message was transmitted in 1971. The next year, Ray Tomlinson created the first email software program and selected the @ sign for email addresses. Email use grew slowly during the 1970s, and it was quite expensive. To send a single message cost a whopping $4. Even so, the first junk email appeared in 1975, and the first emoticon—

"-)"   for tongue-in-cheek

—was introduced in 1979.

Once personal computers began to appear (the Apple II in 1978 and the IBM PC in 1983), email activity began to build. In 1983, Colby College in Waterville, Maine, gave email accounts to all entering students. Soon, other colleges and universities followed Colby's lead and began providing email accounts to their students and faculty.

As Internet use became widespread in the '90s, email use also grew quickly. Today, there are over 569 million email addresses, according to Messaging Online. The average business email user has 1.5 mailboxes, while the average consumer email user has 4 mailboxes. By the end of 1999, it was estimated that 40 percent of the U.S. population had access to email, whether at home or at work.

HOW EMAIL WORKS

Email uses many of the same principles as your ground-based postal service. Each person on an email system has an address, which is made up of an ID or name, domain name, and suffix. (See *The anatomy of an address* later in this chapter.) The domain name is similar to a local post office address plus zip code.

When a message is mailed, it is first sent to the closest email server, where it is forwarded to another server that's convenient. This process may take place several times as the message travels through the Internet on its way to the server that has the recipient's mailbox. There, the message is held until the recipient picks it up.

Email messages are pure ASCII text and contain no formatting. ASCII (American Standard Code for Information Interchange) is the code that allows virtually all computers to talk to each other, regardless of individual platforms. Because the messages are in ASCII format, computers using different operating systems can still communicate easily. Macs, Windows machines, Suns, and mainframes—email works with them all.

Incidentally, the files attached to email are not limited to straight text. They can contain graphics, spreadsheets, artwork, software, video bits, page layouts, and even music. Just be sure that the person on the receiving end has the appropriate software to open the file or has a file viewer program, such as Lotus Notes or Adobe Acrobat.

There are some email negatives. To see if you have any email, you must take the time to log online. In addition, logging on can run up your phone bill, especially if you have to pay toll charges for Internet access.

Email can pile up alarmingly fast. If you find yourself with more than you can handle, you should consider using an email management program. Two popular programs are Qualcomm's Eudora Pro (www.eudora.com) and Microsoft Outlook (www.microsoft.com). They allow you to screen, save, delete, and archive messages. Also, to keep your email from overwhelming you, create separate folders for various projects or clients.

Sometimes email gets stuck. If you're used to receiving frequent messages and the steady stream suddenly dries up, don't assume that you've lost popularity. It's possible that the mail server has a problem. I recently experienced this problem with America Online. After my mailbox was fixed, 34 messages were waiting for me—some of them five days old.

How do you check? Ask someone to send you a message, or, if you have more than one service, send yourself a message. To fix a problem, call the administrator or help line.

HOW MUCH DOES EMAIL COST?

It depends. There are many free email services, such as Hotmail (www.hotmail.com), Yahoo (www.yahoo.com), and Juno (www.juno.com), that rely on advertiser sponsorship to pay for the cost of service. America Online, CompuServe, and other Internet service providers include email as part of a package.

Except for the cost of your telephone connection, there are rarely any additional costs associated with using email. One way to minimize your connection time is to compose your email messages offline. Then, you sign on just to upload or download messages. This way, you can handle your online email duties in a minute or two.

HOW TO GET AN EMAIL ADDRESS

Once you have an online service or an Internet account, you are automatically assigned a globally accessible address and an emailbox. Together, these two items let you exchange email with anyone else who has an email address.

The diagram below shows how an email address is constructed:

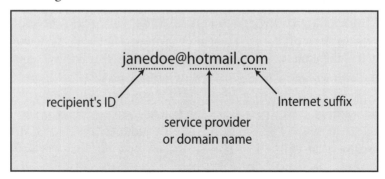

THE ANATOMY OF AN ADDRESS

To send a message to another person, you need to know his or her email address. You can look up the address online, if the recipient is listed, or call him and ask for the address.

All email addresses contain the recipient's ID, his service provider or domain name, and an Internet suffix. The Internet suffixes currently in use include:

.com	Business or commercial organization
.edu	School or university
.gov	Government agency
.int	International organizations
.mil	U.S.-based military
.org	Nonprofit organizations
.net	Internet access providers (ISPs)

Note: Email addresses outside the United States often have a two-letter country code—au for Australia, sg for Singapore, or ve for Venezuela.

To send an electronic message to the U.S. president, you would address it as follows:

president@whitehouse.gov

HOW TO FIND SOMEONE'S EMAIL ADDRESS

Many Internet search engines, such as Infoseek and Yahoo, offer email address searching. There are also email directory services that contain millions of listings.

Useful email directories include:

• Any Who Directory Service	www.anywho.com
• Bigfoot	www.bigfoot.com
• Four11	www.four11.com
• Who Where	www.whowhere.com

IS EMAIL PRIVATE?

Not entirely. Anyone who receives email from you can copy it, store it, forward it to others, and even edit it. As Bill Gates learned during the Microsoft antitrust trial, email may be stored for years as part of a routine disk backup. Therefore, it makes sense to use email prudently. If the information you send must remain private, use an encryption program such as PGP (Pretty Good Privacy—www.pgp.com or 800-338-8754). If you don't encode your electronic mail, use regular snail mail for the really private stuff.

MANAGING YOUR EMAIL

Pitney Bowes recently surveyed the communication habits of corporate and government workers. They found that the average employee sends or receives approximately 190 messages on any given day. Needless to say, keeping up with the sheer volume of e-messages can be a daunting task. The researchers also found that those individuals occupying positions higher up on the organizational ladder felt the most overwhelmed.

Unless you subscribe to an always-on service, such as DSL or cable service, you must log on to see if you have any mail. As I mentioned earlier, going online to check email can eat up your time as well as run up your phone bill.

If you have more than one email address and want to save some time, consider signing up for an email forwarding service. These services allow you to forward all your email accounts to a consolidated mailbox. Some services charge a small monthly fee, but others are free. An email forwarder may be perfect for you if you tend to change email addresses often or want to switch Internet service providers. Among the best-known email forwarding services are:

- Mail Director   www.maildirector.com
- P.O. Box   www.pobox.com
- Prime Mail   www.primemail.com
- Relay Mail   www.relaymail.net

STOPPING SPAM

Once you have an email account, it won't be too long before you start receiving spam. Spam is unwanted email, usually in the form of various get-rich-quick schemes, chain letters, and offers to see lots of naked people. The use of the word *spam* to describe excessive email came from a Monty Python show where a waiter recites the lengthy menu: "We have Spam, tomato and Spam, egg and Spam, egg, bacon and Spam," and on and on.

While spam is surely irritating, it is also costly. According to *InternetWeek* magazine, almost $2 of every Internet user's bill each month goes towards the cost of transporting unwanted email. Most large organizations have spam filters that screen out the majority of the mess.

If you use a private account to get your email, however, you'll need to learn how to set up filters (sometimes called rules) yourself. For example, you could create rules that ignore messages with exclamation points or place all messages from your boss in your priority folder. Many email software programs come with filtering utilities.

To reduce the amount of incoming spam, you should limit the number of people who have access to your email address. Spammers harvest addresses by visiting Usenet newsgroups and member directories. They can get hundreds of addresses at a clip. If you use a free email service, such as Juno or Yahoo, for newsgroup activities, you can keep your primary address relatively spam free. Take a look at the Junk Busters website (www.junkbusters.com) for more ideas.

GETTING YOUR MAIL FROM ANOTHER PC

With a little preplanning, you can send and retrieve email from any PC. If all you need to do is access your mail, you won't have to lug your laptop around when traveling. For example, when I went to Mexico last year, I just dropped in at an Internet cafe, rented a few minutes time on a computer, and handled all my email duties easily. There are a couple of options for picking up your mail from any PC:

- Browser-based email
- POP3 mail

Browser-based email

You can sign up for a free account from Hotmail, Juno, or Yahoo. Then, all you'll need to check your mail is access to the Internet and the URL or web address of the email service. Of course, you'll need to enter your log-in ID and password to actually see your mail.

POP3 mail

Most Internet service providers use Post Office Protocol (POP3) when setting up email accounts. Chances are good that you already have a POP3 account. In order to access POP3 mail from a different computer, however, you need to know these technical details:

- Mailbox server name
- Mailbox user name
- Mailbox password

If you don't have this information available, ask your technical support group for help or call your ISP.

Once you know this information, you can also arrange for a browser-based service, such as Hotmail or Yahoo, to check your POP3 account. Just follow the directions on their websites.

ATTACHING A FILE

Sometimes you'll want to send a fully formatted file to a correspondent. You do this by using your email program to attach the file to your regular email. Attached files are binary, meaning they are not limited to straight text. They can contain special fonts, color, graphics, spreadsheets, artwork, software, page layouts, music, and even video.

When you and your email correspondent use the same service, you can easily attach a file to the message. The attached file will retain its special formatting and arrive on the recipient's desk in the same shape as you sent it. Unfortunately, if you have different email services and your messages must go through a gateway, such as the Internet, attaching files gets trickier.

If you can convince your correspondents to send plain email and paste the text inside, you're in luck. However, if you still receive unreadable attachments, the following tips can help you untangle the mess.

✔ **Pick a common format**
Ask the sender to save the file in a well-supported format before sending. Files with suffixes like RTF or GIF can be opened by just about everyone. Here are some formats that usually work:

EPS	Encapsulated PostScript (drawings)
GIF	Graphics Interchange Format (graphics)
JPEG	Joint Photographic Experts Group (photos)
RTF	Rich Text Format (text files)
PDF	Portable Document Format

(PDF files can be viewed using Adobe Acrobat Reader, which is available for free online at www.adobe.com.)

✔ **Try sending it again**
In order to travel through the Internet, files are broken down into little packets of information. After passing though several servers and gateways, the files are then reassembled at the destination. Sometimes, the bits get scattered or reassembled incorrectly. This problem can usually be solved by asking your correspondent to resend the file.

✔ **Use an alternate method**
For highly sensitive mail, consider sending the document

over a secure server using docSpace (www.docspace.com) or @Backup (www.atbackup.com). These services provide file transfer and storage capabilities over the Web.

OPENING ATTACHMENTS

Often, a file will arrive with a strange name indicating that it is coded in MIME, BinHex, or uuencode. MIME files often have a .mim suffix; BinHex files have an .hqx extension; and uuencode files often end with .uu. To decode these files, you'll need to use a special program. Your email software may be able to unravel some of these codes, but probably not all of them. (Also, see *Try a translator* below.)

Decompress it

Sometimes you'll receive a large file or a group of files in a special compressed format designed to make uploading and downloading faster. You can easily spot compressed files because they will bear names that end in .zip, .sit, and .tar. There are no cross-platform standards here, so you'll need a program such as Windows PKZip (www.pkware.com) to open .zip files and Mac StuffIT (www.aladdinsys.com) to open .sit files.

Try a translator

If you still can't read an attached file, a translator program will usually pry it open. Such programs include Conversions Plus (www.dataviz.com) or Quick View Plus (www.inso.com) for Windows, and MacLink Plus for Macs (www.dataviz.com). These programs allow you to open compressed, encoded, and archived files from just about any platform. They contain translators that will convert files from word processing, spreadsheet, graphics, and database programs so you can read, copy, and print the results.

PASTING AN ATTACHMENT INTO EMAIL

It's best to avoid attaching files, if possible. I often import my file into the message by using my word processor's copy function. I do lose all the special formatting capabilities, and I can't send a really long file without cutting it into smaller messages. Otherwise, though, it works like a charm. Here's how to do it:

1. Fire up your word processor.
2. Open up the file you want to send.
3. Select the copy function, and copy the entire file to your clipboard.
4. Close your word processor.
5. Start your email program.
6. Select the compose mail function.
7. Position your cursor in the message body section of your message.
8. Paste in your file. That's it!

EMAIL FLU

A computer virus is a software program designed to disrupt computer processing. You may recall reading about the Michelangelo virus back in 1992. It was rumored that this virus would shut down all computers throughout the world on Michelangelo's birthday (March 6th) and destroy all data. Fortunately, the rumor alerted most PC and mainframe users, and an unprecedented number of virus detection software programs were sold and installed. As a result of such vigilance, less than one percent of all computer users were affected.

According to the Antivirus Researcher's Report, 150 to 200 new viruses appear each month, and *Computer Economics* reported that the total damage caused by viruses in 1999 came to $12.1 billion.

Your computer could contract a virus if you run a program that is infected. Sources of infected files can be found everywhere: programs downloaded from bulletin boards, the Internet, and other online sources; files you've copied from a friend's floppy or hard disk; even brand-new commercial software. You can also get a virus from an email attachment. Though most viruses only infect your machine if you run a program that contains it, there are exceptions.

Attachments can carry nasty surprises. You can get a macro virus by opening and saving an infected Microsoft Word, PowerPoint, or Excel document attached to an email. Once the virus gets into your machine, it can spread to all future documents created with that application.

Another class of virus grabs your email address book and starts sending out mail from your computer to everyone in your book. This way, of course, it infects your friends, too. The famous Melissa virus infected thousands of computers in 1999 and won the prize for the fastest-replicating virus ever. Several Melissa copycat viruses have since appeared, each a bit more destructive than the last. This class of viruses is especially harmful to servers, causing system crashes from email overload.

Some email viruses are totally evil. For example, the "I Love You" worm virus, which ran rampant in the spring of 2000, was highly destructive. Like the Melissa virus, this worm sends itself to email addresses found in an affected Microsoft Outlook address book. It then spreads itself via Internet chat rooms. If you open an attachment carrying this virus, it will overwrite files on your drives and replace them with the worm source code. The original files are destroyed completely.

To protect yourself, stay vigilant.

- If you receive an emailed file from someone you don't know, don't open it.

- Even if you know the sender, don't open the attachment unless it's expected.

- Avoid clicking on unknown attachments with .sea or .exe extensions. These are self-extracting files and they could unleash viruses.

- Don't click on enclosed Internet addresses (URLs) unless you're sure the sender is legit.

- Always use protection in the form of an antivirus program, such as Norton AntiVirus (www.symantec.com) or McAfee VirusScan (www.nai.com).

New viruses pop up on a daily basis—about 200 new viruses appear each month. Your first line of defense is to get a virus protection program and use it on a regular basis. Among the best are programs from Symantec and McAfee. But, remember, the program you use is only effective in recognizing known viruses.

You can keep your program current by downloading search strings that will help you detect new viruses. (They are found on most online services—use the keyword VIRUS.) Also, you will want to subscribe to regular program updates so that you can safely remove infected programs.

HOW TO RECOGNIZE SYMPTOMS OF INFECTION

There are all kinds of viruses, and some can remain hidden in your system for months or even years. Each virus exhibits different symptoms.

Listed below are some of the most common symptoms:

▶▶ Your system's date and time stamp changes all by itself

▶▶ You notice that your programs keep growing in size

▶▶ Your system crashes more often

▶▶ Your computer seems to be slowing down

▶▶ You see weird or comical error messages, such as "feed me" or "April Fools!"

▶▶ Your disk is wiped clean

How to Avoid Infection

Install and use an antivirus program. Scan both your hard disk and each floppy disk before copying files to your computer or running the programs they contain.

- Keep your antivirus program up-to-date. Subscribe to the program's update service so you can receive new search-and-repair routines as they become available.

- Don't download programs or files with attached programs from bulletin boards or websites not well known to you.

- Don't buy or use pirated software.

- Avoid using software if the package is damaged or shows signs of tampering.

- Back up your hard disk regularly.

- If you receive an email message with a file attached from someone you don't know, don't download or open the attached file.

EMAIL ON THE GO

Email is great for road warriors, too. You can send and receive email worldwide using a variety of tiny devices, such as alpha pagers, palmtop organizers, and notebook computers. Some are wired; some are wireless. When evaluating an email program for remote use, be sure to consider its ability to store several dial-up access numbers.

Many personal digital assistants (PDAs) have email capability. For example, sending and retrieving messages is possible with your Palm or Handspring PDA. These units use built-in Palm Mail software, or you can add email software, such as Palmeta Mail (www.palmeta.com). You could also add a conventional modem or opt for a wireless service, such as OmniSky (www.omnisky.com).

Another way to get your email while on the road is by using PocketMail (www.pocketmail.com). Here's how it works. First, you sign up for PocketMail service. Then, to access the service, you call a toll-free phone number and place your PocketMail device against the receiver of the telephone. The device translates the screaming modem tones into words, just like magic. PocketMail works with devices made by Sharp, JVC, and Palm.

Some mobile phones have email capability. I'm currently using a Samsung phone, with Sprint PCS service (www.sprint.com), that allows me to send and receive emails. The messages appear on a tiny screen on my mobile phone. Though I'm not limited to a specific number of characters, the screen is. It can accommodate only 16 characters across and 4 lines down. So, this arrangement is best for short messages, something I can't always talk my correspondents into.

Several two-way pagers, such as Motorola's Page Writer (www.motorola.com) and Research in Motion's Blackberry RIM Wireless Handheld (www.rim.net), offer another method for handling email on the road. Using a 4 megabyte RIM pager, you can access your POP3 email account via Microsoft Exchange.

There will be times when you find yourself needing to check your email, but have no access to a modular phone jack. If you forgot your laptop or PDA at home, you can still pick up email by using an email-to-voice program such as Mail Call (www.mailcall.com) or CoolMail (www.coolmail.com). Once connected to the toll-free number, a robot-like voice reads your messages back to you.

Warning: If you sign up for a free service, be prepared to listen to some advertising messages as well.

A new a short-range wireless technology, called Bluetooth, holds great promise. (Harald Bluetooth was a powerful Danish king who lived over a thousand years ago.) Soon, Bluetooth email solutions will provide for wireless communications among a variety of mobile tools, such as notebooks, cell phones, and pagers. As Bluetooth chips become universal components in computing and communicating devices, you'll be able to access your email easily from anywhere—at least, that's what the Bluetooth backers say. For example, you could use your Bluetooth mobile phone to wirelessly direct your Bluetooth-equipped laptop to dial out to the Internet. For the latest information, check www.bluetooth.net.

EMAIL WITHOUT A COMPUTER

A host of inexpensive hardware devices now exists that allow you to send and receive email without using a personal computer. Known as Internet appliances, the goal of these devices is to make email activity and Internet viewing as easy as changing the channel on your TV.

For example, I-Opener (www.nepliance.com) features a flat panel display, a keyboard, and a built-in modem. You simply click on a single button to dial up the Internet service and connect to I-Opener's portal. Other appliances to check include InfoGear's iPhone (www.infogear.com) and Pacific Bell's eMessage (www.pacbell.com).

ALL-IN-ONE MESSAGING

Would you like to access your email, voice mail, faxes, and pages through only one service? This is the promise of unified messaging. For example, when you sign up for Onebox (www.onebox.com), all your email, faxes, and voice mail are held in the same incoming mailbox. Users receive a free email address plus a dial-in phone number (with a four-digit extension), so they can access their mail from either a telephone or a Web browser. If you don't want callers to know that they're calling into the Onebox system, you can get your own phone number for $5 a month.

Other services that provide unified messaging are uReach.com (www.ureach.com), GoSolo (www.gosolo.com), and Unified Messaging (www.unified-messaging.com).

☎ In my office

Because I work with editors around the nation, I rely heavily on email. I can't afford to be without email service, even for a day. Therefore, I have several email addresses. If my ISP should happen to be down, I can let my clients and editors know to send me email at a secondary address.

In addition, I have a free account with Hotmail. While traveling, I can access my email by logging onto the Internet and entering my password. I have also set up Hotmail to check my POP3 account. This way, I can get everything in one place.

EMAIL TIPS

Email is great for short messages. For long or complex ideas, though, you're better off using the phone. Dr. Franklin Becker, director of the Cornell University International Workplace Studies program, comments that, "communicating subtleties through email is like trying to pull an anchor line through the eye of a needle."

To improve your "emailability", follow these suggestions:

✔ Reread your message before sending

Doing so will give you a chance to spot errors and tighten your prose.

✔ Don't respond to messages in anger

If you feel like flaming someone, take a break, shut off your computer, and calm down. Once you've sent an angry message, you can't recall it. The damage is done.

✔ Avoid sarcasm and irony

Sarcastic humor is difficult to convey, and it can easily be misconstrued. If you insist on using humor, make your intentions clear by using emoticons.

Emoticons are the visual shorthand symbols used in the online world. Below is a partial list. To view them properly, tilt your head.

:-)	smile
:-(	frown
'-)	wink
:#	my lips are sealed
{}	hug
;^)	smirk
:-\	undecided
:-$	put your money where your mouth is

✔ Keep it brief
Edit thyself. Your correspondents will appreciate crisp, succinct messages.

✔ Preface your message with a subject line
When you answer a message, include a copy of the original message (or the gist of it) so that your recipient knows what you are writing about.

✔ Don't use ALL CAPS
Uppercase denotes SHOUTING in the online world. It should be avoided unless you want to EMPHASIZE a word here and there.

✔ Avoid fancy fonts, color, and other junk
Though your email software may allow boldface, color, large fonts, italics, and other decorations, avoid the temptation to use them. Some email systems will automatically turn such stuff into an attachment, thus making it harder for your recipient to get your message.

✔ Save time by using an address book

Keep frequent email addresses in your online address book. Whenever someone sends you a message, copy the sender's online address to your electronic address book.

✔ Set up distribution lists

If you regularly correspond with a particular group of people, create a distribution list and save it in your address book.

✔ Don't send junk email

Because email is so inexpensive and easy to use, some people have been tempted to send out unsolicited ads (junk email) to hundreds or thousands of recipients. Don't do it. You could be thrown off the network or, if enough people are mad at you, you may be bombarded with prank phone calls, junk faxes, and other miseries.

✔ Check first before sending attachments

Check with your correspondents and ask if they can handle the attachment you propose sending. This gives them the opportunity to suggest a compatible file format or an alternative, such as an FTP site.

RESOURCES

Books

Better, Faster Email: Getting the Most out of Email
By Joan Tunstall
Independent Publishers, 1999

Email@Work: Get Moving with Digital Communication
by Jonathan Whelan
Financial Times, 2000

Email for Dummies, second edition
by John R. Levine (Editor)
IDG Books Worldwide, 1997

Miss Manners' Basic Training: Communication
by Judith Martin
Crown Publishing, 1996

Office Emails That Really Click
by Maureen Chase and Sandy Trupp
Aegis Publishing Group, 2000

Learn how to send the right message in the right format for any occasion. Included are do's and don'ts, sample business emails, email horror stories, e-tips, a glossary, and more.

Websites
Everything Email
www.everythingemail.net

Electronic Messaging Association
703-524-5550
www.ema.org

Messaging Online magazine
www.messagingonline.com

Chapter

11

Internet
. . . .

THE ONLINE WORLD OFFERS something for everyone.

- You can buy office supplies, order a pizza, advertise your business services, buy and sell stocks, conduct market research, make an airline reservation, check out your competition, or visit with a long-lost friend.

- You can check out the latest sports scores, view the winning lottery numbers, get late-breaking news updates, find a job, and even earn a college diploma.

- You can save hundreds of dollars when you download free or inexpensive software, and, whatever your question may be, you can ask for help online from experts in every field.

If you think the time has come for you to join the online world, read on. This chapter will provide an overview of the Internet, discuss several useful Internet services, and suggest some ways you could use the Web to promote your business.

A BRIEF HISTORY OF THE INTERNET

The Internet is really a worldwide network of networks. It all began in 1969 when the U.S. Department of Defense created a communications system known as ARPANET. ARPANET was the forerunner of today's Internet, and its purpose was to link the computers at various universities engaged in defense research at that time. Because it was designed to survive a nuclear attack, the network had no central administration.

By the end of its first year, ARPANET connected four computers (called nodes) located at UCLA, the Stanford Research Institute, the University of California at Santa Barbara, and the University of Utah. For the next decade, the fledgling Internet gradually increased its capabilities—email appeared in 1971, computer-to-computer chat in 1973, mailing lists in 1975, and newsgroups in 1979. In 1980, the first major computer virus outbreak drove ARPANET off the air temporarily.

Then, in 1985, the National Science Foundation created NSFNET, a network designed for the research and education communities. When corporations such as Sprint and MCI created their own networks, they linked them to NSFNET and others followed.

The World Wide Web was invented by Tim Berners-Lee in 1991. The Web gives us a graphical view of the Internet, and it made the Internet a much friendlier place. As a result, the numbers of online users began to grow quickly.

The term "surfing the Internet" was first used in 1992. The White House came online in 1993, and Bill Clinton became the first president to have his own email address. In 1994, the first business transaction took place—ordering pizza from the Hut Online—and the rest, as they say, is history.

Today, there are an estimated 70 million host computers, 17 million websites, and 375 million users worldwide in over 200 countries. According to the *Computer Industry Almanac*, an estimated 490 million people around the world will have Internet access by 2002.

HOW IT WORKS
The Internet is made up of hundreds of thousands of interconnected networks, linked together into a vast web. On the

Internet, you can correspond with a businessperson in Taiwan, download a list of commercial fisheries from New Zealand, visit a newsgroup to discuss the latest developments in marketing, access research data, listen to a radio show, watch a movie preview, or play a business simulation game with participants from around the world. You can hold a telephone conversation (see *Internet calling* in Chapter 3 for details), engage in real-time chat, or take part in a video meeting.

GETTING CONNECTED

To get on the Internet, you need an access account. These accounts are available via an online service, through a telephone company, or directly from an Internet access provider. For a current list of Internet providers, check The List (www.list.com) or look in your yellow pages under Computers-Online Services and Internet.

Prices will vary depending on the number of hours you use, your modem speed, and the type of connection you use. Although you'll pay more for faster services, it may be worth it. *Note*: In some communities you can get free access via a Free-Net. Check the Organization for Community Networks site (www.ofcn.org).

When you sign onto your Internet service provider, you will do so through a telecommunications link, which may be copper wires (modems, ISDN, or DSL), cable, satellite, or even fiber. (See *Ramping up bandwidth* in Chapter 4 for more information about these technologies.) At this point, you'll also need some special software, known as file browsers, that are designed for navigating the Net. Two popular browsers are Netscape Communicator (www.netscape.com) and Microsoft Internet Explorer (www.microsoft.com).

Nowadays, you don't need a computer to surf the Web. Web appliances, such as I-Opener (www.nepliance.com), iPhone (www.infogear.com), Qubit (www.qubit.net), or eMessage (www.pacbell.com), let you send and receive email and view websites without using a personal computer. Though they offer fewer functions than a PC, they cost far less and may be a good solution for you.

You can even use a wireless phone equipped with WAP (Wireless Application Protocol) to access email, engage in chat, and view WAP-enabled websites. Nokia, Ericcson, Samsung, and Motorola currently, manufacture WAP-enabled phones. For more information about WAP, visit these sites:

- WAP. net   www.wap.net
- WAPNet   www.wapnet.com

Experts believe that m-commerce (the name given to remote commerce enabled by mobile devices) is the next big thing. M-commerce isn't just a stripped-down version of e-commerce. Wireless offers unique capabilities that are based on a user's location as well as personalized interaction.

For example, a wireless user equipped with a WAP- and GPS-enabled PDA or phone could find the lowest gasoline prices in an the area, locate a nearby restaurant that matched his pocketbook, or search for an available motel room—all without getting out of the car.

☎ In my office
For the last month, I've been testing the Samsung SCH-8500 mobile phone using Sprint's PCS Wireless Web service. Browsing choices are limited to a few sites that are designed to fit on my tiny screen. Nevertheless, I've been able to access news, weather, shopping sites, financial data, driving directions, even a joke site.

The screen shows only four lines of 16 characters each, so information appears in little nuggets. That's good enough for short emails and quick information searches, but bad for long messages and research. Attachments aren't possible, and because the phone has a limited keyboard, entering text is not much fun. For example, you must press 2 once to type the letter *a*; press 2 twice rapidly for *b*; and so on. At 14.4 kilobits per second, you can really eat up lots of time just waiting for stuff to appear on your screen.

Sprint offers a number of PCS calling plans. The voice plan I selected gives me 500 minutes of wireless Web and voice calls for $49.95 a month. Additional minutes cost 35 cents each. In order not to exceed the allowance, I watch my usage carefully. Otherwise, it's a pretty hefty fee to pay for slow Internet access.

THE ANATOMY OF A URL

To access information on the Internet, you need to know a site's address or URL (uniform resource locator). Your browser will prompt you to either type in the address or click on a button or underlined field. Once you've typed in the address, you'll automatically retrieve the site's home page. Then, you can roam around and explore the information available on that site.

For example, the URL for the U.S. Small Business Administration is:

http://www.sba.gov

Http tells the system that you want to see a document in Hypertext Transfer Protocol, which is the language of the World Wide Web (*www*). The remainder of this address is known as the domain name, and it tells the system where the document resides. In this case, it's a computer (server) named *sba.gov*.

If you wanted to delve deeper into the SBA website and already knew the address of a subsite, you might type something like this:

http://www.sba.gov/starting/indexbusplans.html

This address would immediately take you to an area within the site that was all about starting a business. There, you could access an index of business plans.

BEHIND THE SCENES

When you logged onto your internet service provider (ISP), lots of things happened. Let's imagine that you are located in Portland, Oregon, and that you typed in the SBA's Web address. Let's also assume that you're using an analog modem over a normal phone line.

First, your request goes to your ISP via your telephone connection through the telephone company's central office. Once the modem connection has been made, your ISP server passes the request to a server on the regional network—in this case, NorthwestNet. The regional network then passes the request to the U.S. commercial backbone, which is a network of very high-speed lines running across the U.S.

This backbone is served by a number of network access points (NAPs), and your request is sent on via the NAP in San Francisco. From there, your request is sent to the NAP in Washington, D.C., where it is passed to SURAnet, the regional network for the southeast. Finally, your request is sent to the ISP that serves the U.S. Small Business Administration. If the server is not too busy, it relays the pages you want to see back through the labyrinth to your computer. The whole process usually takes less than a second.

Note: You may have to wait if the server is overloaded, and you may even receive a message telling you that the address is wrong or that the site is down.

Accessing sites outside of the U.S. will require additional steps. Let's say you were trying to take a virtual tour of the Louvre in Paris (http://www.Louvre.fr). In this case, your request would be passed from the NAP in Washington, D.C., to the appropriate NAP in Europe.

USEFUL INTERNET SERVICES

The Internet offers a wide variety of services. We'll limit this discussion to a few that are most useful to small businesses:

- Newsgroups
- Mailing lists
- Mailbots
- Instant messaging
- Web conferencing
- Videoconferencing

You can also read about the following highly useful Internet services in other chapters of this book:

➤➤ Email in Chapter 10
➤➤ Internet phones in Chapter 4
➤➤ Internet paging in Chapter 9
➤➤ Internet fax in Chapter 13

NEWSGROUPS

Newsgroups are loosely organized discussion groups, somewhat akin to an online bulletin board or forum. They are a great way to find and communicate with people from all over the world who share your interests. For example, there are newsgroups dedicated to owners of antique cars or particular breeds of dogs. There are also newsgroups for people wanting to conduct a hostile takeover, improve the fishing industry, or learn about digital photography.

Newsgroups are organized by type: biz (business orientation), rec (recreation), comp (computers), alt (alternative), sci (science), talk (long diatribes), and news. To further differentiate the topic, clues are added to help you find the information you want. For example, comp.dcom.fax has the latest news about fax technology; sci.med discusses medical products and regulations; and biz.comp.accounting is concerned with accounting software and procedures. You can often tell if a newsgroup has a moderator by its title— misc.business.marketing.moderated is a moderated newsgroup.

There are over 30,000 newsgroups that send out thousands of articles each day on all sorts of topics. You can sign up for ones that interest you, listen in for a while, and then start actively participating. In your messages, it's perfectly alright to include information about your business and suggest that people email you for details. Just avoid coming across as entirely commercial—the goal is to establish relationships, not shove products.

Signing up for a newsgroup is simple. All you have to do is follow the directions for your particular software. How do you know which groups to join? Pick up one of the many Internet guidebooks and browse for interesting possibilities. You can also search for newsgroups by using a directory or search engine such as AltaVista (www.altavista.com).

Anyone can start a newsgroup by sending a request for discussion (RFD) to news.announce.newsgroups and to other relevant newsgroups. If enough people vote to use your group, you're official. An even easier way to set up a newsgroup is to join a Web community, such as Delphi (www.delphi.com) or PowWow (www.tribalvoice.com).

In addition to traditional newsgroups, many websites offer discussion groups. For example, Raging Bull (www.ragingbull.com) offers hundreds of discussion topics on stock market performance; and TRIP (www.trip.com) provides TRIP Talk, an opportunity for business travelers to exchange tips, travel news, and horror stories.

MAILING LISTS

A mailing list groups the email addresses of people interested in a common subject. When you send a message to the list, it is forwarded to everyone on the list. Some lists are moderated, but most are not. To subscribe to a list, just send a message to the list manager's email address and ask for a subscription. Then, you'll automatically receive any messages sent to the group in your own mailbox. Hang on to the manager's address, though, in case you want to cancel your subscription.

How do you find mailing lists? You can use a search engine using key words, such as business and mailing list, or take a look at www.liszt.com, which maintains a searchable database of mailing lists. At last look, there were 90,095 listings.

MAILBOTS

If a large portion of your incoming email messages request the same information, such as product literature, research studies, or sample articles from your newsletter, you can use the Internet to send out automatic responses. These response services are known as autoresponders, autobots, or mailbots, and they usually cost from $5 to $20 per month for each mailbot. For that fee, you can fire off the same response to an unlimited number of requests. DataBack Systems (www.databack.com) and AWeber Communications (www.aweber.com) provide autoresponder services. Your ISP may also provide this service.

To set up mailbot service, you'll need an Internet account and a separate email address for each canned response you want to send out. The system will then send the appropriate message every time an email is delivered to its mailbox.

> Mailbots save time answering repetitive questions
> Marcia Yudkin, author of *Marketing Online* (Plume/ Penguin Books, New York, 1995), set up several mailbots to handle inquiries. "I use one mailbot as an electronic brochure," Yudkin notes, "and two others for frequently-asked-question files on freelance writing and small-business publicity."

If you receive lots of email asking for your price list, a mailbot could instantly send the list. If you also get frequent questions on how to join your organization, another mailbot could ship out a membership application. To sample mailbots, visit the AWeber site.

Mailbots also allow you to capture the email address of everyone who writes to you. You can take advantage of this fact when it's time to develop an electronic mailing list.

INSTANT MESSAGING

A favorite activity online is real-time or instant messaging. It's sort of like email on steroids. Groups of people, usually two or three, can communicate by typing in a special window on their browser. Messages appear on each participant's screen and scroll off as more messages appear. Generally, a session begins when someone you'd like to talk to logs onto the Internet and initiates a discussion.

Instant messaging requires special messaging software, such as AOL Instant Messenger, ICQ, or MSN Messenger Service, plus a browser and an Internet connection. Once you've installed the software, you can make a list of the people you want to talk to. Then, when you are online, the messenger service will notify you when someone on your list logs on. AOL calls this private list a "buddy list."

If you feel like chatting, you click the designated name on your list to invite the other person to join you online. If that person agrees, you're connected and can then carry on a private conversation. Some programs will let you run instant messaging as a background application, setting it to "answering machine" mode so you're not disturbed.

Instant messaging can be useful for collaborative work. For example, a committee might work on a common document that one person pastes into the messaging screen. Others can then comment on recommended changes. Many telecommuters use instant messaging to hold fast online meetings with distant coworkers.

One caveat: Instant messaging software is not standardized. Therefore, you can communicate only with people who have the same kind of software that you have.

To get a free copy of instant messenger software, simply visit the appropriate website and download it. These are the most popular programs:

- AOL Instant Messenger   www.aol.com
- ICQ   www.icq.com
- MSM Messenger service   www.msn.com
- Yahoo! Messenger   www.yahoo.com

WEB CONFERENCING

The Web is becoming a virtual meeting place for many workgroups. Specialized Internet sites permit you to host meetings for large numbers of attendees, display slide shows, and even allow the audience to interact with the speakers.

PlaceWare Conference Center (www.placeware.com), for example, provides a virtual auditorium that includes streaming audio and video, interactive audience polls, and question-and-answer capabilities. Other conferencing sites include PowWow (www.tribal.com) and Contigo i2i (www.evoke.com). Many organizations use web conferencing to conduct remote training sessions.

You can also hold small meetings or set up an online forum on free sites, such as eGroups (www.eGroups.com) and Forum One (www.forumone.com). These programs include a number of features that are useful for remote workgroups. For example, eGroups offers group chat, message archiving, a group calendar, and private file space.

VIDEOCONFERENCING

The Internet is an inexpensive medium for videoconferencing, especially if you need to videoconference over long distances.

Computer-based videoconferencing is perfect for situations that require demonstrations or face-to-face meetings. Desktop video is now being used by some companies to cut down on business travel. It's being put to use in a variety of other interesting ways, too, as the following examples show:

- Students at Georgia Tech can attend a Virtual Job Fair that includes video interviews with corporate recruiters.

- Doctors at Kaiser Permanente hold noontime video meetings with their counterparts in other clinics. The company reports saving $1.5 million a year in the cost of their physicians' time.

- Buyers at Minnesota-based Dayton Hudson Corporation demonstrate the latest fashions and merchandise to store managers all over the U.S. via a video link.

- Executives at Converse Inc. headquarters in North Reading, Massachusetts, use video meetings to iron out design and production problems. The result? The shoemaker is getting products to market faster.

- Circuit judges in California's Central Valley now hold video arraignments, thus saving cash-strapped county governments the cost of transporting prisoners.

- Produce buyers in Japan select California produce via videoconferencing. Images of fresh-picked strawberries, artichokes, and other fruits and vegetables are beamed over ISDN lines.

How VIDEOCONFERENCING WORKS

The setup consists of a small camera mounted on top of a monitor, a full-duplex sound card (capable of recording and playing audio at the same time), a modem (analog, DSL, ISDN, cable, or others), software to run the program, a microphone, and a telephone or telephone headset. When a videoconference takes place, the computers are connected via the Internet using a standard analog telephone line or a high-speed connection, such as DSL, satellite, or cable.

To set up a conference, you launch the video software and dial the other computer by clicking on a photo in your graphical phone book or on a private list similar to an instant messaging list. You then start any accompanying application you may want to view, such as a spreadsheet, seat yourself before the tiny video camera, and you're on. Most of the time, only your head and shoulders will on the other participant's screen.

One of the most popular videoconferencing software programs is Microsoft NetMeeting, which comes bundled with Windows 98 and Windows 2000. This program lets you collaborate and share information with two or more meeting participants in real time. In addition, you can share information from software applications located on your computer, control software remotely, keep notes or draw diagrams with an electronic whiteboard, send messages, and send files to participants using the file transfer capability.

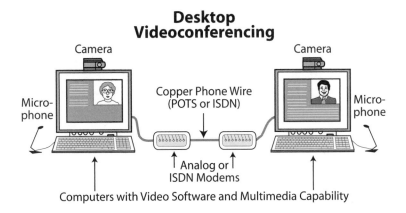

Desktop Videoconferencing

Camera

Camera

Micro-phone

Copper Phone Wire (POTS or ISDN)

Micro-phone

Analog or ISDN Modems

Computers with Video Software and Multimedia Capability

If you don't have desktop video capability, but need to conduct an occasional videoconference, consider renting. Many hotels and office support companies offer videoconferencing facilities. For example, Kinko's copy centers (800-2KINKOS or www.kinkos.com) provide room-based videoconferencing at many of their branches.

FINDING INFORMATION ON THE INTERNET

The Internet's lack of conscious design creates a freewheeling, do-it-yourself atmosphere. Because the Internet grew haphazardly, it can be unorganized and confusing. Fortunately, there are many services that can help you find your way around the Net. For example, you could use a directory, such as Yahoo (www.yahoo.com) or LookSmart (www.looksmart.com). Directories are organized by topic. You select a topic, browse through the titles, and click to go to the next level until you find something that interests you.

Better yet, try using a search engine, such as AltaVista (www.altavista.com), Google (www.google.com), or InfoSeek (www.infoseek.com). When you type a key search term in the online form provided, the engine responds with a list of sites that match your criteria.

Typing the word *patent* brought up 114,285 listings, including articles about recent patent law cases, an example of a patent application (including electronic blueprints), a cartoon about the patenting process, and a video clip from a film on the history of the patent office. It also brought up tons of junk— including the home page of Emily Patent, Wacky Patents of the Month, and loads of useless, poorly informed opinions. You can improve your search by narrowing your cast.

DOING BUSINESS ON THE WEB

Businesses are flocking to the Web in record numbers, looking for opportunities to market and display their wares. The 19th annual Dun & Bradstreet Small Business Survey (March, 2000), found that 40 percent of all small businesses have their own websites (versus 25 percent in 1999) and 70 percent have Internet access (versus 57 percent in 1999).

The opportunity to present your products online to millions of potential customers is very attractive. You can use the Web to increase your business by:

- ✔ Offering new services
- ✔ Increasing accessibility
- ✔ Expanding your market
- ✔ Showcasing your work
- ✔ Generating leads
- ✔ Building community

There are many good books available to help you set up an e-business. Check *Resources* at the end of this chapter.

STEPS FOR BUILDING YOUR OWN WEBSITE

First of all, you'll need a domain name so customers can find you on the Internet. To register your domain name, check with your Internet service provider, or you can find a registrar service on the InterNIC site (www.internic.net/alpha.html).

Next, you'll need your own home page. For a simple site, you may be able to do the programming yourself. To code the document, you can enlist the aid of an HTML editor, such as Adobe's PageMill or Microsoft's Front Page. However, if you want sophisticated graphics, interactivity, or plan to conduct e-business on your site, you'll want the help of a professional. You'll also need software for uploading and maintaining your Web page information, such as a File Transfer Protocol (FTP) utility.

A key component of Internet marketing is information. Your website should attract potential customers to visit, and hopefully, to return. If they find nothing but a bunch of press releases and advertising copy, they won't come back. Spend time developing useful content that answers the needs of your customers. For example:

- Booksellers could relate stories about featured authors
- Graphic artists might provide layout advice

- Travel agents should include packing tips and details on destinations

Pay attention to design. It's best to keep the site uncluttered and easy to navigate. For ideas on what *not* to do, see Vincent Flanders' Web Pages That Suck (www.webpagesthatsuck.com).

You'll want to make it easy for your visitors to leave comments on your site by providing a guest book, a survey, or a comments form. To capture lots of email addresses, offer something free, such as a sample of your electronic newsletter. (Make sure you put your email address on every page!)

An Internet hosting service will provide the tools you'll need for your site. You may want a secure ordering form or cybercash (a kind of e-money). You may opt for a shopping cart service, where customers pick items from a list and an automatic order is created for them. You could also give your customers the ability to download software or files from your site. All these services cost extra, and the prices can vary significantly. According to Larry Newman, a California-based Internet consultant, "This industry is strictly 'buyer beware.' You could easily pay for a Cadillac and end up with a Volkswagen." So, be sure to shop around.

For help finding a reliable Web hosting service, check these sites:

- Web Hosting Directory   www.hostindex.com
- Top Hosts.com   www.tophosts.com

Online ordering can be complicated. There are several firms that offer services to help you get paid. Here are some of the best-known:

- Authorize.Net   www.authorize.net
- Cybercash   www.cybercash.com
- IntelliPay   www.intellipay.com

Once your site is up, you'll need to get the word out so people will know how to find you. Put your Web address on your business stationery, network online, and write articles to post on newsgroups. Send announcements to Web-indexing services such as Zipee (www.web-registration.com) and Yahoo (www.yahoo.com).

Also, to save time, you can use a service such as SubmitIt (www.submitit.com). These services will register your site with dozens of search engines using one simple application. Contact other webmasters and ask if they would be willing to link to your site. Hopefully, if you build it, they will come.

☎ In my office

When planning my website (www.langhoff.com), I made a list of what I thought visitors would be most interested in and designed the pages to reflect those interests. My site focuses on telecommuting, a hot topic and the subject of one of my recent books. I created separate pages to answer frequently asked questions (FAQs), provide advice for wannabes, a list of resources, recent news, an events calendar, links to other useful sites, reviews, and even jokes about telecommuting.

As a service to my readers, I set up a relationship with Amazon.com (www.amazon.com). When a person clicks on a book listed in my bookstore (there are lots, not just my own), they're transported directly to the Amazon site and the page that describes the book. If a customer decides to buy the book, I earn a small finder's fee.

My site was designed by Annie Kook, a professional graphic artist and a good friend. She taught me how to update it, so I now make all the changes. This task takes me a couple of hours each month. I try to add new content to the site on a monthly basis, and I provide a brief "What's New" page for people who visit the site regularly.

The site attracts about 4,000 visitors a month and has brought in requests for interviews, writing assignments from editors, invitations to speak at conferences, lots of book orders, and email messages from around the world. It's definitely worth it.

SECURITY ISSUES

Don't forget security in your rush to get your site online. Work with an established e-business provider to develop security for online ordering, credit card transactions, and the like.

In addition, if you connect via an always-on service such as DSL or cable, you'll want a personal firewall to protect your computer or network from hackers. A firewall provides a buffer between your site, or computer, and the Internet. Firewalls are usually software, but they can have hardware components as well. ZoneAlarm (www.zonealarm.com) is a popular Windows-based firewall; DoorStop (www.opendoor.com) is a well-known Mac firewall. Also, see *Email flu* in Chapter 10 for information on computer viruses and prevention.

RESOURCES

Books
Clicking Through:
A Survival Guide for Bringing Your Company Online
by Jonathan Ezor
Bloomberg Press, 1999

Creating Web Pages with HTML Simplified, second edition
by Ruth Maran
IDG Books Worldwide, 1999

The Consultant's Guide to Getting Business on the Internet
by Herman Holtz
Wiley, 1998

Find It Online:
The Complete Guide to Online Research
by Alan Schlein, James Flowers, and Shirley Kwan Kisaichi
Facts on Demand Press, 2000

How the Internet Works, fifth edition
by Preston Gralla
Que, 1999

The Internet For Dummies
by John Levine, Carol Baroudi, and Margaret Levine Young
IDG Books, 2000

Poor Richard's Web Site:
Geek-Free, Commonsense Advice on Building a Low-Cost Web Site
by Peter Kent
Top Floor Publishing, 1998

Web Marketing Cookbook
by Janice King, Paul Knight and James H. Mason
John Wiley & Sons, 1997

Websites

Learn the Net
www.learnthenet.com

You'll find excellent information at this site for both newbies (people new to the Internet) and those with more experience. Tutorials include mastering the basics, how to build a website, conducting e-business, and more.

CyberAtlas
www.cyberatlas.internet.com

This site provides tons of statistics about the Net, including the top banner ads of the week, the top 50 sites of the month, the reasons teens go online, and so on.

Chapter

12

Modems

. . . .

TO GET ONLINE, YOU'LL NEED A MODEM, a communications line, and communications software. Because modems are a bit tricky to set up, I've included lots of troubleshooting help. Hopefully, this chapter will show you how to get it all together.

A SHORT HISTORY OF MODEMS

The first commercial modem, the AT&T Dataphone, was introduced in 1960, long before the Internet was ever thought of. It transmitted data at 300 bps, or about 30 characters a second, which is laughably slow by today's standards. Commercial modems were very rare, however, as companies had to lease them from AT&T. Then, in 1968, the FCC ruled that phone companies could not prohibit "customer-provided interconnecting devices." This landmark decision, known as the Carterfone decision, opened the door for competition in the telecom industry.

Modem sales were slow until PCs became widespread. In addition, modem costs were high in the early days. For example, when the 14.4 kbps modem was first introduced, it cost $14,400—or one dollar per bit. The 28.8 kbps modem, introduced in 1995, was capable of twice the speed, but only cost around $300. As transmission speeds picked up and sales volumes improved, the price of modems continued to drop. Modems are commonplace today, and, according to industry sources, there are currently over 500 million modems in use around the world.

HOW MODEMS WORK

Basically, a modem takes the digital stuff you're sending and translates it into analog format. Once the information is in analog format, it can then be sent over normal phone lines. A receiving modem sits at the other end of the connection, where the analog information is translated back into digital format so it can be read or stored on a computer.

Unlike most computer equipment, the same external modem can work with either a PC or a Mac. All you need is the correct connecting cord.

CHOOSING A MODEM

To select a modem, you must first determine whether you want an internal or external modem. You must also know how you want to use modem communications (data, fax, voice, or a combination), and you will need to identify what kind of line you will use (analog, digital, ISDN, DSL, or cable). Finally, you'll need to pick a modem speed.

MODEM LOCATION

Do you want the modem to be installed inside your computer (an internal modem), or attached to the outside of your computer (an external modem)?

Internal modem

An internal modem is actually a printed circuit board that fits into an expansion slot inside your computer. You'll have to take the cover off your computer to install an internal modem. This isn't hard to do, but it's not for the fumble-fingered.

External modem

An external modem is usually about the size of a quality paperback and connects to your computer via a cable. They usually cost a bit more than internal modems, but they are handy if you want to move your modem around. External modems feature display lights that provide useful visual feedback about the status of your communication.

Credit card size external modem

If you have a notebook or handheld computer, you can get a credit card size modem that fits in the PC slot that most portable computers have today. These tiny cards perform just as well as full-sized modems and are less hefty to lug around. There's even a wireless version.

TYPE OF CONNECTION

Of course, you'll have to plug in your external modem. You'll use one of these ports:

Serial port

A 9-pin or 25-pin connector plugs into the serial port on the back of your computer. If your modem has a 9-pin connector and your computer has a 25-pin connector (or vice versa), you can get an adapter at any computer store to make them fit.

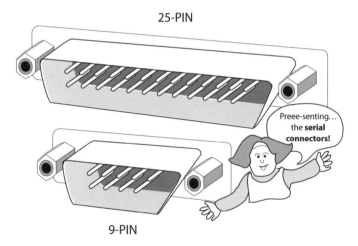

25-PIN

Preee-senting... the **serial connectors!**

9-PIN

On Apple computers, it's easy to find the serial port because it's marked with a phone symbol. Actually, both phone and printer ports operate the same way and can be used interchangeably.

USB port

Many newer modems are designed for plugging into the universal serial bus (USB) port. USB is plug and play—you can add a new device to your computer without installing an adapter card or even turning the computer off. Also, USB-compatible equipment works with any platform, whether Mac, Windows-based, or UNIX.

Ethernet port

DSL and cable modems connect through an Ethernet port and require an Ethernet networking card. This card, standard with newer Macintosh computers, can be easily added to Windows machines as well.

TYPES OF MODEMS

Be sure to get a modem that performs the tasks you want it to.

Data modem

The simplest type of modem is designed to work with data only. A data modem allows you to access online services and bulletin boards, upload and download files (including files containing graphics and sound bites), or log onto another computer and conduct a remote session. About the only thing you can't do is send or receive faxes.

Fax/data modem

For a few dollars more, you can purchase a data/fax modem. These modems have all the capabilities of a data modem, plus you can send and receive faxes. To utilize the fax capability, you must have fax software installed in your computer. For more information on fax communications software, see Chapter 13.

Voice/fax/data modem

These specialized modems are designed to process interactive voice communications, such as audiotext, voice mail, and fax-on-demand. Some voice modems can operate as computerized answering machines. For more information, see *Computer-based voice mail* in Chapter 8 and *Fax-on-demand* in Chapter 13.

Wireless modem

In addition to standard wired modems, there are also wireless types. Many work with your cellular or PCS phones, while others operate with radio signals. These specialized modems send and receive data over the airwaves. They're great if you need to communicate in areas where phone lines are either hard to find or mostly digital.

Dual analog modem

This technology creates a 112 kbps pipeline by bonding two 56 kbps connections together. To achieve the higher speed, you'll need two analog telephone lines. In addition, you will need to find an Internet service provider that supports dual modem connections (also known as multiline analog). Netopia, 3Com, and Ramp Networks all make dual analog modems.

ISDN modem

If you have an ISDN phone line in your office, you'll need an ISDN-capable modem. Alternatively, get an adapter that allows you to attach an analog modem to your ISDN line. Doing this, however, prevents you from taking advantage of ISDN's higher speeds. For more information, see Chapter 4.

DSL modem

A digital subscriber line (DSL) modem will provide an always-on connection to another location. Most people use DSL to connect to the Internet, although some have DSL connections to their office LANs. DSL speeds vary from 128 kbps to about 6 Mbps, depending on the type of DSL provisioned. The modem links to the computer via the Ethernet port on your computer. For more information, see Chapter 4.

Hybrid modem

If you use a variety of phone lines, get a hybrid modem that can support both dial-up and digital connections. Texas Instruments and 3Com produce hybrid modems for ISDN/56 kbps analog and DSL/56 kbps analog. These modems are smart enough to determine what kind of line you're using and adjust to analog or digital transmission as needed. Of course, you pay a premium for all that intelligence.

Cable modem

A cable modem transmits data over coaxial cable, which is the same stuff that carries TV signals. These modems link to your computer via the Ethernet connection on the back of your PC, and they are available through subscription to a cable data service. Transmission rates range from 1.5 to 3 Mbps—that's 50 to 100 times faster than a 28.8 modem. Cable is an always-on shared service. So, as more people in your neighborhood sign on, your service most likely will slow down. For more information, see Chapter 4.

TRANSMISSION SPEEDS

Modems and the connecting phone lines are the slowest parts of the system, therefore it makes sense to get the speediest modem you can get. Modems are rated on the basis of their transmission speed, which is measured in bits per second (bps). A kilobit (kb) is equal to 1,000 bits. The most common modem speeds are 28.8 kbps, 33.6 kbps, and 56 kbps.

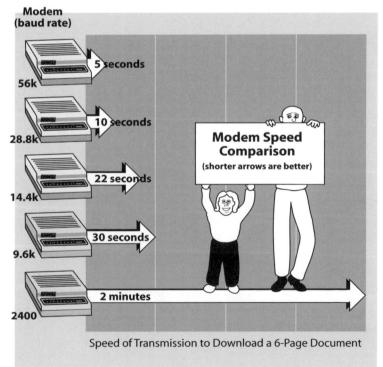

Modem (baud rate)

- 56k — 5 seconds
- 28.8k — 10 seconds
- 14.4k — 22 seconds
- 9.6k — 30 seconds
- 2400 — 2 minutes

Modem Speed Comparison
(shorter arrows are better)

Speed of Transmission to Download a 6-Page Document

Note: A 56 kbps modem can download at 56 kbps speed, but uploads can't go any faster than 33.6 kbps.

COMMUNICATIONS SOFTWARE

To tell your computer how to dial and connect successfully to another computer, you'll need communications software in addition to your modem. Major online services provide specialized software either free or for a very reasonable cost, and most new computers include one or more communications programs pre-installed. If you plan to use your modem to dial local bulletin boards or call your office and download files, you'll need general purpose communications software, such as Traveling Software's LapLink (www.travsoft.com) or Symantec's Procomm Plus (www.symantec.com). You can download Internet access software for free.

GETTING CONNECTED

Hooking up an external analog modem is easy. You just plug the modem into a power outlet and the phone line cord into a wall jack. Then you plug the serial connector on the modem (that's the plug with 9 or 25 gold pins) to the serial port on your computer.

Connecting a Modem

Connecting a PC-card modem is also easy. You simply slide the card into the Type II PC slot making sure the gold contacts are facing in. Be careful that it goes in straight. When you reach what feels like the contacts, press gently but firmly. Then attach your phone cord or dongle connector.

PC Modem Cards

Attaching a DSL or cable modem is equally simple. First, you plug the modem into a power outlet. Then you connect the modem to your computer with an Ethernet cable. Finally, you attach the phone line (for DSL) or the coaxial cable (for cable) to the modem.

DAISY-CHAINING

Your fax machine, phone, answering machine, or other devices can all be plugged into the same wall jack as long as they are all analog devices. This arrangement is known as daisy-chaining.

Just plug your modem into the wall jack using the LINE port on the back of the modem. Then, plug another phone line cord into the PHONE port on the back of the modem and plug in the next device. You can connect up to five devices in this manner.

TROUBLESHOOTING

Modems are relatively easy to use, but you may need to trouble-shoot a problem from time to time. Here are some of the most common problems and solutions.

CONNECTING THE FIRST TIME

If you can't get online, don't give up and don't think that you are stupid or something. The problem may be caused by in-compatible resident programs, such as virus checkers, .ini or .init programs. You may need to modify your communications setup by adding control strings, or special commands, to get the connection right. Try consulting your modem manual, or, if you have an online service, call the customer service people.

It took three different service assistants to help me get America Online to work with my Hayes Accura 28.8 modem on a Power Macintosh. The first technician was helpful, but unable to solve the problem; the second suggested a lot of control strings and finally referred the problem to their tech wizard. After a few unsuccessful attempts, the tech wizard solved the problem by having me temporarily remove all the .init files from my sys-tem folder. These files, which control automatic functions, were somehow preventing the modem from dialing the 800 num-ber.

Another possibility could be a COM port conflict. COM is another name for a serial port, and PCs routinely have two COM ports—COM1 and COM2. Some PCs, however, have four COM ports. In addition to modems, a mouse and a scan-ner also require COM port space. Because most communica-tions software is configured for COM1, you may have to change the COM port to get your modem to work. There's a simple utility from your software that lets you do this. Just look it up in your systems manual and follow the directions.

PROTECTING YOUR MODEM

Modems can get hot and need air cooling to work well. Be sure that you don't block the air vents on your modem with stacks of paper or other stuff. Also, you'll want to attach your modem to a surge protector to avoid the dangers of power spikes. Make sure the surge protector comes with a phone line connection. If you don't, a lightning strike nearby could cook your computer by traveling down the modem phone line.

MODEM SLOWING DOWN

You have a 56 kbps modem, but for some reason, your transmission speed drops to 28.8, 14.4, then 9600, and finally 2400. What's wrong?

There's nothing wrong that you can fix. It may be that your connection is noisy, so the modem has slowed the transmission in order to continue the connection. Standard phone lines are not designed for data transmission. They are often full of noise and other interference that can slow transmissions way down, even causing disconnects.

Sometimes, I find that my 56 kbps modem transmission speed will drop to 26, 24, 20, and even all the way down to 14.4 when noise is encountered on the line—especially when I'm trying to connect from a hotel. If you frequently encounter this problem, plan to dial at night when the phone lines are cleaner. Better yet, get an ISDN or DSL line. Digital lines are noise free.

You could also be encountering a logjam on the Internet. Gateways are the modems operating at the other end of your connection, and they are geared to handle lower speeds only, often stopping at 9.6 kbps. Your modem can operate no faster than the modem at the other end of the line, so your superfast modem has to slow down to match the gateway speed. In addition, if there are loads of users competing for scarce resources, the whole system will slow down. You'll definitely encounter slowdowns at peak times, such as 9 A.M. Monday morning.

Hint: If your modem disconnects suddenly, just dial again. Hopefully, your connection will stay up the next time. Or wait until late at night. Telephone traffic is lightest then, and your chances of getting a clean line are greatly improved.

MODEM AND CALL WAITING—AN UNHAPPY DUO

If you have call waiting on your line, you're in for trouble when using a modem. Call waiting tones can disrupt modem communications and cause the entire connection to be lost. You should disable call waiting on a call-by-call basis each time you initiate a modem connection. This is usually done by dialing *70 if you have Touch-Tone service or 1170 if you have rotary service.

However, if you are on the receiving end of a modem call, you have no way to stop call waiting from disrupting your connection. If you wish to keep call waiting service, I recommend that you get a separate phone line for modem and fax communications.

READING YOUR MODEM LIGHTS

External modems are equipped with status lights that let you know what is happening to your transmission. These lights can be very helpful when troubleshooting. Several internal modems also have software programs that will display modem status lights on your computer screen.

Modem Light Show

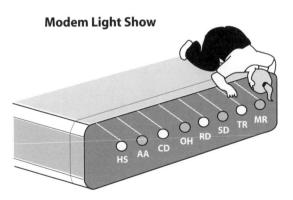

A client of mine, who desires to remain anonymous (read "too embarrassed"), learned what his modem's lights meant after he was slapped with a $527 phone bill for a single call. It turns out his modem didn't hang up when the online software did. He didn't notice that the line was still active until the next time he wanted to dial out online—several days later! Learn to read your modem lights. You'll be glad you did.

Your modem may have only four lights or as many as twelve. The most common are:

HS **High speed** indicates that the modem is operating at its highest speed.

AA **Automatic answer** lights up when you have an incoming modem call. Also, when this light is on, the modem will answer the phone line.

CD **Carrier detect** indicates that you are connected to another modem.

OH **Off hook** shows that the phone line you are using to make or receive a modem call is off-hook.

RD **Receive data** lights up when you are receiving data. You'll notice that this light flashes on and off in short bursts. This corresponds to the packets of information being sent over the line and is quite normal.

SD **Send data** blinks when you are sending data.

TR **Terminal ready** indicates that your computer is ready to make a call.

MR **Modem ready** indicates that your modem is powered on and ready to communicate with your computer.

Warning: Digital Line = Modem Killer

Some hotels, universities, and many larger office buildings have digital lines. When you are traveling, you may run into them. If you're trying to connect your analog modem or other telephone device and it just doesn't act right, it's possible you've run into a digital line.

How can you tell if the phone line is digital? Look at the phone attached to the line. Somewhere on the back of the phone, you should see some text that indicates that it "complies with part 68, FCC Rules." You should also see a ringer equivalence number, or REN. If the phone has a REN number, it's analog. If there's no REN number, it's digital.

Other signs of digital phones are multiple push buttons, visual displays, built-in voice mail, and keypads with special dialing or function buttons. If you're lucky, the phone will carry a warning label saying, "Not for connection to telco lines." You can also test the line (more on this below).

What can you do then? Pay phones are almost universally analog, so you could find a pay phone with a modular connector plug. Or ask to use the fax line. Fax lines are analog unless they're Group IV fax lines, but those are quite rare. Another alternative is to carry an adapter that allows you to plug your modem line into the handset jack. Handset lines are always analog—otherwise, you'd be hearing the digital equivalent of ones and zeros. You can get such an adapter from telecom vendors, such as Hello Direct (www.hellodirect.com) and Teleadapt (www.teleadapt.com).

Fried Modem

If your modem suddenly stops working after plugging it into an unfamiliar wall jack, you may be in for some very bad news. Most modems, including built-in modems and PC modem cards, are unable to handle the higher electrical current that runs over the phone lines of digital phone systems.

When your modem encounters those lines, it burns out. To avoid this problem, get a testing device to check the telephone port before attaching your modem. IBM makes one called the Modem Saver. It's a really easy test—you just insert the test plug into the phone jack. If the light is green, go ahead; a red light means danger. Incidentally, some of the newer modems come with built-in line testers.

Sometimes you desperately need to connect to the Internet or pick up email, but there's only a PBX or digital line available. Luckily, a technology solution exists for this problem, too. LineStein from Hello Direct is an analog-to-digital line adapter that tests the line, learns the characteristics of the connection you're using, and protects the connection if needed. All you do is plug it in. Easy!

MODEM LINE WON'T RELEASE

Sometimes your modem won't hang up, even when you think it has. This situation may occur if your call is interrupted by call waiting, or if your computer gets hung up and you have to reset. Check your modem line to be sure that the line has released. If it hasn't, disconnect the line from your computer and plug it back in. That should do it.

INSTALLING A MODEM ON A TWO-LINE PHONE

If you plug your modem into the same jack as your phone and have a two-line jack, you may find that the modem always dials out on line 1. That's because most modems are prewired to use line 1.

However, you may want to use line 1 for voice calls and line 2 for modem calls. In that case, purchase a two-line splitter. First, plug the splitter into your wall jack. Then, plug your phone into the receptacle labeled line 1/line 2 (sometimes labeled L1/L2) and your modem into the receptacle labeled line 2.

MODEMING INTERNATIONALLY

There are at least 40 different types of telephone connectors used worldwide. Even within countries, you can find variations. For example, Germany uses five different connectors, and Saudi Arabia uses four.

Do some research before you travel to determine which connectors are used where and how to order them. Contacting the hotel where you'll be staying is a good bet. You might also visit TeleAdapt's website at www.teleadapt.com (or phone 408-965-1400). International connections are this company's specialty.

Yet another wrinkle in international modeming are the metering pulses some countries add to their phone signals. These pulses, also called tax impulsing, are counted to determine the length of the call. They really slow modeming down and can cause costly disconnects. You'll encounter tax impulsing in Germany, Switzerland, Austria, Spain, India, Belgium, Slovenia, and the Czech Republic. To overcome this problem, you'll need a special filter that can be purchased from TeleAdapt.

HOW TO DIAL BLIND

Because phone systems around the world use different signals for dial tone, busy, and ringing, you may need to override your modem's configuration to connect successfully. Some modems come with a choice of country configurations. However, many modems designed to work in the U.S. or Canada are not be able to dial out abroad because they don't recognize the dial tone provided.

To get around this, learn how to "blind dial." In effect, you instruct your modem to ignore dial tone. Check your setup file in your modem software to see if you can select this option. If your software doesn't allow you to select blind dialing, you can still accomplish it. Here's how:

1. Change the initialization string in your modem's software. To do this, just add X1 to the end of the string.

2. Disconnect your modem from the phone line.

3. Instruct your modem to tone dial.

4. Listen to your modem. If you hear the series of tones your modem normally makes, you're ready to blind dial.

5. Reconnect your modem to the phone line and dial.

Note: Although blind dialing is rather elegant, it might be easier to dial manually. Then you don't have to mess around with setup strings and pause length—you just dial as if your modem is a phone. If you don't know how to dial manually, read on.

HOW TO DIAL MANUALLY

Modems will dial automatically, but it's often easier to use your modem like a phone and dial out manually. Here's how:

1. Connect your modem to a phone line using a splitter or a duplex phone jack.

2. Connect a telephone to the phone line using the same duplex phone jack.

3. Be sure your modem software is configured for manual dialing.

4. Dial the desired telephone number using the telephone keypad.

5. When you hear the modem's squealing tones over the phone, instruct your software to connect.

6. Hang up the phone.

RESOURCES

Books
Need more help? Some good books to help you though the modem maze are:

Modems Made Easy, second edition
by David Hakala
Osborne McGraw Hill, 1995

Written by the editor of *Boardwatch Magazine*, this book has information on buying, setting up, fine-tuning, and trouble-shooting your modem.

Don't Panic! It's Only a Modem
by Esther Schindle
New Riders Publishing, 1994

Modems for Dummies
by Tina Rathbone
IDG Books Worldwide, 1997

*Next Generation Modems:
A Professional Guide to DSLs and Cable Modems*
by Gilbert Held
John Wiley & Sons (February 16, 2000)

This is a comparative guide to the technologies, capabilities, and costs of next-generation desktop connectivity.

Chapter

13

Fax

DESPITE THE APPEAL OF EMAIL, fax is still highly popular. In Chicago, prospective cooks fax in their registrations for cooking classes; in San Francisco, an agent who books guests for talk shows gets late-breaking industry news over a daily fax feed; in Stamford, Connecticut, commuters fax in orders for home-cooked meals that are ready to pick up at the railway station when the train pulls in.

One out of every four phone calls made in the United States is a fax call. According to Dataquest, more than 6.6 million fax machines were sold in 1999, resulting in an increase of 16.5 percent from the previous year. Also, a recent Pitney Bowes Gallup survey showed fax transmissions rose from 128 billion pages in 1996 to 175 billion pages in 1998. It is expected that the demand for facsimile-enabled devices will continue to grow, and Dataquest has projected sales of 8.4 million by 2004.

Email is less expensive than a fax, but faxes offer a variety of other benefits. They're easy to use and almost always available. Many people prefer faxing over sending an email attachment because incompatible equipment is not an issue. Opening an email attachment is not yet an automatic success. Furthermore, around the world, fax machines are much more widespread than Internet access.

This chapter will cover all aspects of fax technology and use, such as types of fax machines, fax features, fax modems and software, fax-on-demand, and line sharing. Plus, I'll offer you some tips on using fax more effectively.

A SHORT HISTORY OF FAX

Fax technology is actually older than the telephone. It traces its roots to telegraphy and to Alexander Bain, a Scottish physicist, who invented the first facsimile machine in 1842. This early machine picked up signals from a telegraph wire and translated them into words on paper using electrified metal letters.

To do this, the letters were first scanned by a pendulum device and then reproduced at the other end of the telegraph wire by a synchronized pendulum that made contact with a piece of chemical paper. Bain's machine was interesting scientifically, but it was never put to any practical or commercial use. Incidentally, if you're still using a thermal fax machine, you can thank Bain for the smelly, chemically treated paper.

In 1860, an Italian priest, Giovanni Caselli, constructed his version of Bain's fax machine. He named it the pantelegraph. Its usefulness was demonstrated in 1860 when the first long-distance fax was sent from Paris to Amiens, approximately 70 miles. Still, fax wasn't ready for daily use. In order to get the thing to work, Caselli had to use enormous synchronized pendulums that stretched about eight feet high.

It wasn't until 1898 that Ernest A. Hummel, a watchmaker from St. Paul, Minnesota, invented a telegraph-facsimile transmitter. In the same year, his Telediagraph was installed in the office of the *New York Herald*. Soon Telediagraphs were in use at the *Chicago Times Herald*, the *St. Louis Republic*, the *Boston Herald*, and the *Philadelphia Inquirer*. The first picture transmitted via fax was a photo of the first gun fired at Manila during the Spanish-American war. The machine took about 30 minutes to send the picture.

Small improvements in fax technology continued to be made. Transcontinental faxing was achieved in 1907 when Arthur

Korn, an American inventor, used radio waves to transmit pictures between Paris, London, and Berlin. Faxing across telephone lines became possible in 1911. By 1924, fax was so advanced that it only took seven minutes to transmit a 5-by-7-inch photo.

It wasn't until 1978, however, that faxing became common in business. In that year, the FCC allowed direct connection of fax machines to the public telephone network. The first computer fax modem was introduced in 1985, and plain-paper faxing appeared in 1987. Voice was added in 1993, and Internet faxing became available in 1996.

HOW FAX WORKS

With just a few keystrokes, you can send an image over the phone lines to practically anywhere on earth. To use a stand-alone fax machine, you insert a document, key in a telephone number, and press the SEND key. The fax machine first scans the document, reading small areas of the image in succession. It then converts the image into a patterned grid of tiny dots, which are coded into digital signals—0 for light and 1 for dark.

Once the fax machine dials the number you have programmed, it takes about 20 seconds for the sending and receiving machines to perform an electronic "handshake." They do this by exchanging warbling tones that check for compatibility, speed of transmission, and other items before the first page is sent down the phone line.

When the transmitted document reaches the receiving fax machine, the digital signals are reconverted into something resembling the original pattern. The receiving machine then stores the document in its memory or on a disk, or the document is printed out.

Fax technology is divided into two major types—stand-alone fax machines and fax modems. The most common stand-alone faxes are thermal fax and plain paper fax. Fax modems, which

may also take the form of credit card size PC cards, are installed in your computer. These devices combine with your fax
software and printer to perform most faxing duties.

THERMAL FAX

A thermal fax machine uses heat to etch an image directly onto
special heat-sensitive paper. This paper is available in rolls that
are usually 8½ inches wide by 98, 164, or 328 feet long. If
your fax machine has a cutter, it will cut the transmission into
individual pages. Otherwise, you'll receive a long scroll that
you must cut apart yourself.

Thermal fax output has several negatives. The paper is slick and
difficult to write on; it tends to curl up; the image fades if left
in the light; and, because the paper is so flimsy, it tends to get
wrinkled and torn if handled much. In addition, it's not easy to
tell when you're running low on paper. By the time copies
appear with pink edges (indicating the end of the roll), it may
be too late, especially if you're receiving a long fax.

Some marking pens also interact strangely with thermal paper.
You may find that areas marked with a yellow highlighter will
turn into a dark green-gray smear over time, hiding the very
words you wanted to emphasize.

The table below compares the size and capacity of standard
thermal fax paper rolls.

Thermal fax paper capacity

Size of roll - feet	Size of roll - meters	Approx. # pages
98 feet	30 meters	100 pages
163 feet	50 meters	175 pages
327 feet	100 meters	350 pages

On the plus side, thermal fax machines are cheaper than plain
paper fax. Plus, they have a much smaller footprint than plain
paper fax machines, which is important if your desktop real

estate is scarce. You'll find that your thermals faxes really don't fade all that quickly if you file them away in a folder. A check of my files shows that all the faxes I've kept over the years (since 1983) are still completely readable.

Fax manufacturers are also working out the kinks (literally) in paper curling. They have added an anti-curl feature that curls the paper in reverse before output. Incidentally, the larger paper rolls tend to curl less than the smaller ones, and you don't have to replace the paper as often.

Thermal fax is easy to maintain. There are no ribbons, ink cartridges, or toner to replace. From time to time you need to replace the paper roll, a relatively simple process. Operating costs average out to about 6 cents per page.

PLAIN PAPER FAX

Instead of special paper rolls, a plain paper fax machine uses standard 8½-by-11-inch paper, which is the same kind you use for photocopiers and laser printers. You can even use recycled paper. It easy to keep track of your paper supply, and you don't have to worry if you're coming to the end of the roll. Often, plain paper fax machines offer more advanced features, such as broadcasting capability and memory functions.

The cost of plain paper fax machines is about double that of thermal fax machines. Their footprints are also larger—often about the size of a small copier. Costs per page range from 5 to 12 cents.

TYPES OF PLAIN PAPER FAX MACHINES

Plain paper fax machines vary in their printing method.

- **Thermal transfer**
  First the image is etched onto a heat-sensitive ribbon, and then it is transferred onto plain paper. Some of the older models require special rolls of rather costly plain paper— hardly an advantage.

- **Inkjet**
  This printing method is based on the same technology as inkjet printers. It provides nearly laser quality for about a third of the cost, but it is twice as slow as laser printing.

- **Laser**
  The top-of-the-line fax machines are laser. They are fast, reliable, and have the cleanest, sharpest print. However, the quality of the print is determined by the overall quality of the scanned fax image from the sending fax machine. Therefore, the print output will not be as sharp as what you would get from a laser printer connected to your computer.

STAND-ALONE FAX FEATURES

You won't find all these features in every fax machine, nor would you want them all. A list of some of the more common and useful features available today follows:

Activity log

This report lists the telephone numbers, times, and dates of each document sent or received. It is useful for record keeping and cost control.

Automatic cover page

You can program your fax machine with your company name, logo, and phone number, and the machine will automatically create and print a dated cover page whenever you send a document. This is a practical time-saver.

Automatic document feeder

These devices relieve you from the task of standing by throughout the entire transmission and feeding each sheet by hand. Unfortunately, document feeders don't always work as promised. My fax machine means well, but it often grabs two or three sheets when it should have sent only one, thus requiring costly and annoying retransmits. Be sure to insist on testing this feature at the store. I wish I had.

Automatic redial

This feature prompts the fax machine to automatically redial if it reaches a machine that is busy or if the connection fails during the call.

Automatic switching

Many of the newer fax machines come with built-in switching capability, so you can use your fax line for incoming voice calls. With the aid of this switch, your fax machine can distinguish between a voice call and a fax call. However, these devices don't always work as well as you might hope. See *Sharing a line* later in this chapter.

Broadcast capability

Higher-end fax machines can scan a document and send the same fax to a group of recipients. If you regularly fax to a workgroup or a specific set of clients, this feature can be useful.

Closed user groups

This option allows you to restrict the faxes you receive, thus keeping your fax line open for important, expected transmissions. You choose those people you want to receive faxes from. It is the perfect antidote to junk fax.

Color faxing

This type of machine allows you to send and receive color faxes from compatible fax machines. This feature is handy for graphic artists, advertising professionals, and others who need high-quality color comps. HP, Canon, and Brother make such machines.

Copier function

All fax machines can double as copiers, though the copies will be no better than the fax quality supported. Also, the output is slow. The copier function is useful for previewing faxes before sending them. If you're planning to send a complex fax, especially one with dense text or lots of illustrations, you can experiment with fine or halftone mode before actually sending the document.

Delayed transmission

This feature allows you to program your fax machine to automatically send a fax or fax broadcast at a later time. For example, to take advantage of lower phone rates, you can program your faxes to go out late at night.

Gray scale

If you will be regularly transmitting photographs or artwork, you'll want a fax machine with the ability to handle gray scale, or halftones. For most applications, 16 tones of gray are sufficient. However, you can find machines that support 32 or even 64 shades. Gray-scale transmission is much slower than regular fax. It may take up to five minutes to send an 8½-by-11-inch photo. If you are only sending text or line art, you don't need gray-scale capability.

Image enhancement

Some of the more expensive laser and inkjet fax machines can improve the quality of your incoming fax by defuzzing images and smoothing lines and edges.

Junk mail blocking

You can program your fax machine to refuse faxes from specific phone numbers that have been bombarding you with unwanted mail.

Memory

The memory feature has many uses. When your fax machine runs out of paper, memory allows the fax machine to save a few pages of the most recent transmission for printing out later. You can also use memory to scan in a document and then broadcast it to several fax machines.

Memory lock

If you share a fax machine, but want to ensure document confidentiality, the memory lock option can help you. Incoming faxes are stored into memory, but only the intended recipient is allowed to access them via a personal identification code.

Multifunctional

Several manufacturers are selling combos that perform fax as well as other functions. You can get combos that feature a cordless phone, send-and-receive fax capability, and an answering device, or a multifunction device that combines an ink jet printer, plain paper fax, and copier in a single package.

Combo machines are often less expensive than buying the separate components, and they are especially useful if you're short of desktop space. On the other hand, if any one function breaks down, you're really out of luck.

Out-of-paper reception

When your machine senses that it is out of paper, it can save a preset number of pages (about 10 to 20) in memory for printing later. You'll realize how useful this feature is if you envision the following scenario: You receive a partial transmission of a much-needed document, but when you call back to get a re-transmission, you find that everyone is gone for the weekend! Enough said.

Page cutter

Transmitted faxes are cut into individual pages rather than leaving you with one long scroll to cut apart yourself.

Pager notification

This feature automatically dials your pager whenever a document has been received.

Phone

Most fax machines come with a phone, or at least a handset. You may need an attached phone if you transmit to people who don't have a dedicated line or an automatic fax switch. You'll also want a phone when calling a fax-back service.

Polling

The polling function allows you to program your fax machine to automatically call a group of fax machines in sequence and receive incoming fax from them. To take advantage of lower phone rates, you can set your machine for delayed polling.

You might use this feature if you were producing a newsletter and wanted to collect ad layouts from a group of advertisers. Of course, the fax machines at the opposite ends must be set up and waiting.

Polling is also useful if you want to call your fax machine or modem and get faxes forwarded to you while you're on the road. To prevent just anyone from calling and retrieving the fax in the waiting machine, most fax machines offer some degree of security with their polling function.

Remote retrieval
To use this option, you leave your fax or computer (equipped with a fax modem) turned on to receive and store incoming faxes. You can then dial in remotely and instruct the machine to send the fax to the number you specify.

Speed dialing
This feature works just the same as it does on a normal phone. You program frequently called numbers with a one-, two-, or three-button code, and then use the codes to dial out.

Status messages
Lights and/or an LED display tell you know the status of your transmission, the number being dialed, and so on. The display allows you to verify that the number you keyed in is the correct number.

Store and forward
This feature permits you to program your fax machine to receive a document, store it in memory, and then send it on to other fax machines. It is most useful in large organizations that need to get information from one source and rebroadcast it to branch offices.

Transmission speed

Most fax machines today operate at 9600 bps (bits per second) or 14.4 kbps (kilobits per second), but you may encounter older fax machines that run at 2400 or 4800 bps. If you fax frequently, you'll need speed to keep your phone bills under control.

Unless your faxes are all local calls and you don't care how long the line is tied up, buy a fast machine. Just like modems, fax machines will slow down if they encounter noise on the phone line. Also, the transmission speed will be only as fast as the speed supported by the fax machine at the other end.

Transmission mode

The majority of fax machines let you select the quality of the resolution. Standard mode is usually 100 x 200 dots per inch (dpi). Fine mode improves resolution to about 200 x 200 dpi, but it doubles the transmission time. Some machines also support a superfine mode (200 x 400 dpi). These machines often require the receiving fax to have a superfine setting and to be the same brand.

Verification stamp

It's easy to check if your originals were fed correctly by using a verification stamp. The verification mark is printed on the bottom edge of your fax original and tells you how many pages were sent.

FAX MODEMS

If you already have a computer and a printer and you want plain paper capability for cheap, consider a fax modem solution. All you have to do is connect a fax modem to your computer and install the appropriate fax software. Then, you can send any document that is stored on your computer and receive virtually any type of document. You save time, paper, and hassle. Rather than printing out the document and feeding it into your fax machine, you just send it electronically from your computer.

HOW FAX MODEMS WORK

A fax modem contains a standard data modem, plus the telephone signal processing found in a fax machine. To transmit a fax, you use fax software to send your computerized file through the fax modem to a regular fax machine or to another fax modem.

When you receive a fax, the fax modem answers the call and converts the transmission into a computer graphic image. In order to receive faxes, you must leave your computer on and the enable the fax receive mode. Leaving your computer on adds about 20 cents to your electricity bill per day, and wear and tear on your computer is minimal.

Incoming faxes can be viewed, discarded, printed out, or saved for later. Because you can look at them on the screen, you can delete the faxes you don't want to print, thus saving your time and paper. The faxes come in as graphics, meaning you can't edit the words unless you have optical character recognition (OCR) capability. (More about OCR later in this chapter.)

Almost all fax software operates in the background, so you can still use your computer for other tasks. When you receive a fax, you'll be notified via a beep or a pop-up screen. You can then either view the fax on your screen or print it out on your printer.

Faxes sent directly from a computer file via fax modem are much crisper than those sent from a stand-alone machine. They don't suffer any degradation from going through the scanning process.

There are other advantages to faxing with your computer, too. You can archive incoming faxes and save them for editing, printing, or retransmission later. You can schedule delayed faxing to take advantage of lower rates after hours. You can efficiently send broadcast faxes to groups of people just by selecting a stored distribution list. It's also easy to create and access multiple phone books.

Fax modems are great if you normally send documents that were created on your computer. However, if you need to send items that didn't start out as images on your computer, such as newspaper clippings, maps, order forms, or photos, you'll need to add a scanner to the mix.

The image to be sent must be scanned in, checked for accuracy, and rescanned, if necessary, before finally sending it as a fax. This can be a very time-consuming process.

You should also be aware that fax files gobble up disk space. A single page of faxed text is around 60K, and a graphics page is around 200K. Be sure that you have sufficient space on your hard drive to support faxing from your computer.

FAX MODEM ADVANTAGES

- Paper is saved in two ways: (1) you don't have to print every fax you receive, and (2) you don't have to print documents before sending them.
- Time is saved because fax sending is quick and easy
- You get clean, crisp faxes
- You can save faxes for editing, printing, or sending on to someone else
- Broadcast faxing is easy

FAX MODEM DISADVANTAGES

- You must leave your computer on to receive faxes
- It is not easy to fax non-computer-generated documents
- Lots of disk space is used, which can be a problem if you're running out of room
- Fax modems are awkward to implement in a large office setting. Do you want to equip every employee with his or her own fax modem? That could be costly.

FAX SOFTWARE

Fax modems are sold with bundled software. If you've purchased a new computer lately, it likely has built-in fax capability with a "lite" version of fax software. You aren't restricted to
the software included with your modem, though. Almost any
fax software can be used with a standard fax modem.

If you want additional features, such as a choice of custom cover
sheets, OCR, or fax management capabilities, you might want
to purchase a more powerful fax program. One such program
is Symantec's WinFax Pro (www.symantec.com). Make sure that
the software you choose supports both incoming and outgoing
fax. Some of the low-cost versions allow you only to send.

Some fax software packages come with optical character recognition (OCR) capability. OCR software converts incoming faxes
into text files so you can edit the file using your word processing program. Using OCR, an attorney could receive a faxed
contract, convert it to text, port it into a word processor, mark
up the file with a strikethrough or highlighting font, add new
text, and fax back the changes. OCR could be useful for any
business that uses fax for group writing projects, editorial changes,
or publishing.

In addition to text-editing capabilities, OCR has the added advantage of significantly reducing the disk space required to store
a fax. Typically, OCR output has errors, so proofread carefully.
Also, when using OCR, be sure to coordinate with the sender.
The sender will need to send clean, non-photocopied documents without illustrations, underlines, fancy typeface, or hand-
written notes. Text should be in a sans serif typeface, such as
Geneva or Helvetica, and 12 points or larger. All this is a lot of
bother, if you ask me. I'd rather ask the sender to email the file,
or even mail me a diskette.

Fax modems come in a variety of speeds—from pokey 2400
baud models to 33.6 kbps. Although data modems can handle

speeds up to 56 kbps, fax cannot. For more information on selecting a modem, see Chapter 12.

SENDING A FAX USING A FAX MODEM

Faxing from your computer is easy once you understand that your PC is being tricked into thinking it is printing. Here's how to do it:

1. Start up your word processing software.
2. Find the file you want to send.
3. Select PRINT FILE on the menu.
4. Change your printer settings so that your fax software is the default printer. If you have a Mac, you do this with the CHOOSER. If you have a PC, you do this through the PRINT command.
5. Click OK or hit ENTER to indicate that you're ready to print.
6. A dialog box will pop onto the screen asking you to type the name and fax number of the person to whom you are faxing. Answer the questions and select OK.

The software will then convert the file into a fax and dial out. Most software will also give you a report indicating success or failure.

IS A FAX MODEM RIGHT FOR YOU?

To determine if a fax modem is appropriate for you, answer the questions below. If you answer "yes" six or more times, PC or Mac faxing may be the right choice for you.

✔ Do you already have a computer and a printer?

✔ Are most of the faxes you send generated from your personal computer?

✔ Are you the only person in your organization faxing information?

✔ If more than one person in your organization normally sends and receives faxes, are you willing to install a fax board and software on each person's computer?

✔ Do you wish to keep your faxes private from others in your organization?

✔ If you wish to send non-computer-generated documents, do you have or plan to get a scanning device?

✔ Do you need to keep archived electronic copies of your incoming faxes?

✔ Do you need the ability to annotate faxes electronically and forward them to others within your organization or workgroup?

✔ Are you willing to keep your computer turned on all the time (or be unreachable by fax for certain periods of time)?

✔ Do you have sufficient room on your hard drive to accommodate fat fax files? You'll probably want at least an additional 40 megabytes for fax storage.

INTERNET FAXING

What if you don't have a fax machine or fax modem? Or what if the fax machine is busy? You might want to send or receive documents through an Internet-based fax service. These services provide you with a unique phone number for receiving faxes, but it may not be a local number. Toll-free numbers are available for a higher fee.

Your customers simply send faxes to your number in the normal way. The faxes are converted to .tif or .mime attachments and sent to your email address. Most services charge a monthly fee whether you use them or not. The fees you pay will be offset

by potential long-distance phone charges. Here are some services to check out:

- Webfaxit   www.webfaxit.com
- Faxaway   www.faxaway.com
- MessageClick   www.messageclick.com
- Digitfax   www.digitcom.net
- eFax   www.efax.com
- Jfax   www.jfax.com

FAX ON THE GO
You can take fax capability with you in a variety of ways:

Cellular fax
Check to see whether your PCS or cellular phone has built-in
fax capability or whether it can accommodate a PC cellular fax
modem card. For more information on cellular faxing, see
Chapter 7.

PDA attachment
Many palmtops and personal digital assistants, such as the Palm
and Windows CE devices, feature optional fax modem attachments. However, some models can only send faxes and are
unable to receive them.

Satellite fax
These battery-operated fax machines run over the Inmarsat satellite system. They are designed for people who need fax communications from very remote sites.

PC fax modem card
These credit card size devices fit in a card slot on portable,
notebook, and handheld computers. You'll need both a Type II
PC slot and fax software loaded onto the portable computer.

Fax services
You can arrange to have your faxes forwarded to another fax
machine or converted into email.

FAX STANDARDS AND PROTOCOLS

The Committee on International Telephony and Telegraphy (CCITT) sets standards for worldwide fax transmissions. There are currently four international standards for fax transmissions:

- **Group 1**

  This is the earliest standard for fax transmission. Group 1 machines are painfully slow—around six minutes per page. Unless you normally shop for office equipment at your local flea market, you probably won't find a Group 1 fax machine for sale.

- **Group 2**

  Machines operating with Group 2 technology have speeds of up to three minutes per page. Don't get one of these either.

- **Group 3**

  This is the current standard today. Depending on the modem, speeds range from 20 seconds per page to around one minute per page. Be sure to get a fax machine that is compatible with Group 3 (sometimes listed as G3).

- **Group 4**

  This standard is designed for ISDN phone lines. You won't need this technology unless you have an ISDN phone line. Group 4 fax can transmit seven to nine times faster than Group 3.

FAX-ON-DEMAND

Many businesses and organizations are taking advantage of fax-on-demand technology. Customers or clients can call an advertised number (often toll free), listen to a menu of choices, key in a one- to five-digit number to request a particular document, and then enter the fax number to which the document should be sent. Moments later, the fax is on its way.

Another method requires you to call from your fax machine, and the fax is then sent directly to that machine. Instant customer satisfaction!

Fax-on-demand can save you money. You can fax a letter from your PC in about one-tenth the time it would take you to manually print and fax it. Fax-on-demand (FOD), or fax-back, is used in a variety of ways:

- Mail order companies can fax pages from their catalogs, brochures, and price sheets to callers requesting information.

- Travel agents can offer a menu of destinations and prospective travel dates. When the customer makes a selection, a list of restaurants, recreational activities, theaters, exhibits, and business service numbers is delivered.

- Hardware and software firms can provide technical support via fax.

- To pull in an order, booksellers can fax-back catalog information or even the first page of a thriller to prospective buyers.

- Real estate agents can set up a system that briefly describes each property. The caller makes a selection, and the system faxes him a floor plan, photo, and/or marketing flier.

SETTING UP A FAX-ON-DEMAND SYSTEM

To set up an FOD system, you'll need a dedicated computer, a dedicated phone line, a voice/fax board, and software that supports fax-on-demand. Systems are available that will work with only one phone line, but many require a minimum of two lines. Some systems offer the ability to have the sender (you) pay for the outgoing fax call and some—mostly the more expensive systems—have the capability to take credit card orders.

FOD systems range in price from $300 to over $5,000. The higher-priced systems have more features and are preinstalled on their own dedicated computers. However, if you can handle a screwdriver, you can easily install the hardware yourself.

If you're not sure that fax-on-demand will work for you, consider trying it first. You can start out with a fax-back service provider, who will take care of all the details for you. You'll find them listed in your local yellow pages under *Fax Transmission Services.*

CALLING A FAX-ON-DEMAND SYSTEM

Calling a fax-on-demand (FOD) system is easy if your fax machine has a built-in phone. If you're connected to a single-line fax-back system (where you pay for the call), you just dial the number, listen to the voice menu, key in your choices, and press the START button.

If you're calling a two-line system (where the fax machine calls you back), you can call from any Touch-Tone telephone and key in your fax telephone number when prompted.

When using a fax modem connected to your computer or a fax machine with no handset, you will run into difficulty if you attempt to dial a single-line fax-back system. The easiest solution is to plug a splitter into the wall phone jack. Next, plug a telephone into one of the jacks, and then plug your fax machine or fax modem into the other. Call the FOD machine by telephone, listen to the voice choices, key in the documents you want, and press the START key on your fax.

GETTING CONNECTED

Hooking up a fax machine is simplicity itself. You just plug the machine into a power outlet and the phone line cord into a wall jack. Be sure to locate your fax machine in a secure area away from the public eye, but close enough to be able to spot an incoming fax or low paper level.

Connecting a Fax

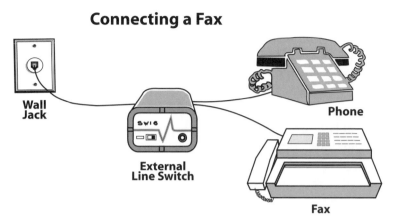

Wall Jack

SWI6

External Line Switch

Phone

Fax

SWITCH FIRST

If you're using an external line switch, be sure the switch is the first device on your line. It should be closest to the wall plug so that all devices, such as phone, answering machine, or fax, are driven by the switch. Otherwise, the device will be unable to switch calls properly.

SHARING A LINE

Most fax machines today come with some kind of line-sharing capability. The simplest machine "listens" for a specific fax tone (called CNG) that is sent out by most fax machines. If no tones are forthcoming, the fax machine rings your phone. Your callers, however, will hear nothing for up to 20 seconds. Unless they have been clued in on how to interface with your particular system, they will most likely hang up.

Some fax machines provide a short voice instruction stating something like, "If you'd like to send a fax, please press 1; otherwise, stay on the line and someone will help you." Another drawback to this type of switch is that CNG tones are not generated during some types of fax calls. Many older fax machines do not emit CNG tone, and tones are not generated during manual fax calls. In these cases, the person sending the fax manually dials your number, waits to hear fax tones from you, and then presses the SEND button. CNG detection is also adversely affected by noisy line conditions—no CNG tone, no fax.

FAX/ANSWERING MACHINE COMPATIBILITY

A better solution is to get a fax machine with an answering machine interface. These interfaces allow you to plug your answering machine directly into the fax machine. The fax machine sits in the background, allows your answering machine to play your greeting, and listens for the incoming fax tones. If it doesn't hear anything after a few seconds, it switches the call to your answering machine.

A word of warning, though—be sure to keep your answering machine greeting short, only 15 seconds or less. Otherwise, the sending fax machine will "lose patience" and hang up. Although you will hear only one ring before the answering machine picks up, your callers will hear three rings at the least. Also, with this solution your fax machine will always answer your line, so you won't be able to use your answering device's toll-saver function.

DISTINCTIVE RING

The best choice for line sharing (if available in your area) is distinctive ring. It is a phone company feature that assigns multiple phone numbers to the same line. Each phone number rings with a different cadence so you can tell what type of call is ringing in. If your fax machine or answering device can support distinctive ringing, it can be programmed to switch one type of ring to the fax, another to your answering machine or voice mail, and so forth. You could also buy a separate distinctive ring switch that serves the same purpose. Distinctive ring detection is highly reliable. For more details on distinctive ring, see Chapter 3.

DAISY-CHAINING

If you need to plug in other devices at the same wall jack, such as a phone or answering machine, you can daisy-chain them. Just plug your fax machine into the wall jack using the LINE port on the back of the machine. Then, plug another phone line cord into the PHONE port on the back of the machine and attach the next device. You can continue in this manner to connect up to five devices.

Daisy Chaining

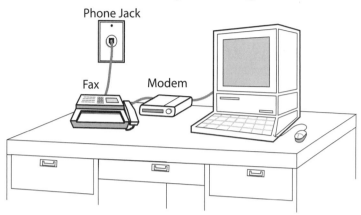

Phone Jack

Fax   Modem

DO YOU NEED ANOTHER LINE?

Before you run out and buy a fax switch, take a hard look at your communication needs. Though you will save some money in phone charges by using a switch on a single-phone line, are you risking the possibility of losing business by sharing fax and voice calls on the same line? Fax calls often take a long time, especially if you have a slower fax modem or a noisy line. If a fax is taking up your only line to the outside world, how can you be sure that potential clients and customers aren't dialing elsewhere?

It's best to install a separate line if you expect to send and receive a lot of fax calls. You'll appear much more professional, and your incoming and outgoing faxes will be less likely to be delayed. What's more, you'll avoid misdirected calls and irritated callers.

FAX LINE HUNTING

If you have more than one phone line and your lines hunt or roll over, put your fax and a fax switch on the last line of the rotary. Besides being less disruptive, this arrangement lets you give out a virtually dedicated fax number to your callers. For example, if you have three lines that hunt—say, 555-1001, 555-

1002, and 555-1003—publish 555-1001 as your voice line and 555-1003 as your fax line. When 555-1001 is busy, your calls will automatically ring on 1002. If 1002 is also busy, the fax switch wakes up and routes the call appropriately. Because the third line is less likely to be busy and fax calls always come in on 555-1003, your fax calls stand a better chance of getting in.

☎ In my office

I originally tried to run both fax and voice over one line on my home office phone. I turned on the fax machine only when I expected a fax. Soon, however, I got tired of scrambling under my desk where the fax is kept, hurrying through calls when I expected a fax, and feeling greatly stressed. So I installed a second line to handle fax and data calls. Occasionally, I use the second line for outgoing calls, but usually I keep it clear for incoming faxes. Now I have peace of mind.

I use PC-based fax for most of my faxing needs, but I also keep an old 1987 Murata thermal fax machine as a backup. That way, if my computer is off, I can still receive a fax. The Murata is also handy for the occasional non-electronic document that I need to send.

Recently, I tested the HP CapShare, a cool mini-scanner for use on the road as well as in the home office. The CapShare lets me capture documents that I can beam to a printer, transfer to my PC for later faxing, or attach to an email. The device is easy to use, runs on cheap AA batteries, and stores up to 50 letter-sized pages or 150 flip-chart pages. Scanning is simple. I just swipe the pages with the device—one pass down, one across, and another up the other side. The CapShare software automatically stitches the scans together to form a complete whole. In just a few seconds, I can see my scan on the screen and know if I captured the image I wanted. It's very handy.

CONNECTING PORTABLE FAX

Except for wireless models, portable fax machines connect to a modular phone jack in the same way that desk models do. If you can't find a modular phone jack to connect to, you might want to invest in an adapter that will allow you to connect to the phone's handset. Konnexx couplers by Unlimited Systems Corp. (800-275-6354) and Road Warrior Toolkit by Computer Products Plus (800-274-4277) are among the variety of such devices available.

DO YOU NEED YOUR OWN FAX MACHINE?

If you need only to send or receive an occasional fax, consider a fax service bureau. You can send an email message as a fax over a modem via online services, such as America Online, CompuServe, or an Internet fax service. Or you could fax from a local business or service, such as Mail Boxes, Etc.

Service bureaus also provide broadcast faxing. You give the document to the bureau along with a list of fax telephone numbers. They do the rest. Prices are usually based on the time of day, and you can often get a volume discount. In addition to fax-sending functions, service bureaus provide fax mailbox services. A fax mailbox could be useful if you're out of town, but still need to get those faxes. You forward your line to the fax mailbox service via your telco's call forwarding feature, and your faxes will be caught and stored for you electronically. You can then retrieve them when convenient.

If you use the same phone line for fax and data, a fax mailbox service can help you out if you anticipate a long online session. Just forward your calls before you log on, and you won't have to worry about missing a fax.

The cost of fax mailbox service varies depending on the number of faxes received and the services you sign up for. Most phone, pager, and wireless companies offer fax mailbox service.

Do the numbers

According to a recent HP survey of mobile professionals, the average business user faxes over 82 pages each month while out of the office at a cost of $164. Keep track of your own usage. If you find yourself spending more than a few dollars a month on fax services, you may find that owning your own machine makes sense.

Be sure to do the numbers

Kim Ecclesine, a Bay Area multimedia writer, took the fax plunge over five years ago. Up to that time, she drove about a mile to the local copy shop each time she needed to send or receive faxes. Kim calculates that she now sends and receives about 30 faxes a month. Based on that figure, her purchase has saved her over $16,000 in fax charges. According to Kim, "I laugh every time I pass that copy shop. I spent $600 to save $16,000. What an investment!"

SENDING FAXES OVERSEAS

Faxing across international borders can be difficult. You need a bewildering assortment of telephone prefix codes; the telephone tones don't always match U.S. tones; and telephone numbers can stretch for miles, or so it seems. Here are some tips to guide you through the maze.

- **Use international codes**

  All international calls originating in the U.S. are preceded by 011, followed by a country code, and then a city code. To dial telephone number 24433 in Berlin, the dialing sequence would look like this:

  011-49-30-24433

011	International code
49	Germany
30	Berlin

  Hint: You'll find a list of country and city codes in the front of your telephone book.

- **Check to see that the number you're dialing is current**
Some countries are updating their dialing plans. Great Britain recently added an extra digit to the city code, and because almost all city codes in the U.K. now begin with a 1, you may need to add a digit. For example, London used to be 71; now it is 171. To dial 123456 in London, the dialing sequence would look like this:

> 011-44-171-123456

- **Change the time-out**
Timing can also be an issue. Some international calls take more than a minute to complete the connection, but, by this time, most fax machines have lost patience and hung up. If your fax software allows you to change how much time elapses before the fax gives up, do so.

- **Call in the experts**
If you find yourself unable to get a fax through, give up and call a fax service bureau. You could also send your international fax through an online service or via the Internet.

TIPS FOR EFFECTIVE FAXING

- Keep a sufficient supply of fax paper on hand. If you use paper rolls, visually check your supply at least once a week and before each weekend. Never allow yourself to run out.

- If fax is your lifeline, consider adding an inexpensive fax machine on the same line as your fax modem. Then, you program the modem to pick up on the first ring and the cheaper machine to pick up on the fourth ring. That way, if your computer is off, you'll still get the fax. This is a good backup arrangement.

- Make it easy for your clients and customers to fax you. Print your fax number on your stationery, business cards, and order forms.

- For the cleanest fax, use a sans serif typeface, such as Helvetica or Univers, and a point size of 10 or more. Also, for faster faxing, avoid underlines and lots of black.

- The 3M Company sells a tiny Post-It fax routing slip that you can affix to the first page of your fax. It saves time, money (one less page to transmit), and trees.

- Use a formal cover sheet when faxing to large organizations or when the information contained is confidential. At a minimum, it should contain your logo, address, voice, and fax numbers, as well as the name, voice, and fax number of the recipient, plus the date and, most importantly, the number of pages you sent. If you want the recipient to call you to confirm receipt, add a simple check box for that, too.

- Create a company policy for fax use. Set guidelines for what kind of information may be faxed, whether urgent, short, or informal communications, and when, such as after hours for long faxes or after 8 P.M. for international calls. To discourage personal use, make sure that your staff knows you will be regularly monitoring fax usage.

- If you have a fax modem, you can still include your signature or logo on a computer-generated fax. You'll need to scan in the logo or signature, save it as a bitmap graphic file, and paste it into each document that requires it. If you don't have a scanner, fax yourself a copy of your letterhead from a local fax service.

- Don't list your fax number in a fax directory. Doing so will probably lead to an avalanche of junk fax mail. When you do receive junk fax, call the sender and ask to be taken off their list. The Federal Communications Commission requires that anyone sending fax ads must include their name, phone number, date, and time of the transmission on the first page of the fax.

- Be careful that you don't cross the line between junk fax and meaningful fax advertising yourself. Tying up a fax line when someone is anxiously waiting for an important incoming fax won't earn you his business. Also, though fax paper is relatively inexpensive, lots of junk fax recipients complain mightily about receiving unwanted faxes and paying for the paper to boot.

- Need to send an extra-wide fax? Architects and designers frequently need to fax blueprints, posters, or newspaper layouts. For this purpose, The WideCom Group (www.widecom.com or 905-712-0505) offers a two- to three-foot wide fax machine.

TROUBLESHOOTING

Fax machines are simple to operate. In fact, most problems seem to be caused by installing paper improperly. Check your manual first.

CALL WAITING

Call waiting and fax transmissions do not mix. If you have call waiting on the same line that you use for faxes, be sure to disable it before sending a fax. You do this by dialing *70 for Touch-Tone service or 1170 for rotary service. Unfortunately, this technique won't help you if call waiting tones interrupt an incoming fax. Because call waiting tones cause the fax modem or machine to disconnect, your best bet is to get a separate phone line for fax communications.

SLOW TRANSMISSION

If you find that your fax transmission is slowing down, don't worry. Faxes automatically slow down when they encounter noisy phone lines or a slower fax machine on the other end of the line. Remember, transmission speeds are only as fast as the speed supported by the fax machine at the receiving end of the connection.

RESOURCES

Books

Fantastic Fax Modems
by John A. McCormick
Windcrest/McGraw Hill, 1994

This book helps you select, install, and customize a fax board for either your Macintosh or PC computer. There are tips on international faxing, secure faxing, and portable faxing, plus listings for hundreds of products.

The Fax Modem Source Book
by Andrew Margolis
John Wiley & Sons, 1996
book and disk

Everything you need to know about fax modems is here, plus some. The disk contains fax source codes and utilities.

Internet and Computer Based Faxing:
The Complete Guide to Understanding
and Building IP and G3 Fax Applications
by Maury Kauffman
Miller Freeman Books, 1998

This text will teach you how to build or buy the most popular PC-based fax applications, including LAN fax server, fax broadcasting, and fax-on-demand.

Chapter

14

Your Phone Bill

J. PAUL GETTY, THE FABLED OIL ZILLIONAIRE, solved his phone bill problems by installing pay phones in almost every room of his mansion. You may not want to go to such extremes, but, with a little effort, you can make changes that will improve your bottom line, too.

Getting a handle on your phone costs requires paying attention to detail. The time you spend analyzing your telephone bills and planning for improved telephone efficiency will pay off in terms of both time and money. In this chapter, I'll discuss how to save money on long-distance charges and how to compare long-distance calling plans. I'll also give you loads of tips on how to control phone costs. My suggestions can get you started, but the rest is up to you.

SAVE MONEY ON LONG DISTANCE

Do you know much you pay for an average minute of long-distance calling? A recent survey showed that 88 percent of the respondents knew what they paid for a gallon of gasoline and 86 percent knew the price of a loaf of bread, but only 38 percent knew the per-minute rate of a long-distance call. It's time to change all that.

TYPES OF CALLING PLANS

Just about every business can save money by choosing a calling plan over basic long-distance rates. Many different kinds of calling plans exist, but they all boil down to one of four types:

Volume discount

These plans give you a discount ranging from 10 to 50 percent that is based on your total monthly long-distance charges. Usually, you have to meet some sort of minimum (often $25 or more) before the discount kicks in. Calls are charged on a per-minute and distance basis.

Consider a volume discount if you make calls at varying times (days, evenings, or weekends) and if you make enough calls to meet the discount threshold. Be sure to compare these discounts to other plans, however.

Time-of-day discount

This option charges you less if you call during off-peak times. Some plans have three calling periods: business hours, after business hours (often from 5 P.M. to 8 P.M.), and nights/weekends. Be sure you understand the carrier's definition of business hours. Some programs define business hours as 7 A.M. to 7 P.M. These discounts are best for residential customers and home-based businesses that can make the bulk of their long-distance calls after the normal business day.

International plan

Most of these plans give you some kind of volume discount to the country of your choice for a monthly fee. They are best for organizations that spend the bulk of their long-distance budget on calls to parties outside the United States.

Flat-rate plan

These plans are popular because the discounts are the easiest to calculate and budget. However, some plans charge flat rates only during specific times of the day. Consider a flat-rate plan if a high percentage of your long-distance calls are coast-to-coast or exceed distances of 1,000 miles. Most flat-rate plans charge a monthly fee, so be sure to factor that into your calculations. If you focus on the low cost of each call and ignore the monthly fee, you may find yourself paying more than you should.

CHOOSING A PLAN

Even if you have local business service, you don't have to sign up for a business long-distance plan. You should evaluate both residential and business plans when shopping for a service.

The Telecommunications Research and Action Center advises you to pick a residential calling plan if you usually spend $75 or less for interstate long distance each month. If you spend between $75 and $200, you should consider either a residential or business calling plan. If your call volume exceeds $200 per month, you'll want a business calling plan.

Your best bet is to get a calling plan that provides fractional billing, where calls are measured in six-second increments instead of full-minute blocks. If you make a lot of short calls, such as voice messages or unsuccessful fax calls, you could save up to 35 percent by using fractional billing.

ANALYZE YOUR CALLING BEHAVIOR

To pick a cost-effective plan, you'll need to analyze your long-distance phone bills. Here's a strategy that works:

1. Assemble your long-distance bills from the last few months and chart the numbers on a matrix or spreadsheet.

2. Determine your per-minute rate. First, add up the total minutes charged on your monthly bill. Then, divide the dollar amount of your bill by the total minutes to find your average cost per minute.

3. Look for patterns. Does one area code get the largest percentage of your calls? What time of day are most of your calls made? Do you make lots of international calls?

4. Based on your calling pattern, narrow your choices to one or two plan types.

5. Do some comparison shopping. Call long-distance carriers and resellers, and provide them with your average monthly usage, the total number of calls, and the total number of minutes. Based on that information, ask each company to quote the best service for your needs, plus their per-minute rates.

6. Set up a spreadsheet or matrix to compare the plans. Plug in the numbers, and note any exceptions, deals, or fees.

7. "Test drive" the service that looks the best on paper. You do this by using the company's five-digit access code before dialing a number. For example, if you wanted to try Sprint service, simply enter 10333 before you dial your number. You'll be billed for the call on your local phone bill.

8. Read the fine print on the service contract, and be sure to evaluate monthly minimums. If you make only a few calls, the plan charging 5 cents per minute with a $9.95 monthly minimum may not be such a great deal. Watch out for hidden charges, too. One plan I know of had a minimum call duration of three minutes, so all calls were billed for at least three minutes. These kinds of charges and fees can add up quickly.

9. Avoid making long-term commitments unless the discount is fabulous.

10. Rates, services, and features are constantly changing, so you should reevaluate your plan every few months.

SHOPPING FOR A PLAN

Shop around for discount calling plans. Don't restrict yourself to the big carriers, such as MCI, Sprint, or AT&T. There are over 500 long-distance resellers in the United States, and you could get a top rate from one of them. These companies are also called switchless resellers, rebillers, or aggregators. They lease phone lines from the major carriers and resell them at a discount to small businesses like you. It's sort of like a co-op bulk-buying service.

Many resellers will even allow home offices to combine billing for residential and business lines in order to qualify for discount plans.

Choosing a Reseller

Be sure to ask the reseller lots of questions. Here's a convenient list you can use:

- Which carrier's service are you reselling?
- How long have you been in business?
- Do you provide 24-hour customer service?
- Are you certified with the state Public Utility Commission?
- Are you a member of the Association of Communications Enterprises?

You can find a reseller by contacting the Association of Communications Enterprises at www.ascent.org or 202-835-9898.

The Telecommunications Research and Action Center, or TRAC (www.trac.org), publishes a newsletter called *Tele-Tips*. This newsletter lists billing plans, peak and off-peak rates, and other features offered by a number of long-distance companies. To get a copy of this newsletter, send a check ($5 for residential or $7 for business) plus a self-addressed, stamped envelope to:

> TRAC
> P.O. Box 27279
> Washington, DC 20005

Comparing Plans

Because features and pricing structures are so variable, it's tough to compare long-distance plans. Rates will differ for interstate, international, calling card, toll-free service, and local toll (those calls made outside your local calling area, but within your local access transport area, or LATA). Sometimes, it seems like you are comparing apples to oranges. However, fruit *can* be compared based on a common denominator, such as caloric value or vitamin C levels. Calling plans can be similarly evaluated by choosing a common denominator.

One of the best ways to compare plans is to examine the average cost per minute. You might want to further break down the cost per minute by time of day or by distance. It's also useful to know what fees and minimums are required, whether the calls are billed on a six-second or per-minute basis, and what hours constitute normal business hours.

Oddly enough, long-distance providers often provide more competitive rates for in-state calls and local toll calls than your local service provider. So, shop for these rates while you're looking at long-distance plans. You may end up with substantial savings.

☎ In my office

In an effort to practice what I preach, I recently analyzed my own long-distance behavior. I gathered three months' worth of long-distance bills and totaled the minutes. Then, I broke the bill down into its components to determine how many minutes were used during business hours, night hours (Sunday through Thursday, 5 to 11 P.M.), and weekend hours. I also looked at how many of the minutes were spent on local toll, interstate, and intrastate calls. Next, I calculated my average monthly bill and the average cost per minute. I also totaled each column. At this point, I could see some patterns emerging.

Sixty-five percent of my calls take place during business hours. Another 20 percent take place between the hours of 5 P.M. and 11 P.M. (Monday through Thursday), and a mere 15 percent take place on weekends or between 11 P.M. and 8 A.M. Also, eighty percent of my calls are out-of-state calls. So, armed with my new self-knowledge, I contacted several long-distance providers and assembled information on a number of calling plans.

The final result? It looked like I needed a new plan, most likely one with a flat rate. To test my theory, I checked out several plans on the WebPricer, a free service provided by Salestar for telephone consumers (www.trac.org/webpricer). The WebPricer compared plans from AT&T, Excel, Frontier, Qwest, MCI, Matrix, and Sprint. I finally signed for a single-rate, seven-days-a-week, 7 cents-per-minute plan with a low minimum monthly fee. My phone bills were immediately reduced by about 30 percent.

TIPS FOR CONTROLLING PHONE COSTS

Here's a bunch of tips that can do wonders in helping you get a handle on your phone bills. Try some out—you'll be glad you did.

Curtail 411 calling

Be careful when calling directory assistance. It's not free anymore, although some plans allow two or three free calls a month per line. Depending on your area, a call to directory assistance will cost you somewhere between 50 and 85 cents. The average charge is 65 cents, but at that rate, just one call a day adds up to nearly $20 per month. According to a 1998 *Consumer Reports* study, Americans spend more than $5 billion on directory assistance each year. Ouch!

If you frequently use directories, buy yourself a disk-based or CD-ROM directory. Select Phone (InfoUSA, www.infousa.com or 800-321-0869) is a computerized directory containing business names, addresses, fax numbers, and Web addresses. You can look up information by name, phone number, or even business type.

Big Yellow (www.bigyellow.com), Bell South's Real Pages (www.yp.bellsouth.com), or SBC's Smart Pages (www.

smartpages.com) are great sources for fast Internet lookups. At these sites, you can search yellow page listings anywhere in the United States by state, name, or business type. World Pages (www.worldpages.com) provides searches of both U.S. and Canadian phone directories. You can also find links to many national phone directories at the Global Yellow Pages site (www.globalyp.com/world.htm).

Call off-peak

If your long-distance plan is based on time-of-day, try to save up your long-distance calls for off-peak hours. Arrange to get to work earlier or stay later so you can make long-distance calls to companies in other time zones.

Warning: Most long-distance companies will bill your call at the day rate if any portion of the call extends beyond the off-hours. For example, if you place a long-distance call at 7:45 A.M. and hang up at 8:01 A.M., the entire call will be billed at the daytime rate.

Fax at night

Program your fax modem or fax machine to send your faxes at night when phone rates are lowest. You can save 20 to 50 percent, depending on the distance involved and your calling plan. To save even more, use email instead.

Shorten your calls

Limit the time you spend on the phone by offering to email or fax a proposal or price list. Then follow up later with a quick phone call. While you may spend ten minutes on a voice call, you may be able to transact the same business with a one-minute fax. If you are paying 10 cents a minute for a daytime long-distance call, you would have saved a buck. It all adds up.

Keep a clock by your phone, or get one of those phones with a built-in timer. You'll be surprised at how much you can save by watching the clock.

Code your calls

Writers, lawyers, and many other professionals have to track reimbursable time spent on the phone. One way to do this is to keep a diary of all telephone calls. However, it's a tedious task, and it's easy to forget. Another option is to use call accounting codes provided by your long-distance company.

However you do it, call accounting is useful for keeping track of your time on the phone. If you use coding supplied by your long-distance company, you can sort your calls and faxes by client name, or you can identify types of calls, such as sales, billing, or publicity. Then, when your bill arrives, you have these tidy codes next to each call. Many long-distance carriers and resellers provide this service either for free or for a small monthly fee.

Another advantage of call codes is that they tend to intimidate your staff into more appropriate calling behavior. Some companies report that using accounting codes virtually eliminated personal calls and reduced phone costs by 10 to 40 percent.

For more information, call:

- AT&T Small Business Services   800-222-0400
- MCIWorldcom   800-727-5555
- Sprint   800-877-7746

Control phone abuse

To stop unauthorized calling by employees, you can get an inexpensive call-blocking device that clips onto the phone line cord. These devices are available at your local electronics store for a few dollars. You can also get a blocker that allows you to restrict calls to particular area codes and prefixes, or even to a specific number.

An alternative is to install a personal pay phone in your employee lounge and require that all personal calls be made on that phone. The revenues from these calls could go into a group coffee or snack fund, to blunt any negative effect on employee morale. Hello Direct carries these phones.

Consider residential service

If you don't need a business directory listing, you may be able to save a bundle by using residential rather than business service. Several telephone companies—including GTE, US West, Sprint, and BellSouth—are allowing residential phone lines to be used for business. More and more state PUCs are allowing this change in tariff regulations. Here are some examples of the savings you could enjoy:

In Minnesota, US West charges $47.63 for a business line and only $18.20 for a residential line. You'd save $353 per line in only one year.

In California, Pacific Bell charges $14.93 for a business line and $11.25 for a flat-rate residential line. In one year, you'd save $44 per line plus all per-minute usage charges in your calling area.

Share a line

If your call volume is low, and if customer service won't suffer when callers experience an occasional busy signal, you should look into sharing a line. You can purchase a switch that will allow you to share a line among your phone, fax, and answering machine. Some equipment comes with built-in switching capability, or it may work with distinctive ring services that are provided by your local telco. You can find line switches in telephone and electronics stores.

Use a prepaid calling card

You can purchase flat-rate, long-distance service via a prepaid calling card. They come in denominations of $5, $10, $25, and the like.

Prepaid calling cards, or debit cards, are very easy to use. First, you dial an 800 number listed on the back of the card; then you enter a PIN number (also printed on the back of the card) plus the number you're calling. Your calls are charged against the card until its value is depleted. When the card value is nearly gone, an automated voice warns you that you have only 30 (or 60) seconds left to wrap up your call.

If you shop around, you can find some very attractive rates. I discovered one plan that charged only 3.9 cents a minute (Big Zoo at www.bigzoo.com). The catch is that the card expires six months after the date you buy it. Also, prices are higher for calls to Hawaii and Alaska. It's still a pretty good deal, though.

You can purchase prepaid cards at stationery shops, electronics stores, or even your local corner deli. They make nice gifts, but be sure to calculate the per-minute cost before buying one. In addition, check for expiration dates. Some expire within six months; others have no ending date. Some cards allow you to "recharge" them—you input your credit card number, then select how many minutes you wish to purchase.

Audit your phone bills

Carefully examine your phone bill each month. Believe it or not, you may be paying for lines or services that should have been disconnected long ago. Auditing is especially important if you took over your company from a previous owner. If you find a discrepancy, notify your phone company and arrange for a refund.

If your phone bill is complex (or you have a lot of lines) and you need help deciphering it, enlist the aid of a telephone bill auditor. Auditors are professionals who will examine your bills, identify discrepancies, and negotiate with the phone company for you. They usually charge a percentage of any refunds they obtain. You can find an auditor in your yellow pages under Telecommunications Consultants, or try contacting the Society of Telecommunications Consultants for a list of members (800-782-7670 or www.stcconsultants.org).

Install a phone miser

MediaCom (www.phonemiser.com) makes the PhoneGenie, a small box that plugs into your phone line and uses least-cost routing to choose the lowest rate for every call. Every time you dial long distance, it scans a directory of discount phone services to find the lowest rates at that moment. Customers are then billed directly (on a monthly basis) by each of the long-distance services that they used in that given month. The added paperwork may be unappealing, but your savings could definitely justify it.

Ursus Productions Inc., a small film production company based in Waterville, Maine, installed the device and watched its long-distance charges drop from $700 per month to $150.

Tackle toll fraud

American businesses lose at least $5 billion a year to telephone fraud. The average cost of just one incident of toll fraud is $44,000—enough to sink many a small business. Because small businesses are usually unsuspecting and unprotected, telephone hackers are especially fond of preying on them. Unlike credit card fraud, where your liability is limited, phone fraud losses are the customer's responsibility. What to do?

If you have a phone system, you might consider installing a fraud detection system. These devices monitor your system and alert you to signs of tampering, such as lots of calls made during nonbusiness hours, a high percentage of credit card calls, or too many busy signals. Some devices will automatically take your phones down at the first sign of fraudulent activity. Toll fraud prevention isn't cheap. Equipment to monitor your system ranges in price from $800 to well over $15,000. Contact your local phone vendor for assistance.

Examine your cellular phone bills extra carefully. Phone cloners and other crooks have many ways of charging their calls to your cell phone bill. For details, see *Wireless fraud* in Chapter 7.

Use a personal number when out of the office

If you tend to make a lot of calls back to the home office when you're on a trip, a personal toll-free number may be cost effective for you. Often, you can get an 800, 888, or 877 number free if you purchase other services from your long-distance provider. Usage fees average around 20 cents per minute.

Arrange for follow-me-service

On the other hand, if your office needs to call *you* a lot, investigate a follow-me-anywhere number, such as Wildfire (www.wildfire.com), Webley (www.webley.com), or AT&T's True Ties (www.att.com).

Control hotel phone charges

Unfortunately, many hotels seem to view their phone service as a for-profit center rather than a service for guests. Therefore, never use the hotel phone service for long-distance calls without checking their policy. Use your credit card instead. If you don't, you may end up paying about 40 percent more for each long-distance call.

Many hotels also charge an access fee when you use your telephone credit card instead of their phone service. These fees range from 50 cents to $1.25 per call. When making reservations, ask whether the hotel charges calling card access fees. If they do, try to stay somewhere else. The Sheraton, Stouffer, and Hilton chains do not charge fees.

In many cases, it's less expensive to use a mobile phone, especially for short calls. For example, if you pay a flat rate of 25 cents a minute, calls under four minutes are less expensive than paying a $1 access fee.

Tip: You can save money on hotel long-distance charges by hitting the pound sign between each long-distance call instead of hanging up. In this way, you avoid paying a calling card access fee for each separate phone call. You have to do this very quickly, however, or you'll lose your dial tone. There's only a two- to three-second window, so have the numbers you want to dial all lined up and ready to go.

Hotels often charge for incomplete phone calls, usually after six rings. To be safe, don't let the phone ring and ring. Hang up after five rings.

Pay close attention to international calling costs

Be careful when making international calls from abroad, especially if you use your U.S.-based calling card. You could end up paying a huge penalty. For example, one family made a one-minute call from Italy to Switzerland, but later found that the call was billed at $10.95. The reason for this was that the call was first routed through the United States, then bounced back to Europe.

Instead, purchase a debit phone card when you reach your destination. You can purchase them in small denominations at vending machines, stores, or post offices.

Another cost-saving measure is to sign up for an international-access calling card from a major carrier, such as AT&T, MCI, or Sprint. When you're abroad, you call your carrier's local access number to connect to a U.S. operator, who then places your call for you. Charges appear on your office phone bill, not on your hotel bill. These cards are good only for calls back to the United States, but you could save up to 40 percent on charges.

Beware of pay phones for long-distance calling

Independent pay phones have been found to charge up to ten times the rate that you'd pay for a long-distance call from home. As reported in *U.S. News & World Report* ("Watch That Pay Phone", 6/26/95), an 18-minute call from Ramsey, New Jersey to New York City cost $21.32 on an independent pay phone. AT&T would have charged $5.53.

To avoid these exorbitant charges, dial 00 before you call and ask the long-distance operator to place the call through your own long-distance provider.

Dial toll free as much as possible

This one is pretty obvious. If you need to find an 800, 888, or 877 number fast, call 800-555-1212 or check out AT&T's AnyWho Info directory (www.anywho.com/tf.html) or the Internet 800 Directory (http://inter800.com).

Dial direct

When you dial direct, your call will cost up to 60 percent less than the cost of an operator-assisted call. In your office, your phones are automatically programmed to use your preferred long-distance carrier. However, if you are out of the office, you must specify your carrier or use the one that is preprogrammed for that particular phone.

Call your long-distance company and ask for its direct dial access code. Use the access code before every call or group of calls whenever you're dialing from a phone outside your office. Some common codes are:

10222	MCI
10288	AT&T
10333	Sprint

Avoid calling collect

Be careful about promises of low rates when dialing collect. For example, MCI's 1-800-COLLECT offers a low rate during off-peak times, but jacks the price up to 49 cents a minute plus a connection fee of $1.79 during weekdays—hardly a bargain.

Use Internet calling

Over the Internet, you can make a phone call to virtually any-one, anywhere, for as long as you wish—and all for the price of a local phone call. There are some disadvantages, however. The quality of your voice connection is not so great. In addition, you may experience delays between the time you speak and the time you hear yourself speaking, especially during peak traffic times on the Net. For more information, see *Internet calling* in Chapter 3.

Cut the cord

According to a 2000 survey conducted by the Personal Communications Industry Association and the Yankee Group, about 2 percent of all telephone users in the U.S. utilize a wireless phone as their sole communications device. You'll probably want to maintain wired service for Internet access, faxing, and data transfer, but you may be able to replace at least some of your wired voice phones with wireless ones. To determine if wireless makes sense for you, compare the per-minute cost of wired and wireless plans and take into account the monthly fees. If you travel outside your service area, be sure to consider roaming costs as well.

COST-SAVING TIPS FROM A PRO

Texas-based Denise Munro is a principal with the Cost Reduction Group. Her firm specializes in analyzing telephone bills for companies with telephone costs of $2,000 per month or more. In a recent audit, she negotiated annual cost savings of $100,000 for a client who had inherited a hodge-podge of services through mergers and acquisitions. Some of the services on the client's bill were unused; others had been previously disconnected, but were not removed from the bill. Such mistakes are not rare. According to Denise, "It is estimated that 70 percent of all business telephone bills are wrong, usually in the phone company's favor."

Though most of her customers have substantial telephone bills, her suggestions are useful for organizations of any size. Her advice follows:

- Invest in a good phone system. Phone systems today are nearly maintenance free. Get one that lets you program it yourself, and ask your vendor to teach you how to set up and care for your system.

- Consider canceling your maintenance agreement. If you had two or fewer service calls last year, your maintenance contract wasn't paid for. The hourly rate for a service call is somewhere around $65.

  Note: If you don't have a service contract, your vendor will not give you priority service. If your communications are critical, you may need to keep the service contract just to get good response times.

- Discontinue any cable protection programs you may be paying for. These cost anywhere from $1.50 to $2.50 per line each month. If you are already paying for a phone system maintenance contract, you're paying twice. Remember, the vendor that installed your phone wiring is responsible for the work.

- If you experience phone trouble, call your vendor first, not the telephone company. Usually, the vendor's service trip charges are cheaper than the telco's. If the problem is with your lines, your vendor can coordinate repair.

- Be sure that your long-distance plan is billed in six-second increments. When comparing plans, don't call just the major carriers. The Big Three may not offer the best plans for small organizations. Look into service from other long-distance carriers, such as Frontier or LDDS Communications, or from a reseller.

- When selecting a long-distance carrier, ask for references and give those references a call. Get the plan in writing. Be sure that you are comfortable with the service programs and have them included in a written contract. Lastly, don't sign long-term agreements—you can always find a better plan.

- Know what you are paying for. Your telephone company can provide a detailed list of the lines and services for which you are being billed. Compare the list to what you know you have and question what you don't understand.

- If you find you are being overcharged or do not know if you are, an auditing firm will pursue your case on a contingency-fee basis. It can also offer recommendations that may result in additional monthly savings.

RESOURCES

Books
Which Telephone Service Provider? The Official Guide to Choosing the Best Local Phone Service Provider for Business
by James Harry Green
book and disk
Flatiron Publications, 1998

Long-distance carriers and resellers
There are over 500 long-distance companies in the United States and Canada. In addition, some areas of the country now allow local phone companies to offer long-distance service.

To find long-distance services in your area, look in your yellow pages under Telephone Companies or Telephone Communications Services; ask your business associates for their recommendations; or contact the Association of Communications Enterprises (www.ascent.org or 202-835-9898).

Additional Resources

· ·

MORE BOOKS ABOUT TELECOMMUNICATIONS

1-800 Courtesy:
Connecting With a Winning Telephone Image
by Terry Wildemann
Aegis Publishing Group, 1998

Whether your goal is to keep customers happy or convince them to buy what you're selling, this book will help you to get the results you want from any telephone interaction.

900 Know-How:
How to Succeed With Your Own 900 Number Business
third edition
by Robert Mastin
Aegis Publishing Group, 1996

Widely recognized as the bible of the 900 number industry, this nuts-and-bolts start-up guide is necessary reading for those who want to be toll collectors on the information highway.

The Business Traveler's Survival Guide:
How to Get Work Done While on the Road
by June Langhoff
Aegis Publishing Group, 1997

Stay connected to your home base from virtually anywhere, including international locations—this handbook shows you how. It is the ideal travel companion.

Call Center Handbook:
The Complete Guide to Starting, Running, and Improving Your
Call Center
by Keith Dawson
CMP Books,1999

Discover the secrets to running an efficient call center. Subjects include the use of interactive voice response, fax-on-demand, email, and websites.

Data Networking Made Easy:
The Small Business Guide to Getting Wired for Success
by Karen Patten
Aegis Publishing Group, 2000

Everything you'll need to know for setting up a network and connecting it properly is clearly explained in this text.

Digital Convergence
by Andy Covell
Aegis Publishing Group, 1999

This book provides a framework for understanding how the convergence of computers, communications, and multimedia is transforming our lives.

The Essential Guide to Telecommunications
by Annabel Z. Dodd
Prentice Hall, 1999

The structure of the telecommunications industry is examined and various industry segments are profiled in this comprehensive survey of telecommunications technologies.

LAN Times Guide to Telephony
by David D. Bezar
Osborne McGraw-Hill, 1995

Written by telecommunications expert David Bezar, this book is designed for information services professionals.

McGraw-Hill Illustrated Telecom Dictionary
by Jade Clayton
McGraw-Hill, 2000

By virtue of over 300 illustrations and several thousand entries, telecom talk is explained completely.

The McGraw-Hill Telecommunications FactBook:
A Readable Guide to Planning and Acquiring Products and Services, second edition
by Joseph A. Pecar, Roger J. O'Connor, and David A. Garbin
McGraw-Hill, 2000

Packed full of engineering diagrams, this book provides a high-level overview of telecommunications technologies.

Mobile Telecommunications Factbook
by Nathan J. Muller
McGraw-Hill, 1998

Topics include: mobile messaging and computing, remote access and monitoring, security, wireless, Web-based remote management, and teleworking.

Newton's Telecom Dictionary:
The Official Glossary of Telecommunications Acronyms, Terms and Jargon, sixteenth edition
by Harry Newton and Ray Horak
Telecom Books/Miller Freeman, 2000

Harry Newton, former publisher of *Teleconnect Magazine,* created this compendium of telecommunications terms many years ago and publishes an update frequently.

Phone Company Services:
Working Smarter with the Right Telecom Tools
by June Langhoff
Aegis Publishing Group, 1997

Phone services are described in detail with advice on how to use them in real-life applications.

Strategic Marketing in Telecommunications:
How to Win Customers, Eliminate Churn, and Increase Profits
in the Telecom Marketplace
by Maureen Rhemann
Aegis Publishing Group, 2000

This book offers telecom professionals up-to-the-minute guidance on how to tackle the tough marketing issues that face them.

Telecom & Networking Glossary:
Understanding Communications Technology, second edition
by Robert Mastin
Aegis Publishing Group, 2001

In addition to providing clearly written definitions of telecom and networking terms, this glossary goes one step further to show you how everything fits together.

Telecom Business Opportunities:
The Entrepreneur's Guide to Making Money in the Telecommuni-
cations Revolution
by Steve Rosenbush
Aegis Publishing Group, 1997

Written by *USA Today* telecom reporter Steve Rosenbush, this book tells you where the money is being made in the evolving, deregulated telecommunications industry.

The Telecommuter's Advisor:
Real World Solutions for Remote Workers, second edition
by June Langhoff
Aegis Publishing Group, 1999

A useful guidebook for telecommuters, mobile workers, work-at-homers, and remote workers of all kinds.

Winning Communications Strategies:
How Small Businesses Master Cutting-Edge Technology to Stay Competitive, Provide Better Service and Make More Money
by Jeffrey Kagan
Aegis Publishing Group, 1997

Read fascinating real-world profiles that demonstrate how progressive small businesses are benefiting from new communications technology.

MAGAZINES

Call Center
www.callcentermagazine.com

This publication focuses on technologies, applications, and advice for running a customer service center, help desk, or sales and support office.

Computer Telephony
www.computertelephony.com

You'll find lots of information within these pages on all aspects of IP telephony voice/data convergence, server-based telephony, enhanced services, application development tools, speech recognition, wireless/WAP, multimedia switching, unified messaging, and customer interaction.

Internet Telephony
www.internettelephony.com

This magazine provides the information you'll require for learning about and purchasing Internet telephony equipment, software, and services.

Mobile Computing & Communications
www.mobilecomputing.com

All facets of mobile technology—trends and developments, new products, and application solutions—are covered in this magazine.

Phone+
www.phoneplusmag.com

This publication reports on the telephone reseller industry.

tele.com
www.teledotcom.com

Here's a magazine designed specifically for the new business and technology managers employed at public network service providers around the globe.

Telecommunications
www.telecoms-mag.com

Service provider technologies and applications worldwide are the subjects treated in this pub.

Teleconnect
www.teleconnect.com

There are lots of buyers' guides included in every issue of this magazine to help readers choose, buy, install, use, and maintain telecommunications products and services.

TELEPHONE EQUIPMENT CATALOGS

Hello Direct
www.hellodirect.com
800-444-3556

Radio Shack
www.radioshack.com
800-843-7422

TeleAdapt
www.teleadapt.com
408-965-1400

This catalog specializes in adapters and connectors for international connections.

WEBSITES

Big Yellow
www.bigyellow.com

This is the Internet's version of the yellow pages.

Global Yellow Pages
www.globalyp.com/world.htm

You'll find links to yellow pages sites around the world.

Salestar
www.salestar.com

To choose a winning telecommunications plan for your organization, use the call pricer located at this site to help you compare long-distance telephone charges.

Telecom A.M.
www.telecommunications.com/secondTAM%20splash.htm

This site summarizes and links to daily telecom news.
Telecom Digest
www.telecom-digest.org

The source for this site is a mailing list that has been in operation since 1981. It contains loads of telecom information.

Telephone History Website
www.cybercom.com/~chuck/phones.html

You'll have access to loads of interesting historical information, sources of old-time telephone equipment, and trivia at this site.

ASSOCIATIONS

Association of Communications Enterprises
www.ascent.org
(Long-distance resellers)

Cellular Telecommunications Industry Association
www.wow-com.com
(The wireless industry)

Electronic Messaging Association
www.ema.org
(The e-business and messaging industries)

North American Association of Telecommunications Dealers
www.natd.com
(Vendors of telecom equipment and services)

Personal Communications Industry Association
www.pcia.com
(The personal communications services (PCS)
and paging industry)

Index